Fifty
THINGS
That Aren't
MY
FAULT

G. P. PUTNAM'S SONS

New York

Fifty THINGS That Aren't MY FAULT

ESSAYS FROM THE GROWN-UP YEARS

Cathy Guisewite

PUTNAM

G. P. PUTNAM'S SONS
Publishers Since 1838
An imprint of Penguin Random House LLC
penguinrandomhouse.com

Library of Congress Cataloging-in-Publication Data

Names: Guisewite, Cathy, author.
Title: Fifty things that aren't my fault: essays from the
grown-up years / Cathy Guisewite. Description: New York:
G. P. Putnam's Sons, 2019.
Identifiers: LCCN 2018005868 (print) | LCCN 2018016509 (ebook) |
ISBN 9780735218444 (epub) | ISBN 9780735218420 (hardback)
Subjects: LCSH: Families—Humor. | CYAC: Family life—
Humor. | BISAC: HUMOR / Form / Essays. | FAMILY &
RELATIONSHIPS / Aging.
Classification: LCC PN6231.F3 (ebook) | LCC PN6231.F3 G85 2019
(print) | DDC 818/.602—dc23
LC record available at https://lccn.loc.gov/2018005868
p.   cm.

Printed in the United States of America
1   3   5   7   9   10   8   6   4   2

Book design by Meighan Cavanaugh

*Penguin is committed to publishing works of quality and integrity.
In that spirit, we are proud to offer this book to our readers;
however, the story, the experiences, and the words
are the author's alone.*

For Mom

♥

Contents

Fifty
THINGS
That Aren't
MY
FAULT

INTRODUCTION

I'm standing in the doorway of my closet, on the threshold of What Happens Next, clutching my last shred of personal power: a great big black trash bag into which I want to dump all my clothes.

Nothing fits.

I don't mean "Ha-ha, nothing fits." I mean *nothing fits*. This is worse than the hot pink bikini that destroyed my twenties in a fluorescent bulb-lit dressing room in a Royal Oak, Michigan, mall. Worse than the blue jeans that broke my heart in my thirties in a charming Santa Barbara denim shop stacked to the hand-hewn rafters with jeans for every female body in the universe except mine. Worse than the go-everywhere black dress upon which I spent a car payment in my forties that never went anywhere because the only time I ever got it zipped was five minutes before handing my Visa card to the hip L.A. salesperson who told me how hot I looked in it.

This is worse than all that. This is my whole life not fitting. My days are too short, my lists are too long. People aren't where they're supposed to be. Everything's changing without my permission. Children are moving away, friends moving on, loved ones leaving the earth, muscles and skin tone not even pausing to wave farewell before deserting me—and after all I've done for them. Just when I think I can't possibly stand one more goodbye, something or someone I thought would be here forever isn't.

Everyone I know is in some version of a great big life shift. Right in the middle of people and things that are changing and disappearing way too fast. An unrequested rearrangement of everything in our personal worlds—as if there isn't enough that feels out of our control right now in the big world. It's unsettling and unnerving. And scary. Impossible to be everything to everyone, to reconcile all that's different, and to keep track of ourselves along that way.

I grip the trash bag. I have an overwhelming, exhilarating need to get rid of things before any more leave on their own.

I stopped my life's work of drawing a comic strip after thirty-four years when the first rumbles of big change in my own life made it impossible for me to hold the pen. My daughter was starting her senior year of high school and I panicked that her childhood was ending before I'd had a chance to be a mom. I wanted, for once in my life, to get to be a full-time mom like the new stay-at-home superstar moms I read about in magazines and also, if I'm completely honest, like the old-school housewife moms I watched on TV when I was growing up. I wanted to get to feel what it was like to make tomato soup in the middle of the day.

That same year, my parents were both approaching their nineties, and I also wanted, for once in my life, to get to be a full-time adult daughter like the patient, loving daughters I read about in books. Graciously, selflessly helping Mom and Dad glide into their twilight years.

None of this has gone as planned.

I became a full-time mom at the very moment my daughter decided to reject all input from anyone over age thirty.

I became a full-time daughter the moment my parents announced they would barricade the front door if I tried to bring in anyone or anything to assist them.

I got older, which I hadn't factored in, and became even more obnoxious and belligerent than my child or my parents, incapable of even committing to exercising five minutes a day.

I thought that when I quit my job, the pace of all the change would slow down. But it didn't. It sped up. Before I knew it, the year zoomed by, my daughter turned nineteen and moved to college, my parents turned ninety, and I turned into a bicoastal hoverer. Commuting between generations. Back and forth between Florida and California so often, I spend the first few minutes of each morning trying to guess which coast I'm on before I open my eyes.

Which is why I'm standing here right now. Trash bag held high. I can control nothing else, but I can control this. I will stuff life as I knew it into this bag and get rid of it. All of it.

The delusional clothes . . . the useless beauty products . . . the plastic food containers with no lids. I will move on to the file cabinets . . . the bathroom cupboard . . . the storage room. I will shred and dump! Delete! Declutter! I will be a role model of clarity. I will do it for my family. I will do it for me. Create a future with absolutely nothing hot pink and strappy holding me back.

I open the garbage bag to stuff in my first triumphant "OUT!"

I reach into the closet and pull out a frayed T-shirt I haven't worn since 1982.

I study it in my hand.

I think how cute it would look paired with an oversize linen shirt, beaded belt, and suede ankle boots. I remember seeing a kicky messenger bag online somewhere with tassels the exact same shade of teal as the faded flower logo on the right sleeve.

I refold the shirt and lay it back on the shelf.

I close the garbage bag.

I march into the kitchen and sit at the table. So many thoughts are stacking up in my head. Big changes . . . little tassels . . . hanging on . . . letting go . . .

I open my laptop to start typing.

Before I can unload the closets, I have to get rid of some of these words.

1.

FIFTY THINGS THAT AREN'T
MY FAULT

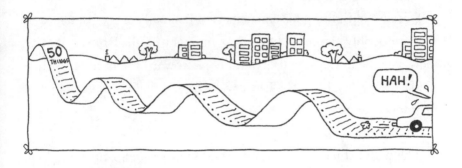

A m I allowed to eat a noodle? I stare at the menu on the wall behind the takeout counter and try to remember.

It used to be so simple.

Noodles were good because they were comfort food.

Then noodles were bad because they were fattening.

Then noodles were good because they were "pasta."

Then noodles were bad because they were carbohydrates.

Then noodles were good because they were fiber.

Then noodles were bad because they were gluten.

Then noodles were good because they were "pho."

Then noodles were bad because they were high glycemic.

Then noodles were good because they were comfort food.

Then what? I have six months of unread healthy-lifestyle maga-zines on my kitchen counter, which puts me six months behind on where the noodle stands.

Paralyzed at the takeout window.

I turn to the line of impatient people behind me and blurt out the one and only thing I am completely sure of at this moment in my grown-up life:

"It's not my fault!"

Decades of fighting for emancipation from all sorts of things, and this is possibly the most liberating moment of all. I repeat it with more volume in case the irritated people toward the back of the line didn't hear. Also, honestly, I just want to feel the words come out of my mouth again.

"It's not my fault!"

The man behind me sighs, loud and exasperated. I turn and look him in the eye. Right in his scowling, unadorned male eye. Not one moment of his morning was spent on eyeliner like mine was, I note. No eye shadow, no mascara, no fine-line filler, no under-eye con-cealer. I look further. No eyebrow shaping no eyebrow tinting no pore minimizer no foundation no bronzer no blush no Botox no blow-dry no straightener no curling iron no root dye no wispy lay-ers no highlights no ear jewelry chosen to match his outfit.

I stop at his neck. No need to move on to his outfit. In four sec-onds, I've already calculated that if I add up the hours, days, weeks, and years of his life starting from when he didn't play dress-up at age three like I did until this moment in this line at this takeout counter, he's had approximately eighteen thousand extra hours of time on earth to do all sorts of things that I haven't. All of that is also not my fault.

"IT'S NOT MY FAULT!" I proclaim even louder, right at his non-lip-lined, non-lipsticked, non-lip-plumped lips.

He glares and takes a step backward. I turn back to the cashier, place a non-noodle order, and strut down the counter to pay.

Life is just different for girls.

Life is more time consuming.

Life is more complicated.

Life is overflowing with expectations and obligations that use up our time, energy, and spirit and leave us feeling exhausted, insecure, and alone.

And I Have Had It.

I dig through my ten-pound purse for my two-pound wallet.

It's not my fault that my wallet contains one credit card and nineteen bonus club cards to stores in which I could get a discount if I could ever find the card.

Not my fault I have to carry the bonus club cards in my wallet because I didn't get my phone number registered to the accounts.

Not my fault that when I try to register my phone number to the accounts, I'm told my user name already has a membership associated with it and that I have to enter the password, which I don't remember and didn't write down for fear of identity theft.

Not my fault that I haven't reset my passwords, because that would involve checking my email to get the reset codes, and when I check my email, I have to face the little bold print on the upper right of the screen that says I have **7,038** emails I haven't answered.

The disgruntled gentleman who was behind me in the ordering line is now behind me in the paying line. I feel his eyes boring into me, his ungroomed eyebrows raised at the spectacle of the insides of my wallet and purse, which are dumped on the *Pay Here* counter.

Again, I slowly turn to face him. His flat one-ounce, bonus-club-card-free wallet is gripped in his unmanicured fingers like a manly badge of superiority. Membership badge to a detail-free club to which a girl will never belong.

"IT'S NOT MY FAULT!!" I roar.

I drive home with the windows of self-righteousness wide open. I breathe in the possibility of innocence. Big, freeing gulps of it. I barrel past mini-mall eateries and jammed parking lots, a Los Angeles suburb full of people hungry for dinner and a taste of what just happened to me in the takeout line.

What just happened was the opposite of who I am.

I am from Dayton, Ohio, and Midland, Michigan: I apologize for holding up lines. I don't scream in public or at strangers.

I am my mother's daughter: I take personal responsibility for everything and everyone on the planet. I look for those I can help, not those I can blame.

I am a member of my generation: I proudly own all my life choices.

I'm all of that—the Midwest's gracious values plus Mom's deep sense of responsibility plus my generation's triumphant empowerment. I'm courteous, compassionate, and personally accountable for every speck of everything.

But not today.

"IT'S NOT MY FAULT I WAS RAISED TO THINK EVERY-THING IS MY FAULT!" I yell out my wide-open window.

Hah!

I barrel down the road toward home, indignation rising up in me, soaring, pouring out of me like lyrics of the perfect songs I can never find on the car radio.

"It's not my fault I can never find songs on the car radio because

I haven't had three hours to learn how to program the simplified digitized car radio menu screen!"

I'm on fire.

"It's not my fault I just paid someone to make me a sandwich because it's become too complicated to buy a loaf of bread!"

"Not my fault I drove to the takeout place in sweat pants because all my blue jeans hurt!"

"Not my fault the sweat pants also hurt because someone decided women's workout wear should be clingy and sexy to show off the hot 'after' body, not the non-hot, actually-needs-to-work-out 'before' body!"

"Not my fault that women's magazines have covers declaring we should embrace our beautiful natural curves, but sixteen articles inside on how to get skinny—and that even if *I'm* over it, I still need to spend hours and hours navigating the hypocrisy for my daughter!"

"Not my fault I can't call my daughter on the $700 phone I bought her to discuss it because 'voice is over'!"

"Not my fault that the man behind me at the takeout place will never understand because he never had to navigate any of the body-issue contradictions for himself or his son!"

"Not my fault I'm thinking about that man again!"

It's all right there as I scan the memory of him and imagine the different universes in which he and I live. The million tiny things between us that use up women's waking hours, leaving us frustrated and frazzled, holding hands with frozen donuts at 11:00 p.m.

Men are the same size all day. They don't have pre-breakfast, post-lunch, mid-afternoon, and after-dinner bodies requiring different wardrobes for each part of the day and phase of the moon.

Men are the same height all day. All the pants in a man's closet are the same length because all the heels of his shoes are the same height. Men don't spend one speck of their lives deciding how tall they'll be before they commit to buying or hemming their pants. They don't need six different styles of black pants in four different lengths to go with nine different heel heights of black shoes for fourteen different types of occasions.

Men are the same shape all day. They don't need to decide which direction to mold which body parts before they put on clothes.

Men are the same age all day. Their faces are their faces.

When a man needs a white shirt, he buys a white shirt. A woman does a three-mall, six-department, two-hundred-style-fabric-cut-size-price-manufacturer, multi-dressing-room search. Ditto underwear. Ditto T-shirts. Ditto jeans. Ditto sweaters. Ditto socks. Ditto shoes. Ditto workout wear.

Ditto the worst of the worst . . .

When a man needs a swimsuit, he grabs trunks his size off the rack. A woman dives into the deep end, the vortex of insecurity. Eleven and a half months of dynamic, twenty-first-century female confidence building, all undone by a one-second peek at our beautiful natural curves in eleven inches of spandex under a fluorescent dressing room bulb.

It's not my fault we're still supposed to stuff ourselves into someone else's version of what we should be because there are zero realistic alternatives!

IT'S NOT MY FAULT THAT THINGS THAT SHOULDN'T MATTER STILL MATTER, AND THAT EVEN THOUGH I HELPED PIONEER A GENERATION TO THINK COMPLETELY DIFFERENTLY, I'VE SOMEHOW RAISED A DAUGHTER WHO SOBS IN THE SWIMWEAR DEPART-

MENT DRESSING ROOM JUST LIKE I DID—*WITH ME STANDING RIGHT BESIDE HER!*—HER SELF-ESTEEM CONSTRICTED BY A WHOLE NEW WORLD OF SASSY LITTLE STRAPS!

I turn down the wrong street on purpose so it will take me longer to get home.

There are support groups for the big problems. Unequal pay, unjust treatment, unfair practices, global inequality. Harassment. There are politicians, movements, organizations, public forums. There's honor in raising one's voice about the big problems.

There's no honor in mentioning what happened last night with nine "100 Calorie Packs" of Mini Oreos. No one to put into perspective the thousand extra pressures, time saps, and mini confidence wreckers that added up all day and left me feeling so exhausted and useless and small at 9:00 p.m. and then so huge at 9:06 p.m. No sympathy for the minuscule things that prevent me from doing the big things. That stop me from getting through the next five minutes.

I remember the thrill of being a twenty-two-year-old new working woman in my first advertising job. Ecstatic that I had a job, the respect of my coworkers, and the blessing of the world to succeed in ways my mom never dreamed possible. I remember the morning of a big meeting when I couldn't get my "fat" skirt buttoned. Couldn't get anything buttoned. Nothing fit except my bathrobe. All of life out there for me to conquer, and I had to call in sick because I literally couldn't walk out the front door.

I remember my insecurities being so ingrained that I parked across the street from a party and watched what other women were wearing before I was brave enough to leave my car and walk in myself. I remember it like it was yesterday.

Because it *was* yesterday. For all that's changed in me over the years, so much of the ridiculousness is still there. Stuck on my DNA like the frosting swirls on a Hostess CupCake.

It's not my fault that when the doors of possibility for women opened, the role models got so incredible and the comparisons became so impossible. Suddenly women weren't just getting jobs. They were becoming dynamic career women, financial wizards, nurturing home-makers, enlightened involved parents, environmental activists, com-munity leaders, self-assured, self-expressed, self-supporting global change makers, loving equal partners, weekend yoga instructors, on-line entrepreneurs—and size 5's all at once. When the message is that all women can do anything, it's hard not to get the feeling that all the *other* women are doing something and I alone am stuck in the same old ruts.

It's not my fault that even guilt has too many options. I used to eat a muffin and have calorie guilt. Now I have calorie guilt, carbohy-drate guilt, fat guilt, sugar guilt, gluten guilt, nonorganic blueberry guilt, manufacturing process pollution guilt, non-biodegradable-wrapper guilt, carbon footprint guilt. Nine entire guilt categories per muffin. Multiply that over the whole food chain.

Not my fault that I carry all the new guilts on top of all the old guilts. Bulk guilt. Multigenerational guilt. I bring a pre-thank-you hostess gift to the dinner party. I send a thank-you text when I get home. I write an email thank-you the next morning in which I say a proper thank-you note will follow. I search for paper upon which to compose the proper note and a pretty thank-you card into which to tuck it. I hunt for a postage stamp with a design element that coordinates with the pen color, which matches the lining of the en-velope. Violet. No. Plum. No. Eggplant. No.

Etcetera.

My skirts button now, but I can no longer leave home for fear of how long it will take me to express gratitude if someone does something nice for me.

I turn down another wrong street on purpose.

It's not my fault I have bonus guilt. I had the amazing platform of an internationally syndicated comic strip, which some people said I should have used to voice triumphant stories of unwavering feminism, but which I instead used to voice the insecurities, relationship frustrations, mother-daughter angst, career grief, and food blunders under which so many of our triumphant dreams get squashed. Some people thought my work reinforced the negative stereotype of women being obsessed with shopping, weight, and love, but it wasn't my fault we still live in a world that partly judges women by what we wear, how much we weigh, and whether or not and who or how we love. Not my fault that with every glorious new possibility for women came an extra sense of isolation when we not only couldn't keep up but were told we shouldn't talk about the things that held us back.

Many days I wanted to say, *Hey, it was kind of humiliating to admit what I did in the comic strip today, but this is the truth of what's tangling everything up for a lot of us, and it makes us feel even more alone because we're not supposed to admit we're vulnerable to any of it! You only looked at the subject matter but didn't notice the small personal victory that wrestling with the subject matter included! My message was meant to be one of compassion and hope! The powerful female spirit rising above the muck!*

I spent days researching the fashion trends of the season, for instance—how women are portrayed, the convoluted sexism sold in women's magazines that's billed as "fearless fashion." Images like that of a sultry executive leaning against her desk in a one-button blazer with nothing on under it (*"This season's feminine touch!"*) undermining decades of efforts for women to not be viewed as sex objects in the workplace and inviting confusion at best and sexual harassment at worst. I would try to sum up days of research and perspective and the real-life experience of living in this culture into four tiny newspaper comic strip boxes with a bit of hope in the last panel . . . and would be heartbroken sometimes, honestly, when some people would say, "There she goes, writing about shopping again."

I wanted to write notes to all the people who were unhappy with my work and explain myself. I wanted to write notes to all the people who were happy with my work and tell them how deeply grateful I was that they let me know I wasn't alone.

I still owe all those notes. Thousands of them. It's all on the list.

It's not my fault I just ate my whole sandwich at the last stoplight out of self-pity.

Not my fault I'm circling completely different neighborhoods now.

Nor that I've started yelling out the open window again.

"It's not my fault I could have had a nice dinner with friends tonight but turned down the invitation because I'm eight hundred episodes behind in my television watching and can't hold my own in dinner party conversations anymore!"

"Not my fault the headlines were so depressing this morning, the only way I could reclaim some personal power was to go online and buy another pair of shoes!"

"Not my fault that all the time I've gained from owning a smartphone has been lost searching for my smartphone!"

"Not my fault that my selfies no longer resemble myself!"

"Not my fault I still pay monthly dues to a gym I haven't gone to in a year because I'm too embarrassed to call and cancel my membership!"

"Not my fault I keep running out of color ink when I only print in black!"

"Not my fault I look completely different in the store mirror than the home mirror!"

"Not my fault that when I open my mouth to say something to my child, my mother's voice comes out!"

"Not my fault that even after all the times my heart's been broken, I can still be seduced by the promises of hair products!"

"Not my fault I can summon the energy to run to the kitchen and make a hot fudge sundae, but not the energy to strike even one yoga pose during a commercial break!"

"Not my fault I used up another half hour of my life last week trying to figure out which pack of plain white paper to buy!"

"Not my fault I have so many passwords in my brain, I can't remember the names of friends!"

"Not my fault that I can go so quickly from restorative meditation to shrieking at a voice on an automated answering system!"

"Not my fault that no matter how many times I've repeated yesterday, I believe with all my heart that I will be completely different today!"

"Not my fault that every now and then, the most positive thing I do for myself is rip up all the affirmations stuck on the front of my file cabinet!"

"Not my fault that almost every time I've listened to my body, it's told me to do the wrong thing!"

"Not my fault that now that everything has a link to more information, I never, ever feel I've finished anything!"

"Not my fault that my ego soared just long enough to convince me I'd remember what was on the fifteen full memory cards I tossed in my desk drawer without labeling!"

"Not my fault I can't share my dreams with friends because they'll ask how it's going and expect me to have made progress!"

"Not my fault it seems best to skip the positive self-image books at this point and simply start shutting my eyes in the shower!"

"Not my fault that I believe my wants and needs are more deeply understood by Amazon Prime than by 99 percent of the men I ever dated!"

"Not my fault that some days, even with all I know and have done, I still measure my self-worth in fat grams."

But not today.

I've been driving in circles for an hour, and now I'm heading down my street, a changed woman. I've breathed in the possibility of innocence, great big gulps of it, and I feel good.

I pull up to the garage that's too full of stuff for a car to ever fit in it. I squirt anti-bac on my hands and breath spray in my mouth so my dog won't notice I ate a sandwich without giving him the chance to beg for a piece.

I open the front door. Am tackled by the dog. My life is exactly as I left it an hour ago, but it feels completely different. I drove an hour and ten miles out of my way to get to back where I belong—to a place of perspective, freedom from the past, and renewed belief in myself.

I look at the handsome four-legged guy who's waited so long for me to return, and say the one and only thing I am completely sure of at this moment in my grown-up life:

"It's not my fault the fastest way back to me was to take the really long way home."

2.

WHY THERE'S A LIFELESS BODY IN DRESSING ROOM NUMBER TWO

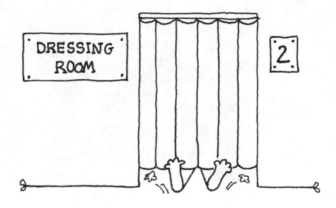

This is being written from a four-foot-by-four-foot dressing room in a Top 10 Sporting Goods store. Not written, actually. I'm dictating it to my iPhone, as I only have the use of one finger to press the little microphone icon. The rest of me is trapped in a sports bra. Not the Sexy Sports Bra of my daughter's world. This is a normal sports bra made for normal women.

These could be my Last Words. My Audio Goodbye—just in case this is the day I actually die of strangulation from underwear. On the odd chance that my sole beneficiary, my nineteen-year-old Sexy Sports Bra Princess, doesn't pluck the iPhone from my dead hand

and sell it on Craigslist without even listening to my big speech, I'm leaving this for someone else to hear.

I've been stuck in this sports bra for seventeen minutes. Have contorted my body every way possible to get out of it. Tried to wrench it upward, tug it downward, pry it away from my crushed rib cage.

The bra is now lodged halfway between my chest and my chin, with my left arm and hand squashed flat under it. The lower half of my right arm is sticking up out of the neck hole, which is how I got to the microphone icon—by bending over and poking at my purse on the floor with the index finger of my right hand until the phone fell out and I could jab the screen.

Before I black out, I need to be heard. More pressing than the primal urge to scream for help is the primal urge to explain why it's a size L in which I'm stuck. This is not the classic "If I must die, please, God, let them find my lifeless body wearing an S." Or even the "Let the paramedics all be men, because humiliating though it will be for them to find me like this, at least they won't peek at my size tag." This is more urgent than all that.

I'm trapped in an L, not an S, because I couldn't stretch the size S wide enough to get it over my head. I couldn't have stretched it wide enough to get it over my daughter's old American Girl doll head. The S sports bra is not made for *any* female, plastic or otherwise. The L barely got over my shoulders, then sprang back around my chest like a rubber tourniquet, where it will apparently stay until it's removed by the surgical scissors of whoever finds me passed out on the Gatorade logo that's embedded in the linoleum floor of this dinky room. I'm briefly bizarrely cheered by the fact that if someone bothered to embed a Gatorade logo in the linoleum, it must mean they planned for people, like me, to be upside down in underwear staring at the floor while speaking Last Words into an iPhone. I'm not the only one!

The cheer ends. Of course I'm not the only one. If a small person can't get into an S and a small person can't get out of an L, what are 99 percent of the world's women, who are medium to extra large, supposed to do? This is why I have to speak up before my battery or I expire.

There are at least six hundred sports bras in this store—proud symbols of athletic emancipation, opening a universe of sports and exercise to women because we're finally supposed to be comfortable doing sports and exercising when we wear one of these. This is what we come to buy when we're committing to feeling good about ourselves. But as far as I can tell from the times I've shopped for one, every sports bra is only going to make the woman who tries it on feel horrible about herself.

I want to scream, but in my current condition, how much do I really want anyone to come running? I want to rally like-minded women to protest with me . . . but my kindred spirits are all stuck in their own individual four-by-four Top 10 Sporting Goods dressing rooms, trapped just like me in underwear that was supposed to set us free that we can't get out of. Part of a huge, liberated, utterly immobile group, each member of which feels completely, half-nakedly alone.

I stare down at the Gatorade logo. It's making me thirsty. Also it's reminding me how much I wish I'd used the ladies' room before I came in here. I remember the Top 10 corporate policy of "restrooms for employees only" from a previous unhappy visit. I start calculating if there's any chance I could escape the sports bra, get dressed, apply for a job, and get hired in the next three minutes so I could qualify to use their bathroom. Frustration rises like the tide, a giant wave of discomfort and injustice rushing over . . .

I instantly regret using a water metaphor. As so often happens in the crusade for change, the urgency of the greater cause is washed away by the urgency of the needs of the moment. More water imagery. Fewer minutes remaining of anything good happening in this room. I give one last panicked, futile squirm, after which I vow to not move one muscle until I'm hopefully unconscious for the rest of the day.

I think of our foremothers in their laced-up corsets. I think of the centuries of underwear injustices, of athletics that were so out of reach they weren't even a dream; of the millions of strong, defiant female voices that never had a chance to be heard because women couldn't even imagine speaking up about such a thing. I think of my frostbitten ancestors, trudging to the outhouse in ankle-length bloomers and non-sports corsets in the middle of winter. I think of all the areas of life that appear to have been transformed for women, but with innovations that missed the mark just enough to leave us stifled in new and different ways. I think of how far we've come only to be stuck where I am right now. Mobilized but paralyzed, incensed but silenced. Incarcerated a mile away from a public ladies' room by a puny chartreuse sports bra.

One day, I promise, someone will go to all the women's dressing rooms, gather up the cell phones of my generation, and transcribe our voice memos. And then, finally, we'll have ourselves a real revolution.

3.

DRIVING LESSONS

ant me to drive?"

"Sure!" I say as brightly as possible through a jaw spasmed shut in horror.

It's a sunny Sunday afternoon and we're starting from the safest possible place—a carport wide open on three sides with a nice long driveway that leads to a quiet residential street.

Still . . .

I get in the passenger seat and shove it as far back as it will go so I won't be crushed when the nine airbags deploy. Strap on the seat belt. Calculate how my arms can shield my face from shattering glass without being lacerated themselves. Legs better off bent? No. Straight ahead. No. Bent. No. One bent, one straight, giving a fifty-fifty chance of needing only a cast, not a wheelchair, after our half-mile drive to the market. I'm gripping the inside of the door so tightly, I might self-inflict a stress fracture before she even gets the car out of the carport.

"AAACK!"

"WHAT?" She snaps her head toward me, glaring.

"You lurched!" I snap back.

"I lurched because you screamed!"

"I screamed because you lurched!"

"Do you want to drive?"

"No! I want you to drive! You're doing a great . . . AACK!"

"WHAT?"

"You lurched again!"

"Do you want to drive??"

She slams the gearshift to P.

So far we've moved twelve inches and I've aged eleven years. I try to uncurl the clenched fingers of one hand with the paralyzed fingers of the other, assessing damage. I'm not being self-absorbed here. If I'm injured, there will be no one to take care of her. Just like strapping the oxygen mask on myself first on the airplane.

"No!" I say. "I want you to drive! You're doing a great job!"

I turn to give my "great driver" the visual of my reassuring face to go with my perky words of encouragement, but I don't see the driver. My seat is shoved so far back and hers is shoved so far forward that when I turn, all I see is the back of her headrest.

"Um . . . aren't you sitting a little far forward to be safe?"

I hear the oh-so-familiar Big Frustrated Exhale. "Do you want to drive?" she asks.

"No! I want you to drive! You're doing a great job!"

"Here! Go ahead!" She tries to yank the key out of the ignition without turning off the motor. "Want to trade places?!"

"No! I do NOT want to trade places!"

"Yes, you do. You want to trade places."

"No, I don't!"

"Yes, you do!"

WE ALREADY TRADED PLACES!!!

I didn't need to scream that last one out loud. Mom knows as well as I do where we currently sit.

Mom. Yes. It's not my teenage daughter at the wheel. It's my beloved mother. I'm in Florida for one of my many new regular visits to "see how everyone's doing," and right now I'm seeing how Mom's doing. Mom, who safely drove me from birth to 2013. Who drove me through blizzards to get to birthday parties and piano lessons. Who drove me through thunder and lightning to compare thirty different pairs of black open-toed pumps at twelve different shoe stores at three different malls. Who braved icy roads in the middle of the night for emergency chocolate supplies to fix my broken heart. Mom, who drove me to every "first," her eyes all watery and blurred with panic and pride—first day of school, first sleepaway camp, first dance.

She never got a scratch on the car. Never lost her way. Not even when I was the one with tears—weeping in the passenger seat that life was over because an eighth-grade girl was mean to me, wailing that I couldn't go to school because my hair looked stupid. Not even when I was sulking and silent and Mom had to read all the road signs in my teenage mind . . .

Mom was always the expert: judging when to veer around an emotional pileup, when to go slowly over every bit of buckled ego, when to do a U-turn and point us toward the nearest Dairy Queen.

The truth is, I was never safer than when Mom was behind the wheel. I was free to tell her anything when we were on those drives, just the two of us. I could confess all my secrets and share every dream in the sanctuary of Mom's passenger seat.

She steered me safely through it all. Then she steered me right into my life's work. I started working as an advertising copywriter in Detroit after college and was already quite successful by the time I was twenty-five. Mom, a picture of reserve, had always taught me to keep my feelings private, and there was a lot to feel confused about in those years. I was trying to live up to two role models—the homemaking Betty Crocker of my youth and the liberated Betty Friedan of my future.

Heeding Mom's advice, I didn't talk to friends about the angst of feeling stuck in the middle. Instead, I wrote in my diary and ate. I gained forty pounds with one Betty's Triple Chocolate Fudge Cake Mix while trying to digest the other Betty's *Feminine Mystique*. Frustrated by the Bettys, I sought guidance from M&M's. Ultimately, I summed up my confusion in crumb- and candy-covered scribbled drawings, which I sent home to Mom in letters to let her know I was coping without sharing my feelings with anyone.

In spite of a lifetime of teaching me to keep things private, not to mention the fact that I didn't know how to draw, Mom insisted that these humiliating scribbles should be published for millions of people to enjoy. She researched comic strip syndicates at the library and announced she was going to send my "drawings" in to someone with a nice note from Mom if I didn't. Just to make her not do that, I mailed some to Universal Press Syndicate, the first name on the list she'd typed for me. Within days they sent me a contract to draw *Cathy* for the rest of my life along with a note saying they were sure I'd learn how to draw if I had to do it 365 days a year.

I loved my advertising career and it was crazy to think I could support myself being a cartoonist, so I kept both jobs for a year and a half, working all day on one job and most of the night on the other, until I was finally exhausted enough to quit one of them.

Mom was clear which one it should be. She said I should leave what was safe and secure and leap into the impossible. Women were just starting to have the chance to try anything and be anyone, and Mom cheered me on to do it all, to see how far I could go.

Even when I decided to go three thousand miles away from her. When I was thirty, Mom did half the driving during the five-day trek that brought me to California. It had been two years since I'd left my advertising job to do the comic strip full-time, and I was feeling brave enough to also leave everything else that was so safe. A beautiful home, a boyfriend, friends, family, the Midwest—none of it could compete with the lure of the rest of the world. Newspapers and magazines were full of stories of women who were doing things that used to be impossible, and emboldened by Mom, I couldn't wait to try it all, completely by myself.

Mom helped me squash my drawing supplies and half of my closet into my two-seater sports car. I made a bed for my sixty-pound dog on top of everything we'd piled behind the two seats, and Mom lovingly pointed the three of us toward the complete unknown.

"I'm helping you go as far away from me as you can get," Mom joked as we pulled out of my cozy neighborhood in suburban Detroit and headed for Los Angeles, "without having to jump in the ocean and start swimming." I didn't see the irony in the fact that I was launching my triumphant cross-country quest for independence with Mom nine inches away in the driver's seat.

I also didn't see what Mom surely saw down the road. She had to know with each passing mile that she was driving me farther away from the hope that I'd ever live near Dad and her as a grown-up, of having grandchildren close by, of family Sunday dinners at their house. We went through Illinois . . . Oklahoma . . . New Mexico . . . all the pages of the AAA TripTik, with me so excited about what might lie ahead and Mom so aware of what I was leaving behind. She still did it—rock solid behind the wheel, driving for days across America with love, enthusiasm, and the pure motherly joy of helping her girl go chase her dream.

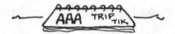

That's what a great driver Mom was. That's how safe I was with her behind the wheel . . . right up until a few years ago, when without so much as a blinker to warn us, we changed lanes in the middle of life.

Every visit home since, the shift has been different. Mom has seemed slightly smaller and slower behind the wheel, and I've sat up straighter and been more alert. This visit, I'm bolt upright, in a full body clench—able to only make one-syllable yelps or those little stifled sounds that used to come from the bottom of Mom's heart when I was young and at the wheel and she was teaching *me* to drive. As we sit here twelve inches out of her carport, it's painful to see how far we've come.

I wanted to drive with Mom today so I could "assess her competence." In spite of how cheerfully I've reassured her what a great driver she is, she knows she's being assessed and I know she knows she's being assessed and it's possibly added a bit of tension to . . .

"CONCRETE STANCHION ONE INCH FROM THE RIGHT FRONT BUMPER!!!"

"Do you want to drive?!"

"No. Sorry, Mom. You're doing a great job."

"Would you like me to go back in the house and get your father and have *him* drive?"

This snaps me out of my reverie. My ninety-year-old mom is a little bit lurchy now, but my ninety-year-old dad has much, much more going for him behind the wheel: spinal stenosis, macular degeneration, double hip replacements, arthritic knees, and occasional episodes of briefly passing out.

"Let's not get Dad."

Mom completes her backup. Turns around and aims for the neighbor's yard. I do my best to pretend I'm relaxing in what is the perfect metaphor for my place in life right now: the passenger seat. The place that used to be so safe but isn't anymore. The position from which I see everything, try to direct everything, and can control absolutely nothing. The position from which I'm doing the exact same thing in opposite directions: trying to help my own nineteen-year-old daughter get safely on the road of life and trying to gently steer my ninety-year-old parents safely off of it.

I'm equally worried for all of them, and they're equally as belligerent as each other. Nineteen- and ninety-year-old versions of the exact same need for independence, the exact same belief that they have it all under control. Nineteen- and ninety-year-old versions of the exact same rejection of my opinions and advice. For this tiny window of time, I'm the powerfully powerless guardian of them all.

All I can do is be grateful for the brave mom who got me here. Say my prayers for what will be. Position my brain away from the airbags and buckle up.

4.

IN LOVING MEMORY OF
THE LEGS I USED TO HATE

Gradually, graciously, I've made peace with myself from the waist up.

I've learned to appreciate my evolving face like a poem, one fine line at a time. A slow, gentle morph into a slightly older version of me. My eyes have adjusted to my maturing hands and arms too, little by little, like they adjust to the sun. I no longer have to squint when I look at them, not blinded anymore by what I see.

But this. What I'm looking at now. This came from nowhere with no warning.

The legs I've always hated have overnight been replaced by Grandma's legs. The young legs I used to think were so horrible have suddenly, irrevocably, turned into old-person legs that actually *are* horrible. I stare in disbelief.

I want the legs I used to hate back! I want my untoned, overweight young legs! The legs I hid from public view most of my life! Come back, horrid fat young legs! Come back! I am ready to love you now!!

Another silent scream into a mirror. Another Celebration of Me Day ruined by getting a good look at me, and I am *ticked*. I do not deserve this.

I didn't wear skirts or shorts for years because I thought my legs were too ugly. Didn't wear a swimsuit for decades because I thought my legs were too fat, too flabby, too cellulite-y, too stretch-marky. My legs humiliated me. They ruined all my outfits. They destroyed my self-confidence. They made me cry when I tried on boots. I hid them behind muumuus, long skirts, and jeans. Today, for the first time, I was finally ready to accept them exactly as they are. And now they aren't what they are anymore.

The mirror that just ruined my life is in the dressing room of a store I've previously refused to enter because I was offended by the mannequins in the window. Mannequins with long, slim, perfectly sculpted plastic legs. Mannequins that walk all over a woman's sense of well-being like a parade of seven-foot-tall Barbie dolls.

I was feeling too good about me to boycott today. I strode in on real-life legs I was finally mature enough to accept and love after all these years of being ashamed. I am through hiding, I declared this morning. Finished feeling "less than" because of some delusion that my lower half is "more than." I strode right past the perfect plastic legs in the window, right up to the summer shorts display, plucked a few cute pairs off the rack and was shown into a dressing room. The first pair I put on fit perfectly. I joyfully turned to the mirror to begin my Celebration of Me.

And here I am. Not celebrating. I'm staring at the worst my legs have ever looked in my life with the full, sick new knowledge that this is the best they're ever going to be. Fat legs can get thin. Cellulite-y legs can get smooth. Flabby legs can get toned. Old lady legs can't get anything except worse.

I want the legs I used to hate back! I want my untoned, over-weight young legs! The legs I hid from public view most of my life! Come back, horrid fat young legs! Come back! I am ready to love you now!!

My fat young legs don't come back. Neither does my skinny young salesperson, who swore she'd be back to get me anything I need. Why do they even offer? There's never anything women need when we're in a fitting room except for someone to shove some answers under the door.

Why are there 5,000 products to prevent eye wrinkles and nothing to prevent thigh wrinkles?

Why is there a zillion-dollar industry to deal with the aging of a few inches of face skin, but zip to deal with the aging of the many, many, many, many, many, many, many, many, many inches of leg skin?

Why are there clinics all over the globe to "plump" the lips, yet only shame if we on our own plump the hips?

I stare at my new old legs in the mirror. Swimwear has just been destroyed for an entirely new irreparable unthinkable reason, trumping the hundreds of ways legs have already destroyed swimwear for me up until now. This one can't be dieted or exercised away. Nothing can make old lady legs sticking out of a swimsuit look like anything but old lady legs sticking out of a swimsuit. Ditto shorts. Skirts and dresses would be possible, except we liberated ourselves from the tyranny of pantyhose years ago, and now have to display our age from at least the knee down when we wear them. The only thing that can possibly make old legs look worse is old legs in pantyhose worn to try to disguise old legs.

Even the wonderful Spanx Revolution missed the point. Old-fashioned control-top pantyhose used to control the top and then politely control and cover everything all the way down to the toes. Spanx stop above the hemline, leaving everything from the hem up looking youthful and smooth and everything from the hem down looking as if it's attached to an elderly relative.

Since the invention of stockings, no other generation of women has been expected to wear skirts and dresses with bare, aging legs. A complication of life that no one's protested because all the time we gained from not having to shop for pantyhose is now spent trying to figure out how to get out the front door without pantyhose. Longer skirts. Drapey capes. Self-tanners. Taller boots. Huge scarves that direct the eye to the neck instead of the knee.

I think of my mother, who used to apologize for giving me her thighs. Thighs I would be overjoyed to see again. Thighs *Mom* would be overjoyed to see again. She never talked about the day hers changed. Never shared the trauma of realizing how beautiful and perfect her legs used to be when she noticed they weren't beautiful and perfect anymore. She suffered in silence. Was it too horrible to mention? Did she want it to be a surprise?

I think of my daughter, who hates the perfect young legs she has right now. I want to shake her. I do not want to be silent. I want to show her my legs to warn her of the future. But showing her my legs would involve showing her my legs. Much as I love her, I've already suffered enough.

I put my pants back on without trying on the other pairs of shorts. I walk out without saying goodbye to the salesperson, walk away without even glaring at the Barbies, who are still showing off in the window.

In time, I'll accept my changed legs just as I've accepted all the other changed parts of me. I'll quit being sad about the places I didn't take them and the cute clothes I didn't buy them when I could. I'll forget how perfect they were back when I hated them. I'll even forget how bad they look today, because by then they'll be older and they'll look even worse.

I walk into a shop down the street. For today, I'll focus beyond the legs. I'll celebrate other parts of me. There are at least ten parts I can think of that are still stubbornly, heroically, mercifully un-changed by time.

"May I help you?" the woman asks.

"Yes," I say with pride, "I'd like to buy my lovely young toes a pedicure."

5.

THE ATTACK MOM

H i, Mom!"

I've waited two months to hear those words in person, to see my sweet college girl. I weave my way through the mass of people and their stuff in the Los Angeles airport baggage claim toward her waving hand popping up over the crowd. Only a mom's ears could hear "Hi, Mom!" through so much chaos from so far away.

The last time we were together, the sound coming from my daughter wasn't nearly as cheerful.

She said I treated her like a child. I said she shouldn't have left her new $65 sweat shirt wadded up on the living room floor.

She said I was too picky. I said if she leaves a half-eaten plate of macaroni and cheese on the counter for thirty-six hours and then puts it in the dishwasher without rinsing it off, it will not get clean.

She said I was controlling. I said I would disconnect her video game system if I found out she still hadn't started her psych paper.

She couldn't wait to go back to school. I couldn't wait for her to leave.

And now we can't wait to see each other.

My heart almost stopped when her caller ID popped up on my phone last week. She was calling instead of texting. Reaching out in the ancient verbal communication style of my people instead of the hip, silent, misspelled one of hers. She missed me . . . needed me . . . I grabbed the phone.

"Hey, Mom." That's all she had to say. I'm a mom-linguist at this point—can translate four hundred slightly different inflections of "Hey" and "Mom" into four hundred completely different meanings.

"I'll book you a flight home," I answered warmly, and heard many, many words of relief in her "Okay."

I'm weaving through airport people now as fast as possible. I've had time to rest and reflect, and have two months of things built up that I want to say. I can't wait to tell her how proud I am of how she's making it through her first year of college. How amazed I am by her bravery and determination. That I understand how hard she's working to figure out who she is independent from me.

I finally get through the crowd to where she's standing.

I stop to catch my breath, so grateful to see her. All my love and longing, my pride and admiration, my eagerness to have a relaxed, happy visit this time . . . It all wells up, ready to pour out. I put my hands on her shoulders to pull her close.

I listen, in sick disbelief, to the first words I say:

"Did you brush your hair today, honey?"

She stops smiling and glares. "MOM."

Incredibly, I continue. "It kind of looks like you just got out of bed." Every single thing is working in my brain except the off switch.

She takes a step back, leaving my loving hands poised in the air holding shoulders that aren't there anymore. Says flatly, "I like my hair."

"But it's kind of tangly and wadded up," I say, using my midair hands to gesture toward her mop. I'm watching myself as if in an out-of-body experience, doing exactly what I wasn't going to do. I hear myself make it even worse, if possible, by lifting my voice to a high, happy range so my words will sound light and loving and she won't interpret my criticism as criticism. "Why not just pull your hair up in a ponytail?" I singsong. "I have a brush in my purse if you want to—"

"You. Are. *So*. OCD." She cuts me off, scowling, and digs more deeply in to her side of the invisible line that just got redrawn between us.

"I was OCD enough to spend $145 on a salon appointment and

special shampoo for you before you returned to school last time!" I scowl back. "Is it too much to ask you to spend five minutes brushing your hair before you leave the house?"

"*Five minutes?* It does *not* take *five minutes* to brush hair, Mother!"

Her luggage hasn't even landed on the baggage carousel and we've already arrived home. Right back in our magical mom-daughter dungeon, where the deepest love on earth can instantly transform into a nit-picking free-for-all.

She pulls her phone out of her back pocket to get far, far away while she stands right next to me. I watch her disappear into her world and stop to catch my breath again.

—ð♡ε—

I fell in love with her long before she was born. I had been pregnant for forty-one years with the dream of her the day I first touched the tummy of her birth mother, who was eight months pregnant with the reality of her. One day before, I'd been quietly filing something in my office when a phone call knocked me to my knees.

"A birth mother came in today who'd like to meet you."

"What?" I choked back. I was single and terrified. I'd only signed up with an adoption facilitator a couple of months earlier and was still wrestling with whether I could or should really do this on my own.

Suddenly there I was, twenty-four hours later, with my hand touching the rest of my life through the shirt of an equally scared, unbelievably trusting stranger. In one day I'd gone from the dream of having a daughter "someday" to being half of a miraculous meeting of two moms—one who was bringing a little girl into the world; one who would take her through it.

I would say it isn't possible to describe the bond that grew between my daughter's birth mother and me in the four weeks that followed, except it felt to me, and I'm pretty sure to her too, that our bond was deep and immediate the minute we met. I will never be able to comprehend the selflessness of her love that made it possible for her to seek a life for her child she knew she couldn't provide. I can still hardly breathe when I think of the faith she put in me to be the mom she couldn't be. I drove my daughter's birth mother to the hospital when she went into labor. The admitting nurse asked if we were sisters. *So much more than that,* I've thought a million times since that night. We are so very much more than that.

I held her birth mother's hand while our daughter was being born. I fed the baby that suddenly belonged to both of us tiny bottles in the hospital nursery day and night until she was ready to come home. I made sure our daughter and her birth mother had time alone together in the hospital, and that the three of us had a little time together, too. Then I drove our daughter home by myself, just the two of us. I was so overwhelmed by the impossibly complicated emotion of driving her away from her birth mother, the incomprehensible joy and responsibility of becoming her life mother, that I couldn't stand to have anyone else in the car. I was on my own and thousands of miles away from any family. My daughter and I locked around each other deeply and completely, and have been each other's world ever since.

—❦♡♡❦—

I look at her now, engrossed in her iPhone with the two thousand Facebook friends she'd rather be with than me. I would do anything for my child. I would crawl across the earth on my hands and knees to help her. I would die for her. I would give her anything—my food, my blankets, my bed, my air, my home, my life. She is my life. I would do anything for her.

Anything, it turns out, except keep my mouth shut.

"Pull your shoulders back, honey. You're all slumpy." I've lost all ability to screen outgoing messages. I continue . . .

"Pull your tank top up! The world doesn't need to see your underwear. Suck your stomach in! You look . . ."

Her head whips up from her phone. "What? *Fat?* I look *FAT??*"

"No! Just . . . suck your stomach in!"

I've not only ruined our reunion, but probably the rest of the day. Still, I keep going . . .

"Don't chew on your nail! The airport's full of germs. Don't leave your purse unzipped! You could get robbed. Don't wipe your nose with your hand! Use a tissue."

I'm scanning her like a one-woman Homeland Security squad now. Scanning in reverse for all the unacceptable things she's brought off the flight with her, seeing every possible infraction with my X-ray mom eyes. Her jeans are too ripped, her flip-flops are too flip-floppy, her sweat shirt's dragging on the ground, disorganized papers are sticking out of her purse. And now, after months of my desperately missing her, she's texting someone instead of talking to me.

"Don't text someone instead of talking to me!"

"Duh . . . I was just letting my boyfriend know I got in okay."

"Don't say 'Duh'!"

"God, Mom."

"Don't say 'God'!"

"JEEZ."

"Don't talk with your mouth full!"

She doesn't have anything in her mouth. I'm simply on auto-attack. Too much is pent up, too little has sunken in. Also, I'm angry with myself for not instilling all the things I wanted to instill when I had some power over her. I had nineteen years to create a meticulously groomed, perfectly organized, impeccably mannered young woman, and I'm staring at . . . well, a nineteen-year-old. I'm angry with myself for ruining our reunion. Angry that I do this every single time I see her, even though every single time I see her, I promise I won't do it again. Do I have any choice but to stand here and attack?

Another big breath. Yes, it turns out. Yes, I do.

From the deep reservoir of maternal instincts, I manage to pull out the one concept guaranteed to create new life from the rubble of this moment. I think of the one thing I could say that promises to take this bad day and parlay it into something else.

Something much, much worse:

"Let's stop and get something to eat on the way home."

Ta-da.

I will take this highly combustible mother-daughter moment and throw the highly combustible issue of food on top of it. Under the guise of "comfort" I'll toss thousands of calories and carbohydrates and two hundred years of rejected rules of etiquette on top of the drama I've already created in our first five minutes together. I will go for explosion.

"Don't take such big bites!"

"Put down the fork while you chew!"

"Napkin goes on your lap!"

"No more rolls!!"

"Sit up straight!"

"That dressing just added five hundred calories to your salad!"

"Dessert? Really?? You think you need dessert?"

"Elbows off the table!"

"NO TEXTING WHILE WE'RE EATING!!!"

Attack Mom Smorgasbord. All she can eat, all I can critique.

We're not quite there yet, however. We're still standing in baggage claim, still waiting for suitcase number one. I look away from the restaurant scene I'm imagining in my head long enough to look at my daughter, who's apparently looked away from the screen on her iPhone long enough to read my mind.

"Um . . . Maybe I should just Uber home next time instead of having you pick me up, Mom."

I, having just destroyed our reunion and our day, and having thought of an event that could wipe out the rest of our visit, smile at my beautiful girl and answer as only a loving mom can:

"Don't be silly, sweetie," I say. "It might not be safe."

6.

THE DAY I OUTGREW
ALL MY SHOES

No warning, no slow dissolve, no preparation whatsoever. In the middle of the night, the unthinkable happened:

My feet outgrew all my shoes.

I went to bed a size 7. Woke up a size 8.

Went to bed Cinderella. Woke up Drizella, the big-footed stepsister.

The one and only part of my body I could count on to not get bigger—grew. The only things in my closet that fit perfectly no matter what—don't.

My feet are too big for them all.

I'm still reeling from the morning I woke up to the news. And it was supposed to be such a beautiful weekend . . .

Saturday, 9:00 a.m.

"We're leaving for the gym in three minutes!" I call to my daughter as I run down the hall. "I just have to put on my shoes!"

A sleepy groan comes from behind her door: "Mo-o-o-m . . ."

"NO GROANING!" I cut her off. "You've been blobbing on the couch watching TV this whole visit home! Come on! I'm just getting some shoes!"

"Why did you make me get up so early if you're not even dressed yet?" she grumbles.

"I'm just putting my shoes on!" I proclaim, shoving my foot into a workout shoe. "One sec!"

The shoe doesn't go on. It's too tight.

I loosen the laces, stick my hand inside to check for obstacles. Shake it out. Retry. Still too tight.

I grab a pair of comfy non-workout sneakers. Too tight.

I pull off my socks and try my happy run-around espadrilles. Too tight.

"How long does it take to put on a pair of shoes?!" she yells.

"CAN'T YOU GO BLOB ON THE COUCH AND WATCH TV LIKE A NORMAL TEENAGER??" I yell back, much more frustrated by the two great big new problems in front of me than I am by her.

I hear her little victory whoop as her rear lands on the couch. The TV clicks on.

The parenting books say a good mother always includes the child in challenging times so she can be a role model of how to cope with adversity. *How true,* I think.

I run to my bedroom door, yank it shut, and lock it.

I'm not a good mother. I'm a mother with big feet. There will be no modeling of roles in this happy house today. I march back to my closet. I reach in and cautiously lift one of my happiest go-everywhere, do-anything little slip-ons off the shoe shelf. I lower it to the floor and ever so gently slip it on and . . .

I stare down at the cold, barefooted truth.

It's too tight.

Saturday, 9:06 a.m.

I start ripping shoes off the shelf.

My feet are too big for the stunning red patent leather Valentine's Night pumps that I never actually had a chance to wear on Valentine's Night, but *still could someday!*

Too big for the sparkly New Year's Eve stilettos upon which I so hopefully perched.

Too big for the gladiator sandals that helped me march away from three stupid relationships.

Too big for the peep-toe wedges that strutted me right back into the arms of someone even worse!

Drizella gone mad. I squeeze my eyes shut. Momentary solace in blackness. I open them. *BROAD DAYLIGHT DISASTER IN BLACKNESS!* My feet are too big for all my beloved black shoes! Black flats . . . Black boots . . . *NOT THE BLACK HEELS!*

Yes! Too big for all eight pairs of virtually identical, yet completely unique, beloved black heels! Each one just distinct enough to make a totally different statement. Eight dialects of Black Shoe Speak, the language of Black Shoe Land—the minuscule inflection of heel height and strap placement and sole thickness . . . the meaning-specific amount of toe reveal . . . the precise degree of pointiness . . . The language handed down generation to generation, modified season to season . . . The complex subtleties of a thousand tongueless tongues that send a million powerful messages to the men who will never have any idea that anything's being said!

All that. All over. Every single pair too small for my giant Drizella size 8 boats.

Saturday, 9:17 a.m.

I pull a big open box from the back of the closet and hug it to me. A tear plops down on the magnificent all-weather fleece-lined riding boots inside the box, which never saw a stirrup, a horse, a barn, or a raindrop. I wipe it off. A flicker of pride that the tear didn't leave a salt or water mark since I spent $12.99 on a can of All Weather Leather & Suede Protector when I bought the boots, even though I had no intention of ever letting them touch the ground if it was wet or dirty out.

I stare at what's left in the closet. Grief stares back. My happy shoe shelves, now a footwear cemetery. All the other things in the closet that are too small—even the miniature jeans, even the insane plum-colored stretch-velvet holiday tube skirt—they all could be given new life with a little two-to-five-year commitment to the gym. Outgrown shoes are just dead. Shoes that don't fit anymore are never, ever going to fit again.

How poignant, suddenly, that so many are in funeral black.

"What are you *doing* in there??" My daughter rattles the locked doorknob.

Drizella on turbocharge. I speed-crawl to the bedroom door, lunge at the lock above the doorknob, and turn it. Click!

"Did you just do the *dead bolt*, Mom??"

"GO BACK TO YOUR FROOT LOOPS AND TV!"

"What are you *doing*??"

Well, she doesn't need to know, does she? Also, she doesn't need to see the spectacle of what could appear to be complete hypocrisy:

feminist mom kissing her hooker heels goodbye. I've spent almost two decades lecturing my daughter on how a person's value has nothing to do with what she wears. I don't have the energy to explain it's only *because* I'm a fully realized, triumphantly whole woman—who does not buy into the superficiality of footwear—that I can be so sad about . . .

"Mom?"

"GO AWAY. I DON'T NEED OR WANT MOTHER-DAUGHTER TIME RIGHT NOW!"

I hear her stomp off.

I crawl back to the shoe cemetery, pull out my phone, autodial *my* mother, and dump the whole morning on her.

"Oh, yes," Mom says with a knowing chuckle, "I remember when my feet suddenly got too big for all my shoes."

"*What?*" I say. "This happened to *you?*"

"I went to bed a size 7, woke up a size 8. It happens to all of us! I thought you knew!"

"How would I know *that*, Mom??"

"I thought they'd have a film or something about it in school."

I say goodbye to my mother and shake my head at her generation's trust in the public school system to teach girls the facts of life with cheerful films.

Saturday, 9:25 a.m.

I silently recommit to a life of open, loving heart-to-heart disclosure with my daughter—the one I've dead-bolted out of the room. I flash back to our first beautiful, emotionally honest facts-of-life session.

It was nine years ago. "You look all weird, Mom," my preteen daughter said.

I was sitting on my bed. My bedside table was preloaded with supplies: a single long-stemmed red rose, a stack of liberated-librarian-recommended Change of Life books, a box of tissues, a pint of mint chocolate chip ice cream, two spoons, and a DVD of *The Sound of Music.*

I patted the bed next to me. My daughter sat. "Yes, well—" I choked while ceremoniously laying the rose across her lap.

"OUCH!" she yelped after grabbing it and getting stabbed by a thorn.

"This is a special evening . . . " I continued as she wrapped her injured finger in one of my conveniently located tissues, "and I want to share some special books with you."

Anticipating how emotional the ceremony might get, I had pre-viewed all the books, highlighted some passages, and stuck colorful sticky notes on the many pages that had illustrations I wanted to thoughtfully explain. I lifted the stack of books tied together with a pretty pink ribbon and placed it between us. "The pink ribbon is for the childhood you'll soon be leaving behind, and the red rose is for the woman you'll soon become," I began.

My daughter skipped right over the symbolism and stared at the sticky notes sticking out from all sides of each book.

"Seriously, Mom?" She looked at me with totally-over-it preteen eyes. "Another one of your sticky-note talks?"

I lovingly ignored her lack of gratitude, untied the pink ribbon, put my arm around her shoulder, and bravely read *The "What's Happening to My Body?" Book for Girls* aloud.

"I want you to know you can ask me anything, honey," I said, closing the book, fighting back tears. "Anything. Do you have any questions right now?"

There was a long silence. And then . . . "Why all the books, Mom?" she asked. "They had a film about all this in school. Can I go watch TV now?"

I stayed in bed alone the rest of that evening. I put *The Sound of Music* in the drawer. I ate the pint of ice cream by myself, one spoon in each hand. When I was done, I reread all the books.

In case she ever had another question, I would be ready.

Saturday, 9:33 a.m.

I turn back to my shoe wasteland, metaphor for this special time of life. A closet full of pointy stiletto thorns stabbing my delusion that nothing's changed.

I pick up my open-toed, open-sided, open-backed, dainty ankle-strap-wrapped heels, which gave me shin splints and back pain and threw my whole body out of alignment, but which were going to make Rick Somebody or Other love me.

I pick up my first "career girl" pumps, which not only promised to give me the cool, professional authority of the big boys in the office, but which took three inches off my thighs.

I pick up my beloved royal blue satin sling-backs. I remember the night I committed completely enough to finally step off the carpet in them, the exact spot on the sidewalk where I felt the first scratch on their soles. It was the moment that made these shoes mine forever. Unreturnable. Like a first kiss. I remember how after that, I could walk into any room fearlessly if these sling-backs held my feet.

They aren't just shoes, after all. They're mini-marriages, performed in that most perfect wedding chapel, the shoe department. The only place on earth that has mirrors that only show the body from the knees down. Marriages cheered by shoe department strangers: *"Cute!" "I LOVE those!"* Blessed by friends and family, at least the female ones: *"Where did you FIND those?!" "They're PERFECT! PERFECT for you!"* Over a lifetime, hundreds of sacred ceremonies for the feet. Vows of commitment. Rationalizations recited like wedding poems.

Nobody told me the bride would wake up one day with middle-aged bone spread and have to walk away from every pair in giant fickle naked feet.

I hold up my silver Cinderella wedding shoes. I glow inside, remembering the one-mother-two-sisters-five-girlfriends-three-month-fifty-seven-shoe-store search for them. I parted with the man I married— but I will never ever part with the shoes that walked me down the aisle. Is that so wrong?

Then again, when have I ever given shoes away? The really worn ones have been down way too many roads with me. The hardly worn ones are still waiting for their big chance. The piles of shoes in between have exactly fit who I was the day I fell in love with them, an irreplaceable diary of my heart written in saucy boots, no-nonsense pumps, shiny stilts, goofy wedges.

Whose feet could I ever trust to walk in all these memories and dreams?

Deep breath. It takes a while . . .

Maybe my beloved shoes have brought me exactly as far as they should.

Maybe, I think, they've walked me right to this new rite of passage.

Saturday, 9:45 a.m.

Finally I call my daughter in.

I silently lead her to my closet. I was wrong to lock her out before.

This is exactly the time to share what's ahead more fully than my mom was able to share it with me.

I look at my great big little girl and her innocent nineteen-year-old size 7 feet. I put my arm around her and gesture toward my closet. On this dark day when all my shoes are lost to me, I see the light in her. My legacy. With my love and guidance, she can literally walk in my shoes.

And so I offer it all to her. My soul. My soles.

"Honey . . ." I start. "I want to talk to you about some big and beautiful changes, let you know it's not so scary, it's just part of life. Someday . . ." I pause. I'm so overwhelmed, I can barely speak. "Someday you'll stand at your closet just like this with a daughter of your own and you'll remember this moment with me. I'm passing all I know on to you, honey, just like you will one day pass it on to your daughter. That is, if you have them." I gesture tearfully. "Would you . . . would you like my beautiful shoes?"

She squints into my closet.

"Those?"

"Yes," I choke. "Remember when you were little, how your tiny three-year-old feet wobbled in my heels? All you wanted to do was pretend you were me." I gently nudge her toward the closet. "They're for you now, baby."

She squints more deeply. *"Those??"*

"Yes," I say tearfully. "All yours."

She leans down, peers at the closet floor, wrinkles her oh-so-cool, teen-fashionista nose.

"Eww," she says.

I snap out of my moment, certain that I misheard. "Excuse me?"

Her nose is still wrinkled, head shaking side to side.

"Eww."

I silently lead my daughter out of my room.

Close the door. Lock the doorknob. Flip the dead bolt.

Click.

Saturday, 9:59 a.m.

I walk back to my closet and sit back down on the floor.

After a while, I gently lift my beautiful silver Cinderella wedding shoe and hold it up in the light. The tiny pretend jewels on the strap sparkle like diamonds. I place part of one giant Drizella foot into it. I shut my eyes and dream. About all that came before and all that will come after.

I think about my mom.

Then I think about my girl. I smile.

One day her feet will outgrow all her shoes, but she will not have heard it from me.

7.

I WOULD WASH MY HANDS
OF THIS IF ONLY I COULD

n the prime of my life, at the pinnacle of my personal power, I have been rejected by another automatic hand-washing system in the ladies' room.

I wave my hand under the faucet to activate the water. Nothing.

I move to the next sink and wave. Nothing.

I move back to the sink that worked perfectly for the woman who used it right after it didn't work for me. Nothing.

I try the automatic soap dispenser. Nothing.

I glare at the towel dispenser but do not wave. I won't give it the satisfaction.

Powerful though I am, I apparently don't emit enough of an energy field to make the ladies' room sensors think there's a human in front of them. In this girl sanctuary, where women come to do many things, including reapply our self-esteem, I'm not even registering as a life-form.

I step away from the row of sinks.

I watch a four-year-old on tiptoes wave her tiny hand under the faucet and get water. Watch a mom wave a baby's even tinier fingers under the soap squirter and get soap. Watch an elderly woman wave two frail, almost transparent hands at the water, soap, and paper towel sensors and get everything she hoped for.

I step back up and try with a more can-do attitude. Nothing.

The public ladies' room has always been a humbling place. Waiting in the endless lines . . . praying that the toilets will flush . . . witnessing all the prettier women primping . . . *she's thinner, she's curvier, better hair, better clothes, better shoes, better everything* . . . facing the mirror ourselves . . . doing makeovers . . . rehearsing speeches . . . recovering from tears . . . checking, rechecking, checking, rechecking . . .

We go through enough in the ladies' room. No one should ever be rejected by the sink. We go through too much outside of the ladies' room, too. Way too many other situations in which things work completely differently for everyone else than they work for us. Way too many things over which we have no control—even tiny, insignificant things like this.

I glare at the faucets in front of me. Ashamed that I spent even one second letting them get to me. Ashamed that I spent one second feeling ashamed for letting them get to me. That's how it adds up. Sometimes at the end of the day, when I feel diminished and discouraged and don't know why, I think that what happened was the equivalent of a lot of little faucets in the world not working when I tried.

I reach into my purse, pull out a small plastic bottle, and squirt antibacterial hand sanitizer in my palms. Rub it in, give one last defiant look to the sensors that didn't sense me, and head for the door.

I'm almost out the door when I stop myself and turn around. I march back in and place my anti-bac bottle on the counter. Leave it there for the next victim of the sink. This is the ladies' room, after all. No lady should ever feel alone in here.

TOP FIVE REASONS
I DIDN'T EXERCISE TODAY

1. I don't want to admit how easy it would have been to start ten years ago.

2. I feel too fat.

3. It's too confusing to pick my activity.

4. I can't find a hair tie.

5. I exercised yesterday and I don't look any different.

8.

CAREGIVER STANDOFF AT
THE ICE CREAM PARLOR

MOTHER FATHER DAUGHTERS

S
ome families spend summer weekends at their cottage on a
lake.

Some go on annual retreats to a mountain lodge.

Some picnic under a favorite tree in the neighborhood park.

Beloved places and traditions that anchor a family in memories
and one another . . .

Our family comes here.

∂—◊◊◊—◊

Dad welcomes my two sisters and me with a sweeping gesture
and a proud voice, as he does each time we visit this place—as if he's

pointing out the captain and first mate deck chairs on a family sailboat.

"I'll be *there*, and Mom will be right *there!*" he announces.

But Dad isn't gesturing toward deck chairs. There's no boat. We're standing at the ultimate eternal vacation destination: the Family Plot.

"Um . . . nice, Dad!" one sister says, looking down at the big blank double patch of grass between other people's headstones with all the appreciation she's learned to muster from our previous hundred visits to the plot.

"Such a pretty place," the other sister echoes on cue, but looking up at the trees, not down at the grass under which Dad is so enthusiastically reminding us he and Mom will be planted.

They've been bringing us here for years, so we're more than a little numb to the emotion of it. We know it's a great comfort to them to have their affairs in order. Even more, we know it's a comfort to them to know it will be a comfort for us to have everything in order. We understand that's why they've not only made us visit this place, but the Whole Situation, over and over. They've thought of everything, arranged everything; planned for the end of life the same way people plan a wedding.

"Can we go home now?" the third sister—that would be me—mumbles.

"No need!" our joyful mom answers. "I brought the Folder in the car so we can stop for ice cream and review the details!"

Most people do some kind of end-of-life planning, but this is abnormal, I think, as our family gets situated at the large round umbrella table outside an ice cream shop in Sarasota, Florida, where we come after every plot visit. Dad with the double scoop of butter pecan ice cream he always orders, Mom with the modest scoop of raspberry sherbet she always has, my sisters and me with great big bowls of all the flavors of "we do not want to talk about this again." In the middle of the table, next to the tidy stack of extra napkins Mom always remembers to pick up, is the Folder—containing their neatly organized last wishes, cell phone number of the priest, funeral instructions, headstone inscriptions, drafts of their obituaries, the location of important records, donation preferences, and much more.

Dad's specific requests, like Dad, are exuberant, detailing lists of invitees and people to notify; noting that Milky Way candy bars and chocolate milkshakes should be served at the reception following his funeral. Mom's requests, like Mom, are reserved: one Bible verse, one short poem, and one "FOR HEAVEN'S SAKE DO NOT WASTE YOUR PERFECTLY GOOD MONEY ON A PARTY FOR ME WHEN I'M GONE! ABSOLUTELY NO PHOTO BOARD FULL OF PICTURES!" written in such large type it fills up a whole page.

Mom and Dad met at Kent State in their freshman year. Mom was a quiet first-generation college student from an Eastern European immigrant community in Cleveland. An earnest journalism major, with a love of books, ballet, opera, and art. Deeply devoted to her family and community, Mom took a bus home most weekends to help her parents in the small neighborhood restaurant/bar they owned. Dad was a song and dance man, creator and star of Kent State theater productions, part of a well-known local two-man comedy team—Guisewite & Mouse—and president of his class. He swept Mom off her demure little feet, just like in the movies. And here they are a lifetime later, just like in the movies. Mom's graciousness and Dad's gregariousness blended somehow into a team that has ushered my sisters and me through life with a way of looking at almost everything with hope and humor.

This explains why the dreaded grief-filled Folder that's lying in the middle of the ice cream parlor table in front of us is labeled "The Grand Finale!" in cheery bright red pen. As though it contains the program for a thrilling event, not the details for one of the most dreaded ones. Details our parents have meticulously planned so my sisters and I will never have the wrenching experience of not knowing what to do because no one could stand to discuss it.

After a few bites of sherbet, Mom puts down her spoon, picks up the folder, and begins the familiar review for my sisters and me.

"Do NOT let them talk you into an upgraded casket!" she proclaims. We've heard this speech so many times, we could recite it in unison. "We've prepaid for cheap ones! Nice, basic, cheap! Don't let them prey upon your emotions and talk you into something with a bunch of frills we don't want!"

"We will not care how the casket looks after we've croaked!" Dad adds. "Also, don't let some overeager funeral director convince you to spring for an expensive celebration-of-life venue! No kickbacks to fancy caterers and florists! The church social hall is just fine!"

"But not for me!" Mom reminds us, flipping to her No Party page. "Remember: Under no circumstances is there to be a big party for me!"

"Of course they'll have a party for you! Your girls love you!" Dad counters, as he always does.

"My instructions clearly state NO PARTY!" Mom replies, as she always does, waving the page in the air. "I will NOT stand for a party!"

"Well, you won't be standing, but if I'm still here, there's going to be a party for you! A beautiful party with pictures and a video!" he insists with a charming song-and-dance-man grin, reaching over to give his bride a loving squeeze.

"NO!" Mom protests, waving her page more vigorously in the air. "NO PICTURES! NO VIDEOS! NO MAUDLIN SONGS! Absolutely no sneaking around behind my dead body!"

This devolves into the regular discussion of which one of them is likely to "croak" first . . .

Which devolves into a new round of promises that the sisters will listen to the wishes of the deceased parent, not the wishes of the non-deceased one . . .

Which wraps up, finally, in a long, long, long review of where every single piece of paper pertaining to anything important is located. Followed by a rereading of their wills and powers of attorney. Followed by the whispered verification that we've all memorized the location of every hidden key as well as the secret combination to their safe, which contains duplicate copies of everything we've just discussed for the hundredth time . . .

My sisters and I come to Florida often to visit Mom and Dad. We usually come separately so we can have our own time with them, but also so our trips will be spaced out and there won't be long periods with no one seeing how they're doing. They're both amazingly healthy, but every birthday makes us more nervous to live so far away. We had a sister conference recently and decided to make this visit together so we could bring our own uncomfortable topic to the ice cream table. We rehearsed how to present it with the flair and good nature we learned from our parents. Surely these optimistic, pragmatic people, who have so carefully planned for everything, who are so open to discussing all the icky topics, will appreciate what we want to do just as we appreciate all they do to protect us.

Mom is tucking the last pages of their end-of-life review back into the Grand Finale! folder. I exchange a nod with my sisters, open my oversize purse, and pull out a folder the three of us have prepared.

"You're doing so beautifully, Mom and Dad," one sister begins.

"You've thought of everything for us, and now we've thought of something for you!" the other sister continues.

"And now," I say, proudly, holding up our folder labeled in an equally cheery bright red pen, "we present 'The Next Adventure!'"

Mom and Dad go blank. Before I can stop him, Dad plucks the folder from my hand and pulls out one of the several pamphlets inside.

"Assisted-living facility?" he asks, staring at the pamphlet, looking as stunned as he sounds.

"No, no, Dad!" I answer, trying to speak with even more lilt in my voice. "Let's think of it as the *Next Adventure!*"

"Graduated care community??" Mom asks, sounding equally stunned as she picks a different pamphlet out of the folder.

"It's nothing you need *today*, but things could start to change, and we think it's time to plan for the Next Adventure!" I whip my head toward my sisters, silently imploring them for backup. *"Don't we??"* My sisters are useless. Caught off guard and struck mute by our parents' bad reaction. Either that or they're simply relieved that I, not they, have the floor and are happy to let me flounder on my own.

I try to summon the inner resolve I had when I was preparing my daughter for the beautiful life changes that awaited her, but I'm no match for the parental unit. Mom's ninety years of experience have somehow enabled her to achieve a geriatric glare and a preteen stink-eye at the same time, so it's as though both my mother and my daughter are staring at me through the same face.

I wince and look at Dad, which is even worse. World War II Veteran, Eagle Scout, Man of the House, Rock of the Family, Provider Extraordinaire, Protector and Defender of Everyone.

"What do you think we can't handle in our own home?" Superman asks flatly.

"Um . . . it's just that you and Mom have worked so hard taking care of a big house by yourselves your whole lives," I try. "It might be wonderful to live someplace where you could have some help now."

"We don't need help," he answers curtly.

"It could be fun to look at some options." One sister finally rallies and opens a pamphlet on the table.

"We don't want options," Mom answers without even glancing down.

I look at the pretty pamphlet my sister spread out. It's logical and colorful and uncomplicated by emotion. The residents in it are happily doing group craft projects in one shot, gratefully hugging the children who helped them relocate into such a nice safe place in another. So easy. So worry-free. So not how our situation is unfolding.

"There are so many resources for older people!" My other sister comes to life and accidentally blurts out the worst possible thing.

Without a word, Mom stands, gathers everyone's trash, marches inside the ice cream shop with it, returns with a squirt bottle of multisurface cleaner and paper towels, and cleans the tabletop. Dad rises from his chair without any of his usual effort, his arthritic back, knees, and hips suddenly as strong and flexible as a young man's. He grips his Grand Finale! folder in front of him across the table from where I grip our Next Adventure! folder. We stare at each other's cheery bright red words.

Caregiver standoff at the ice cream parlor.

And then our dear parental units, who've spent the last twenty years preparing themselves and us for the end of life, who've made us sit through hours of agonizing reviews, who've hauled us to the Plot . . . Those beloved college sweethearts head back to the handicapped spot in which their car is parked and make their discussion-ending victory statement over their shoulders:

"We'll get back to you when we're older."

9.

CORDS

Bring your laptop to the dining room, Dad! I'll help you set up bookmarks!"

Having verified that our parents will not be moving to an independent living community any time soon, my sisters returned to their homes in different states. I've stayed behind to try to help Mom and Dad at least be more efficient in this house.

"Are you coming, Dad?" I call again.

No response. I walk down the hall to the home office Dad shares with Mom. Command Central for all the critical business of their days. It's half the size of a spare bedroom, with two desks, two swivel chairs, two file cabinets, two computers (one desktop, one laptop), reams of paper, multipacks of tape, staples, pencils, file folders, and many "pending" piles. A room so full of meticulous records from the past and supplies for the future that if one parent's sitting at one desk and the other wants to get to the other desk, they both have to stand and sort of twirl around for the second person to squeeze through. The dance they've done a million times in their sixty-five-year marriage. The dance I would have done with my husband a maximum of two times before renting office space across town.

I look in the doorway.

Mom's staring at the most recent 50 of 25,384 messages in the email in-box on her desktop monitor. Deleting an electronic note from someone—even a nice invitation to a shampoo sale at Walgreens drugstore—seems as rude to her as throwing a thank-you note from a grandchild in the trash. Filing an email is out of the question—*I'll never find it if it's in a file! It has to be right here in the in-box!*—which partly explains why so many of their careful record-keeping systems are out in the open, covering every surface of the room.

Dad doesn't trust his computer's memory to remember anything, so he's writing notes to himself on the back of a used envelope. Two seniors squashed into their mini-headquarters with sixteen gigabytes of available disk space and zero inches of any other kind of available space.

I've learned to appreciate the hustle and bustle that goes on in this little office that gives my parents purpose: Get the birthday card off to the nephew! Double-check the arithmetic on the bank statement! Confirm dental appointments! Start worrying about holiday dinner reservations in June!

I've even learned to appreciate the unfinishedness of it all. My proud mom and dad are surely not going to pass away any time soon and leave this big mess for someone else to see. I smile at the piles that must be helping keep them healthy enough to avoid *that*. But there are a couple of things I can upgrade . . .

"Bring your laptop to the dining room table, Dad!" I say, stepping into the overflowing room. "We'll have more space to work in there!"

Dad stares at me. Stares at his computer. Stares back at me.

I reach to pop the power cord out of its magnetic port on the side of his laptop.

"DON'T UNPLUG THE COMPUTER!" he cries out, looking as horrified as if I were about to disconnect life support.

"It's a laptop, Dad." I laugh, reaching for the plug again to demonstrate. "Remember? It doesn't have to be plugged in!"

Dad swivels to block me with his full five-foot-five, 130-pound mass, arms outstretched. "THE BATTERY WILL GO DEAD!" he declares.

"The battery can last for seven hours!" I shake my head with another little laugh.

"THE BATTERY MIGHT NOT BE CHARGED!" he insists.

"It's been charging for three years!"

"IT'S ALL HOOKED UP TO THE PRINTER!"

"Look, Dad," I say, leaning in again, "you can simply unplug the . . ."

Dad rises up now, all ninety years of How Things Should Be aimed right at me. *"DON'T UNPLUG THE PRINTER!"*

Without even turning from her email screen, Mother plucks the portable blood pressure monitor off the shelf next to her and hands it behind her back to Dad—a gesture as familiar as passing a tissue after a sneeze.

I take a step back and continue as gently as possible. "The printer doesn't need to be plugged into the computer at all, Dad! It can be wireless! We could change the settings and you could print from anywhere in the house!"

Why I think expressions like *wireless, change settings* and *print from anywhere* are appropriate to use with a ninety-year-old already taking his blood pressure, I'll never know. I must be so pleased to be the computer expert in the room, instead of the computer idiot I am when I'm with my daughter, that I'm interpreting Dad's frozen look as rapt attention, not the panic that it actually is.

"You and Mom don't even have to have your own printers for your own computers!" I continue. "You could both be connected to one printer that's not even in the office! You could print wirelessly from the hall closet!"

This causes Mom to grab the *OS X 10.3 Made EZ* library book she checked out off the shelf and start furiously flipping through the pages trying to look up what on earth I'm talking about. Dad's retaking his blood pressure.

His laptop isn't merely plugged in; it's locked down. He "installed" the laptop on his desk by anchoring the power cord to the desktop with duct tape fifteen minutes after my sisters and I presented it to him three years ago. The laptop hasn't moved an inch one way or the other since. Certainly has never gotten near Dad's lap. We bought it for him when he was sick a few years ago, thinking it would lift his spirits to be able to track weather disasters and stock market plunges online right from his bed.

"Look, Dad!" we said, placing the laptop on the bed next to him, "you can track weather disasters and stock market plunges online right from your bed!"

"THE BATTERY WILL GO DEAD!!" Dad exclaimed, eyes wide and worried.

We plugged the laptop into the outlet behind his nightstand.

"IT WON'T WORK IN HERE!" he announced, propping himself up against the pillows and gesturing down the hall. *"THE INTER-NET IS IN THE OTHER ROOM!"*

We patiently explained that the Internet is flying around in the air somewhere.

"THE NEIGHBORS COULD GET ON OUR SYSTEM AND LOOK AT OUR PRIVATE FILES!" he protested.

We closed the bedroom blinds to trap the Internet indoors.

"THERE'S NO PLACE FOR THE PRINTER!" He waved his arms hopelessly. *"THE PRINTER HAS TO BE ATTACHED!"*

Dad finally became so frustrated by our lack of knowledge about how things work that he rose from his sick bed, marched down the hall to Command Central, planted his new laptop on his desk, and secured the cords in position with duct tape, and that was that.

And now this is this. Dad has taken his blood pressure four times in a row, which he knows full well—but has forgotten—will give false readings and make his blood pressure actually go up when he sees the inaccurate numbers. Mom accidentally hit some key with her elbow that made her entire email in-box disappear and is flipping even more furiously through *OS X 10.3 Made EZ*, trying to figure out where it went. I'm about to assert myself and take charge when the phone rings.

When the phone rings in Mom and Dad's house, everything stops.

Meals. Conversations. TV shows. Naps. Baths. Dishes. Everything. They've never once "let the machine get it" if they were home. Superman can't stand to not pick up in case it's an emergency and he's needed to save somebody. Mom can't stand to inconvenience the answering machine when she's perfectly capable of answering it herself. Also, she doesn't like to "fill up the tape" in case someone needs more space in the future for a longer message, should she ever let anyone leave one.

Mom leans over some papers to grab the telephone receiver attached with a curly cord to the base unit attached to the landline cord attached to the phone jack on the wall behind her desk. Dad jumps up and hurries down the hall to grab the phone that's screwed into the wall in the kitchen. They like to both be "on" at the same time. My sisters and I have bought and returned four different cordless phone systems over the years. We've presented each one with love and rationale.

US: Look! You could each keep a receiver near you! You could both be "on" from your chairs in the living room! So much safer than jumping up and running to another room when the phone rings!

THEM: *THE BATTERIES WILL GO DEAD!*

US: You could answer calls from the bathroom!

THEM: *CALLERS ARE NOT ALLOWED IN OUR BATHROOM!!*

US: You could walk around doing other things while you talk! You wouldn't have to stand two feet from the wall or desk to have a conversation!

THEM: *WHY WOULD WE DO OTHER THINGS WHILE WE TALK ON THE PHONE?*

And there we have it. The great big disconnect.

I stand in the hall between the office, where Mom's on, and the kitchen, where Dad's on, and try to remember the last time I was on a phone when I wasn't also doing other things. I used to keep my friends' phone numbers and birthdays in my head. Now I keep a mental list of which friends will and won't be offended when I'm washing dishes, doing errands, or checking email while we talk. At least I know the people I irritate.

My daughter is friends with a universe of strangers, people she's never met in countries she's never been to: great big global groups of Facebookers, bloggers, and gamers. Attachments are fragile and fickle, and all in the air. Landlines don't exist. Single-tasking is ancient history. Human contact is to be avoided whenever humanly possible.

Mom and Dad make weekly pilgrimages to the bank to visit the people guarding their money. They know their bank tellers' names and wedding anniversaries and how it's going with the recent foot surgery. My daughter never goes inside a bank. Has never even spoken to a drive-up teller. Money comes out of an ATM on the sidewalk; money goes in by snapping photos of birthday checks on the kitchen counter and clicking *deposit*.

Mom and Dad shop in stores, eat in restaurants, and buy tickets for upcoming plays and ballets at the theater box office in person. Dad doesn't even like to drop mail in the mailbox that's in front of the post office. He likes to park, go inside, and hand his letters right to a U.S. Postal Worker he knows by name.

My daughter shops, returns, buys tickets, pays bills, and orders takeout online. She scans and bags her own groceries in the self-check-out area at the supermarket. She's been in a post office once, when I tried to force her to learn how to buy stamps for the thank-you notes I forced her to write by hand. Never even made it to the counter. "They have machines, Mom!" She pointed and, before I could stop her, ran to the self-serve machine in the lobby and came back waving a sheet of generic metered first-class postage stamps over her head like a millennial victory flag.

"But you can pick out pretty stamps at the counter!" I implored, trying to pull her toward the long line of people my age and older who were waiting for a person to wait on them. "The postal worker can show you all the pretty stamps and you can pick the ones that match the sentiment of the notes you're sending!"

My daughter looked at me with the same sick disbelief as the day the credit card reader wasn't working on the gas pump where she stood trying to fill the tank of her car.

"The credit card thing isn't working on the gas pump!" she wailed through the window of the passenger seat where I sat.

"Walk inside the gas station and give your card to the person behind the counter," I answered as patiently as I could.

"WHAT?!" she recoiled.

"There's a *person* inside! Give your credit card to the *person!*" I said less patiently.

"WHAT?! I'm not dealing with some random dude!" She got back in the car, slammed the door, and started the engine. "I'll drive to a different station where things work! Seriously, Mom? The *person??!*"

Mom and Dad are brick and mortar. Face-to-face. Grounded. When Mom and Dad are with friends, no one's twitching to check text messages or Instagrams. People are fully there when they're there, plugged in to the moment and one another. Relationships are anchored, connected by all those visible and invisible cords. Is that why the friendships, marriages, and sort of everything else, including all the cars and appliances made by their generation, seemed to last a lot longer?

I think a little wistfully that the last cord that connected my daughter to something that really mattered was the umbilical one. What will keep the people in her world attached to each other or anything else when the people in my parents' and my world are gone? I want my daughter to know the strength and clarity of not wandering that far from the base unit that's helped make my parents' relationships so solid and my life so secure. I want her to stay connected to the power source of principles, values, faith, and family that will help her be grounded and safe.

But I also want my parents to experience the thrill of unplugging. They might not ever be ready for the wonder of carrying the *Encyclopedia Britannica* in a smartphone in their pants pockets and aprons, but they could at least experience the freedom of taking a phone call on the front porch with the World Wide Web on their laps.

I want, for one minute of my life, to not feel right in the middle.

Mom and Dad are off the phone now and have returned to their respective posts in Command Central. I watch them get back to work, resuming the business of the day with the tenacity of busy young executives, a ten-year supply of paper clips, rubber bands, and manila envelopes stacked on the shelves beside them. I'm moved to tears by all that's come out of this little room and the great big plans for the future still being dreamed up by the two people working away so diligently at the items on their lists.

I take a moment to collect myself and to gather a couple of things I suddenly need. I walk back in and reach toward Dad's laptop again.

"Here, Dad," I say, cutting a long piece of duct tape from the roll I picked up on my way in. "It's been a long time since you got those cords anchored down. Let's give them a nice fresh layer of tape."

10.

AT LEAST I DIDN'T EAT A DONUT

Morning. 10:00 a.m.: Walk to the kitchen and open the refrigerator, where I keep my bag of organic raw almonds. Carefully count out fifteen almonds and place them in a little treat cup to carry back to my desk for the good-for-me snack that will keep me focused and productive for two more hours until lunchtime.

10:01: Toss all fifteen almonds in my mouth and eat them before the refrigerator door closes. My feet never even move.

10:01:30: Hate myself.

10:01:35: Forgive myself. The recommendation is for "a handful of almonds per day," and I have smallish hands, so I probably should have had twenty almonds, not fifteen. I help myself to five more.

10:01:45: Pause to consider the possible meanings of "handful." A small pile in the middle of a small hand? A medium pile in the middle of a small hand? A large pile in the middle of a medium hand? Might my hand be medium, not small? I eat ten more almonds to make sure I'm nutritionally complete.

10:03: Hate myself.

10:03:15: Scrutinize the Nutrition Facts panel. The label says *Serving size 33g.* It's a 16-ounce bag. *13.7 servings per container.* I throw six more almonds in my mouth to compensate for the aggravation of having to read numbers that make no sense.

10:03:45: Pour the rest of the bag on the counter and divide the remaining almonds into 12.7 small piles, since there are supposed to be 13.7 servings per bag and I probably already ate one serving this morning. I subtract the number of almonds I might have eaten in the previous days I've owned the bag, and eat any almonds which could affect the math:

Broken almonds must be eaten because they don't count as full almonds.

Over- and undersize ones must be eaten because they throw off calculations.

Oddly shaped ones must be eaten so they don't feel rejected.

10:04:30: Nine perfectly matched almonds remain. Nine is nowhere near anyone's version of a serving size, but seems appropriate for a much-deserved celebratory snack for all my effort. I scoop the nine almonds into my treat cup. Quickly seal the top of the cup with plastic wrap to prevent the almonds from accidentally spilling into my mouth on the long five-second walk back to my desk.

10:05: Never mind.

10:06: Sit at my desk. Glare at my empty treat cup. Check my stats on my Fitbit app: I've walked thirty-seven steps. Eaten approximately 1,100 calories. Burned seven calories. One hour, fifty-four minutes until lunch.

At least I didn't eat a donut.

11.

THE BUILD-A-BOOB WORKSHOP

Yesterday, the Build-A-Bear Workshop.

Today, the Build-A-Boob Workshop.

How much can one mom take?

"We were just *there*," I say wistfully to my daughter, hoping she'll turn and look where I'm pointing in the mall—two stores down and eleven years back in time. "You were staring through the Build-A-Bear window, begging for tiny pink outfits for a little teddy bear!"

My daughter isn't turning and looking.

"Remember?" I say, smiling warmly, hoping to draw her back to the hundreds of precious hours we spent holding hands in this mall, browsing for dreams, negotiating her childhood. "Remember how you cried and cried when I wouldn't buy that last little pink tutu for your bear because you didn't make your bed all week?"

She isn't remembering, isn't smiling, isn't drawn back.

She's in a teen trance, staring through the extremely different store window in front of us at tiny pink outfits for extremely grown-up humans. This isn't the first time we've been here, but it never, ever gets easier. I reach out to put a hand on her shoulder to remind her how deeply we're still connected . . . but before my hand can land, my baby rushes away from me, through the store door, into the arms of a mostly naked mannequin.

Come back! I silently scream after her. *I'll buy you the tutu for the bear! I'll make your bed for you for the rest of your life! JUST STEP AWAY FROM THE HOT PINK PADDED PUSH-UP POWER BRA WITH MATCHING MAGENTA MICRO-THONG!!!*

I would be screaming out loud and hauling her to the exit except she's nineteen. I can't lift her. Also, there's that preparing-to-be-deserted, pre-grieving-mom part of me that's just so grateful to still be included in anything. Even if what she's dreaming of decorating today is as far from a teddy bear as my mortified mom-brain can imagine.

She wouldn't have heard me anyway. She's already turned from the mannequin and is under the spell of a Victoria's Secret Sales Hottie. A Sales Hottie holding out a giant black mesh bag she wants to help my baby fill with "Cu-u-ute!" things more provocative than my wedding lingerie. Nothing, absolutely nothing, a mother can hold out at this point to compete with that.

"What size boobs do you want?"

The Sales Hottie doesn't actually use those words, but that's what she means.

In this bustling fantasyland, one can turn perfectly nice, God-given As into sassy Cs. Lovely Bs can become dramatic Ds. The alphabet can go on and on . . .

I look at my grown-up little girl gazing at the Sales Hottie with the same sparkly, believing eyes that used to gaze upon Snow White at Disneyland. I try to comprehend how this is happening. It isn't just the shock that she grew up. It isn't just the grief that the world lost its innocence and modesty right when my baby's launching into her first fragile years of womanhood. It isn't just the guilt that my generation of women is the first in history to have the freedom and resources to point our daughters in a whole new direction and that our daughters are choosing to rush en masse to sexy lingerie.

Well, yes. Actually, it is sort of that last one. I have enough on me without also having to feel responsible for helping create the freedom for my little angel to think it's a statement of self-worth to spend $70 on a bra that makes her look like the other kind of "angel," the one in a lingerie catalog. All those years she curled up on my lap at bedtime, the thousands of times I whispered to her sweet, sleepy head as I kissed her good night that anything was possible . . . was I supposed to be more specific?

I try to find a place to stand. Too close and I humiliate her. Too far away and I humiliate myself by appearing to be shopping for something for me. There's absolutely no direction I can look without making eye contact with the fact that life as I knew it is over.

The Hottie is pulling out enhancement choices, as if the only universal wish is for bigger. There isn't one bra on display that doesn't embellish someone's size and make the shopper, at least subconsciously, feel that exactly who she is isn't enough. This is *not* what my proud generation meant by a woman having more choices.

The Hottie is demonstrating to my baby that she can not only pick what size and shape she'd like her womanhood to be, but exactly where on her chest she'd like to position it. This is *not* what we meant by options!

The Hottie is showing her how to make her own powerful personal statement by changing the angle of the flirty straps in back so she can change the angle of the flirty situation in front—as though nothing my generation said about a woman not being defined and valued by the size of her cleavage got through. As though enough of a woman's money and brainpower doesn't already get wasted trying to get a guy's attention.

I shut my eyes for a minute to regroup. I try to erase the memory of all the money and brainpower I've wasted trying to get a guy's attention. I try to eradicate all memory of all men.

And yet who can stand here in this underwear emporium, surrounded by these sultry getups, and not think of men? Provocative scenarios start racing through my mind:

What if men had a store full of the equivalent of padded push-up bras for their manhood and peer pressure from their entire generation to shop there? Hah.

What if most of men's clothes were designed for their manhood to peek out a little bit and men had to spend time each day recalculating which piece of their underwear wardrobe would reveal the appropriate amount of themselves to everyone at the office, PTA meetings, and church? Hah.

What if a man with the equivalent of a God-given A bought lingerie that made him the illusion of a dramatic D, and then got to the part of the evening where he was supposed to take his clothes off???? HAH!

"You look all sweaty, Mom," my daughter says, glancing over from the Bombshell Bra—Adds Two Cup Sizes! she's squishing between her fingers like Play-Doh.

"Yes, well, I was just . . ." I start to answer, but never mind. She doesn't want to hear my fantasies any more than I want to hear hers. We're honoring the Mother-Daughter Code of Silence today. She knows it's best not to share how excited she is to be shopping for Really Big Girl Underwear. I know I can't share how mortified I am that she's doing it or any of my opinions about the cultural collapse I believe the entire women's underwear industry represents.

Either truth would ruin what we have, which is this last little sliver of time on earth when she's still young enough to want my approval almost as much as she wants my credit card. This sweet, aching time when she needs and wants me to give her permission to grow up.

I've spent nineteen years arming my daughter with a sense of self-esteem built on the values of hard work, integrity, and kindness. I enshrined every good report card on the refrigerator door, recorded every heroic science fair effort. I wept at the dance recital when, after four years of trying, she was finally brave enough to tiptoe onto the stage. I showered her with praise the day she wrapped a favorite doll to give to a sick neighbor, cheered and cheered the day she made the honor roll.

The Sales Hottie has spent thirty seconds teaching her how to make her boobs double in size.

My daughter likes the Hottie more than she likes me now. She'd go home with her if she could. The Hottie is not all awkward and weird like I vowed I wouldn't be but still am. The Hottie feels no need to pair each bra with a speech about how women foster sexism with the mix'n'match messages they wear. She announces style numbers into her magic headset in a loud, nonconflicted voice, summons miracles from the secret back room, pulls non-God-given cleavage out of cute little drawers.

I hate her.

I try to peek around to see if there are any kindred spirits in the store, but I still don't want to look as if I'm looking at anything, so I peek out the sides of my eyes without actually moving my eyes to the sides, which must make me appear even more insane than I feel. So often all I'm ever searching for at the mall is someone like me. Someone who matches me.

ISN'T THERE ANYONE IN THIS STORE WHOSE INNER CONFLICT IS THE SAME SIZE AS MINE??! I fought for a universe in which women aren't sexually repressed, but I didn't mean *THIS.* I prayed my daughter would have a healthy body image, but I didn't mean in *THAT.* I rally against . . .

"Mom, will you come in the dressing room with me?"

Everything stops.

I've been invited into the Room.

I turn toward my daughter and nod quickly, too moved to speak. I follow silently, winding past displays and, finally, through the Door. I watch the Sales Hottie take my little girl's fantasies out of her giant black mesh bag and display them on the wall. I watch my daughter lock the door after the Hottie leaves and turn to me with a nervous smile.

She wiggles into item number one and I instinctively reach to help. I look at my hands adjusting her lacy hot pink straps, and for a second I see my own mom's hands—carefully sewing tiny loops in the shoulders of all my summer tops to save me from the embarrassment of someone accidentally seeing a tiny white bra strap. For another second, I'm back in a department store dressing room with Mom, way back when underwear was underwear, dying of embarrassment that my mother was even seeing me in a bra.

Could life be any different now? I watch my baby fuss with the tiny hooks and bows. It isn't just my blessing she wants. She needs me to help her fit. Literally, help her fit into a world that's as far away as I can imagine from the one in which I grew up. A world that seems so much more complicated and scary now that my generation has freed hers from the repressive rules that were so clear and so safe.

She turns to face the mirror.

Our eyes meet in her reflection. Hers are all sparkly, just like when she saw Snow White at Disneyland. Mine are so full of so much, I can hardly see.

All I can think is how much I wish we could go two doors down and build a bear.

12.

INFIDELITY

I woke up with the exhilarating urge to cheat on my Fitbit fitness tracker.

What if I sneak outside and start walking without wearing it on my wrist? I could walk anywhere and it won't know. I could stop after an eighth of a mile, sit at an outdoor café with a 450-calorie cold-pressed mango smoothie, and watch YouTube videos for twenty minutes.

It won't note my slowed heart rate. It won't obsessively calculate calories or track pounds gained or lost based on the "profile weight" I entered, which may or may not have resembled what my profile weighed the day I started. It won't note anything because it won't *know.*

I stride out the front door. Scroll to the Fitbit app on my phone and laugh right into its little dashboard. "HAH! I am cheating on you today! I'm going for a walk without your tracking one thing about me. I left my wristband on the kitchen counter! I'm free!"

My eyes flash, wide and triumphant.

The wide, triumphant flash causes my left bifocal contact lens to dislodge. I blink to keep it in place, which makes both eyes get teary, which makes both lenses swivel. By the time all the blinking and swiveling is done, the bifocally part of the lenses is positioned better than before, and when I squint back at the screen I realize I've just delivered the whole life-affirming speech to my frozen yogurt loyalty app icon.

No matter. I'm liberated. The first steps are giddy. I'm walking on my own two feet and no one's keeping track.

Block number two: I look around. Is anyone watching how I'm walking with no one watching me walk?

Block three: I do a tentative little hand wave. *Look at me! Nothing on my wrist! I'm walking without anyone watching me! Someone look at me!*

By block four, it's all I can do not to scream out to complete strangers. *LOOK! I'M CHEATING ON MY FITBIT WHILE MY FITBIT APP'S RIGHT HERE IN MY FANNY PACK! IT'S BOUNCING ALONG WITH EVERY STEP BUT IT DOESN'T KNOW IT BECAUSE I LEFT THE WRISTBAND AT HOME! IT WILL NEVER EVEN SUSPECT! LOOK AT ME!!*

Is it possible to experience anything in the twenty-first century without an audience? This is what I wonder in block number five.

I stop to Google the question, hoping that if passersby aren't amazed that I'm walking without tracking, they'll at least give me credit for pausing for a runner's cramp. Before I can click Google, I see a new message from Fitbit: *"One step at a time! Get moving!"*

I sit on the curb.

"Runner's cramp!" I call toward six women in Tour de France spandex who streak past on skinny little bikes pretending they're not impressed.

"I *have* been moving!" I hiss to the iPhone screen. "I already walked five blocks!"

Another message from Fitbit bings in. *"Motivate your day!"*

"I don't need motivating!" I hiss back. "I've been walking without telling you!"

"Take a quick 250! Let's go!"

Now I *am* screaming out loud. "I WANT CREDIT FOR CHEATING ON YOU! I WANT CREDIT FOR CHEATING ON YOU!"

I glance up. A woman pushing a stroller careens sharply to steer her baby to the non-me side of the street, her Chihuahua racing beside her too terrified to bark.

"DON'T BE AFRAID!" I shake my phone in the air toward the frightened family. "I HAVE A CRAMP! I HAVE A CHEATING-ON-MY-TRACKER CRAMP!!"

I look down the street. Even the cars have quit coming this direction. Waze must have sent out an alert that there's a lunatic sitting on the curb.

I'm all alone. At the end of block five. Zero witnesses. Zero accountability.

One hundred percent unobserved, unsettling freedom.

I try and fail to embrace my emancipation. With nobody watching, it seems so empty to go on. What's the point if no one will know?

I consider downloading a different app that tracks directly from the phone without a wristband and recording my walk from here . . . but I wouldn't get credit for the five blocks I've already gone. I consider going home, putting on my Fitbit wristband, and starting all over, but even to me, who's spent the last nine minutes of my workout sitting on a curb, starting over would feel like quitting.

I think about the years ahead, with all the people and places changing and the likelihood that I'll need to take many, many steps with zero possibility that anyone will care to record them. I think of the millions of things in life I've been afraid to try alone so far. I think of all the people who forge ahead on all kinds of dreams without a tracker, an app, or a support system.

I feel a familiar wave of total inspiration and complete disgust.

I turn my phone all the way off. Stand up. Boldly head toward block six. All by myself, but *really* by myself this time. I walk with a new commitment to own my own minutes, to do something just because I said I would. In this century of astounding, triumphant personal accomplishment, I am succeeding at this: putting one foot in front of the other without telling anyone else. Going down one little road by myself. Boldly, bravely, walking into the rest of my life.

I feel a brand-new happy rush of endorphins. I feel my heart wake up. No fitness tracker on earth could measure how far I've already come today.

And now, rounding the corner by myself to block seven, I pause to give myself a nice little round of applause.

13.

NOBODY WANTS TO HEAR ABOUT
YOUR NICE CLEAN CLOSET

She had the cool, worldly aura of someone who'd just traveled to the neighborhood Goodwill and dropped off eight garbage bags full of her life. The dewy glow of a Decision-Maker. I should have trusted my instincts and sneaked out the back door of the restaurant before my friend saw me waiting at the hostess stand. I could have called from the parking lot, said I was stuck in traffic and would have to reschedule lunch for another day when . . .

Too late. I'm hugging her hello.

"Hi!" we both chime. "You look wonderful!"

I step back from the hug and scan my friend's face for why she looks so much more wonderful than I do. What has she done to herself that she didn't tell me she was going to do? Why the dewy glow? Surely she would have mentioned if she were planning . . .

But the evidence is all over her.

I look into her clear, sparkling eyes. I see unwrinkled blouses lined up by color on matching hangers.

I look at her youthful smile. I see a neat stack of blue jeans that were the same size as her rear end when she got out of bed this morning.

I catch a whiff of hibiscus, which I thought was perfume when we hugged, but which I now realize is the smell of fresh Bed Bath & Beyond shelf paper.

I can't believe it. Another girlfriend has sneaked off and done it without telling me: Botox of the closet. Storage-room peel. She's given her entire home a deep cleanse and rejuvenating lift.

I could have been so happy today, eating a peanut butter sandwich on Wonder Bread made with a leftover IHOP grape jelly pack from the bottom of my purse while leaning on my kitchen counter. Could have been with a friend who's still like me: me.

Way too late. We're led to a patio dining area edged by a picket fence and locked down like inmates under rutabaga-striped woven flax napkins. Prisoners of Lunch. We live in drought-ridden California, so the waiter interrogates us about our commitment to hydration before filling our glasses with water. We're handed menus listing $20 rations of locally grown chard and raw root vegetables. I hunger for Skippy Super Chunk. I hunger for the day before yesterday, when I could have told my friend I had other plans.

I take one try at the conversation I thought we were going to have today:

"How was your trip to Paris?" I ask hopefully.

"WE CANCELLED PARIS!" my friend bursts back.

I knew it.

"WE DECIDED TO HAVE A STAYCATION INSTEAD SO WE COULD ORGANIZE OUR WHOLE HOUSE! I DROPPED THE LAST BAGS OF STUFF OFF AT GOODWILL ON MY WAY HERE!!" she exudes, plucking her iPad from her tidy purse. She clicks *play*. Not only did she spend her staycation organizing her whole house, but she organized the photos of the organizing. Before and after shots set to soaring victorious music. Liberation of the Linen Closet. Arc de Underwear Drawer. A slide show of the Trip Through Stuff that she and I have been cheering each other on to take the last few years but neither of us could ever stand to start. We've pored over "Simplify Your Life!" articles together as if they were exotic travel brochures. Laughed about trying to scale the mountains of belongings we no longer need. Laughed with relief that there was someone else we could count on to never actually do it.

"Look! That's my kitchen cabinet!" She points at the iPad and exclaims, "My spices are in alphabetical order!" . . . "Look! I redid my whole bathroom!" . . . "And my *closet!* I got rid of every single thing that doesn't fit!"

"Wow," I say. It's the only word I can get out. I was prepared to feel a twinge of envy when she showed me shots of her wrapped around her sweetie under the Eiffel Tower in the moonlight. I was braced for lovebird selfies on the Seine. This is worse. Abandonment extraordinaire. *I want to get rid of everything that doesn't fit in my closet! I want to travel to the bottom of my bathroom cabinet! . . . I . . .*

I take a gulp of my precious California water, then another. And another. Something besides jealousy is stuck in my throat.

My friend taps the pause button long enough to glance up at the waiter who just arrived and deftly order a red quinoa and oak leaf salad with persimmons and cashew ricotta crumbles, pomegranate vinaigrette on the side, warmed buckwheat bun—tapenade, no butter—without even asking me what I'm having. Without rummaging through all the menu choices together like we always do, trying everything on ourselves and each other before we decide to wear the exact same thing in our stomachs and on our hips. Without turning the menu into a Great Big Food Closet like girlfriends do, which is half the fun of lunch. She's moved on from ritual. Moved on from me.

I glance around the patio. I could still escape, except if I try to leave without finishing my water I'll be arrested. I grip the menu and order the kale and shaved Brussels sprout special in as defiant a voice as I can muster, pretending that I too have decision-making skills that don't include the other person at the table. But that other person is too busy showing off her simplified new world to care that I've just chosen food without her input.

"Look at my T-shirts!" she exclaims as her slide show and music soar on. "If I hadn't worn one in six months, it went out!" . . . "I got rid of *boots!* Can you believe it?! *Boots!*" . . . "I tossed out old files, greeting cards, pens with no caps, plastic food containers with no lids!" . . . "I feel so *FREE!* I got rid of all that *STUFF!* I have so much *SPACE!!*" . . .

"Wow," I say again. Her happy pictures hurt my eyes. But why? The lump that isn't jealousy is still stuck in my throat. What is it? My friend and I have spent hours coaching and counseling each other to get out of ruts. *"You have to let go!"* we tell each other. *"Free yourself from the past so you can move on!"* This is exactly what we dreamed of doing. Why aren't I thrilled for her?

Her slide show zooms dramatically into a shot of the pristine pencil drawer in her kitchen. Six nice fresh pens—with caps!—all pointing the same direction, cute compartments full of untangled paper clips and rubber bands, a fresh roll of tape, two pairs of scissors. It isn't that she cleaned out a kitchen drawer and I didn't, I think. Isn't even that her whole house looks like this and mine doesn't.

It's what else I see when I look at her pictures. My mind zooms in like her camera. It goes right through shots of my friend's perfect kitchen drawer, through images of my own jumbled kitchen drawer . . . to a mental view of the desk drawer in my daughter's bedroom: broken kindergarten crayons mixed with souvenir pens from college tours, butterfly stickers, tearstained SAT practice quizzes, Professor Snape's wand, a class photo with all the boys' faces scribbled out. One drawer in a roomful of drawers full of a thousand goodbyes to my child's childhood that I know I have to face but am still nowhere near ready to start.

My friend's slide show has moved on to a slow pan of her tidy linen cabinet. It makes me think of what's waiting in the overflowing linen cabinet in my parents' house: "perfectly good" towels from 1955, afghans crocheted by my great-aunt, Dad's stiff olive-green World War II army blanket, doilies from the village where Mom was born, the chenille bedspread from my grandmother's house that can with one touch transport my sisters and me back to being five years old. Shelves packed with things too special to use, too precious to give away, that will all have to go somewhere else, sometime in the near future. One cabinet in a houseful of cabinets, in a lifetime of cabinets full of a million goodbyes I can't stand to think about.

That's what I see when I watch my friend's slide show—the giant job ahead. The huge rearrangement that starts with a kitchen drawer and leads to the dismantling of life up until now. Now I know what that lump is that's still stuck in my throat—it's What Comes Next.

I take a $3.50 mouthful of the kale that was just delivered, hoping to dull the overwhelmingness of it all. Big mistake. Kale doesn't dull anything. Chewing all these superfood nutrients to the tune of my friend's super-healthy ability to streamline her world just makes me hyperaware of every sense. The more antioxidants I swallow, the more ill I feel.

I can't watch her show anymore. For all my talk about wanting to organize and simplify, I'm not ready to look at the big picture my friend just opened up. The great big closet full of changes, decisions, and goodbyes. *The* Big Life Closet. I know how to buy trash bags, plastic storage boxes, and cute trays full of little compartments. I know how to turn up dance music on Saturday morning and make *in* and *out* piles. But I don't know how to do what she did—undo a life I'm nowhere ready to have undone.

I don't want my daughter's room to ever look like she didn't grow up in our house. I don't want to downsize my parents' big, wonderful lives into a shoebox of special things. I don't want to face the nice clean empty shelves of the future—drawers without Mom's scarves in them, closets without Dad's neckties, a room without twenty stuffed animals on the bed. I know the people I love need me to help escort them to the next stage, and I will do anything for them. But I can't stand what else that means: that I'll be helping them disappear. I can't stand facing the great big pristine blank pages of the calendar ahead when they're gone, when I'm not needed to help with anything, not necessary for anyone.

Where are the books on this? I want to ask my friend. *Where are the cheerful magazine articles on how we're supposed to sort out all this??*

I don't ask. I'm too afraid she'll answer with the truth. Will say what we've always said to each other: *You have to let go! Free yourself from the past so you can move on!*

She's too busy humming along to the grand finale of her presentation to answer questions anyway. "Ta-da!" she sings to the last shot of her bathroom cupboard. "I even got rid of all the half-used shampoos and conditioners!"

She clicks the end of the slide show, beams, and tucks her iPad back in her purse. I squeeze my friend's hand and tell her how proud I am of her. Kale remains are carefully boxed up to throw out at home. Water glasses are drained and surrendered. The check is split and paid. Dessert menus are rejected.

"No dessert for me!" my triumphant friend says. "I fit into every pair of jeans in my closet!"

"No dessert for me, either!" I announce.

"I may never eat dessert again!" she proclaims.

"Me either!" I echo "I am done with dessert forever!"

I drive home. Open the front door. Eat dessert.

I would have eaten dessert on the way home but for fear that my friend would have, by some horrid coincidence, stopped at the same 7-Eleven and seen me in line with a frozen ice cream sandwich. I've had all the girlfriend input I can take for now.

I walk through my house—past the closed door of my daughter's intact bedroom . . . past pictures of Mom and Dad in front of the home that's still packed with their lives . . . past all my own cupboards and cabinets full of decisions I'll make some other time. I change into my sweat suit, toss my lunch outfit on the bed, clip the leash on my dog, and leave the house for a nice long walk without even opening the closet door in my room.

I got a good look in the Big Closet over lunch. I've seen enough for one day.

14.

NO COMMENT

o. I do not wish to rate my latest transaction.

No. I will not take your short survey.

No. I will not help improve customer service by commenting on my experience.

No. I will not remember to go online when I get home and share my thoughts.

No. I will not write a few words about how it was to receive or try your product.

No. I will not tell you if I'll be recommending your product or services to friends.

No. I will not give any hints on what you could do better.

No. I do not want to earn bonus points or even 5 percent off my next purchase by volunteering a few moments of my time to share my views on the last person who assisted me.

I do not have enough moments left on earth. I need all my moments to try to convince someone I already know to accept my opinion on anything. My child rejects my opinion. Other family members argue with my opinion. Friends act as if they need and agree with my opinion, and then go off and do something completely different. Overhaul their whole lives with no input from me whatsoever. Based on my track record thus far, getting someone I know to appreciate my opinion will take all the time I have left. The rest of you are on your own. I am 100 percent finished spending time giving opinions about anything to anyone else.

And that, I think as I get into bed, is exactly how I feel about all of that.

I lay my head down on my pillow and close my eyes. I'm about to scroll down to *Sleep* when I pause to open the self-survey of how I think I did today in my mind.

I click the little box on the far right: "Extremely Satisfied."

15.

HELICOPTER DAUGHTER

*D*on't climb on that! You'll fall and break your neck!

Don't walk with that! You'll trip and poke your eye out!

Don't go downstairs without holding the rail! You'll slip and crack your skull!

Don't cross the street without holding my hand! You'll be run over!

Don't go outside without a jacket! You'll catch pneumonia!

Don't wear socks on the wood floor! Your feet will go out from under you!

Don't touch the hot pan! You'll scald yourself!

Don't walk with scissors! You'll stab yourself!

Don't take such a big bite! You'll choke!

Don't read in the dark! You'll go blind!

AND DON'T ROLL YOUR EYES! THEY'LL STICK LIKE THAT!

As exhausting as it is to be a helicopter parent, it's even worse to be a helicopter daughter. Hovering over a stubborn two-year-old was child's play compared with hovering over two stubborn ninety-year-olds. Like supervising twins. Cherished, challenging Mom and Dad Twins. They're bad listeners, both of them. They say *NO!* to everything. My sisters and I make rules to keep them safe, but as soon as we aren't looking, our parents do whatever they want.

There's very little my sisters and I can do except worry when we all live far away in different cities. After our last unproductive visit, we talked many times on the phone and finally agreed on one simple solution that's helped lots of families. We decided to order an emergency alert call system so Mom and Dad could simply press a button on a pendant if help was needed. My sisters and I cried together, so sad that we'd reached this point in life, but grateful there was something we could do. We pledged our love and support of one another, and then hung up and began our own online research from our own homes.

After way too many hours on our own, squinting at way too many options, reviews, and testimonials, trying to guess which "Number One Bestseller!" would actually get help there in time to help Mom and Dad . . . After all that, my formerly unified sisters and I re-emerged as rivals. Came back at each other on a long distance conference call as the opposite of how we started: three exasperated experts on emergency alert systems; three advocates for three completely different ones.

Mom would never wear one that looks like the one you picked!

I spend a lot more time with Mom than you do. I think I know what she'll wear!

Can I help it if I have a job and kids at home and you're more free to travel?

I'm busier than you are and I make time! I call every day!

Dad's not going to wear a necklace! I picked a system with a wristband!

It's a pendant, not a necklace! You always make things worse than they are!

Me?? You're the one who ruins everything!

Etcetera.

In our quest to keep Mom and Dad safe, we threw one another under the bus. Every ancient sibling grievance relaunched and magnified by the current grief of knowing Mom and Dad are now at this stage of life. The sadness that should unite us mixed with worry and guilt and all the other things that tangle families up . . . until finally the loudest, bossiest, and most obnoxiously self-righteous sister won.

I enjoyed the thrill of victory for five full seconds before I realized winning meant it was now my job to present the Emergency Call Button System to the Twins. Our beloved, belligerent, noncompliant nonagenarian Mom and Dad Twins.

Which is why I'm sitting at their kitchen table in Florida today with a package hidden under my chair. Outnumbered and all alone.

"Come sit at the table, Mom and Dad!" I call cheerfully. "I have a surprise!"

"WE DON'T WANT ANY SURPRISES!" comes the stereo response from the other end of the house. I forgot they've gotten a little sensitive about the S word after the series of "Surprise!" home health care interviewees one of my sisters arranged for Mom and Dad to meet.

"It's not really a surprise!" I try again. "It's a *gift*!"

"WE DON'T WANT ANY GIFTS!" they yell back.

Right. I also forgot the G word was ruined with the "Gift!" of a raised toilet seat my other sister wrapped and had under the tree last Christmas . . . also the "Gift!" of a nice new set of bathroom safety bars the three of us tried to give them for their anniversary.

I need backup. I pull out my phone and start to dial, but who? My sisters are mad at me and my dog never answers when I call. I put the phone away and gather all my grown-up resourcefulness, all my finely honed take-charge life skills. I summon all my strength and steely will and funnel it into one loud wail:

"I NEED HELP!"

It would be total manipulation if it weren't so true. I do need help. I need my parents to help me take charge of my parents. I hear them drop their guard, just as they've always dropped everything to rush to my sisters' or my aid. As though I'd been stung by a bee just now, not stung by the frustration of trying to be a mom and dad to Mom and Dad.

Dad scurries the length of the house without shoes, socks, knee braces, or his cane. Mom hurries down the hall in slippery slippers, balancing a cup of coffee on top of a stack of newspapers. The sight of so many pending disasters terrifies and empowers me. They need the system I'm about to present to keep them safe. So many, many things could happen when my sisters and I aren't here.

"What's wrong??" they ask, coming right up to either side of me, "What can we *do*??"

I look from one to the other, overwhelmed with love for these amazing people who have spent their lives keeping my sisters, our children, and me safe. Even with pacemakers, hearing aids, hip surgeries, and all the other life-altering events of the last several years, they're still the guardians of our family. Everyone's training wheels came off decades ago. Mom and Dad, in every possible way they can, still run alongside all our bikes.

Mom still reads the newspaper with a pair of scissors in one hand so she can cut out articles that might help one of us. She spends days trying to research things on the computer for us, writes long, thoughtful notes of advice by hand if her radar senses someone's having a problem. Greets us at the door with her sewing kit, file folders full of guidance, and a kitchen full of goodies to help fix anything that might be wrong.

Dad worries about everyone's tire pressure, every smoke detector battery that needs changing, and every dead bolt that needs tightening. Even now, when we're old enough to have grown children of our own, he slips a twenty-dollar bill in our hands each time we leave for the airport "just in case," and will not sleep until we let him know we're safely home. Even now, in this moment when I've come to protect them, they've both rushed to protect me.

"Thank you, Mom and Dad," I say, wiping a not-so-pretend tear from my eye. "Just sit with me. Help me figure something out."

"Anything!" they say, sitting close, each laying a reassuring hand on my shoulders. "We'll do anything to help!"

"This is so hard for me . . ." I begin. And now it really is hard. "You're both so healthy and strong. *I* know you can handle everything," I continue, "but . . ." I pull the bag from under my chair and clutch it in my lap.

I take a deep breath. No turning back now. No pretending this moment isn't what it is. No shirking the responsibility I fought for and won. No not doing what I need to do. I pull the box from the bag, lay it on the table, and blurt out the truth of why I'm here:

"My *SISTERS* think you need to wear emergency alert call buttons!"

Mom and Dad reel backward with horror. "NO!" they answer in their great big Mom-Dad twin voices.

"Yes!" I say. "Can you believe it?? *They* think you need help! *They* made me come here to set up this device and outfit you with call button pendants!"

"NO!" they repeat, leaning away from the box. Leaning so far back in their chairs, I note, they could easily topple over backward and crack their heads on the kitchen floor. And yet . . .

"Yes!" I continue, shaking my head with disbelief and commiseration. "That's what my *SISTERS* want! *They* want you to wear emergency call buttons!"

I look toward Mom and Dad helplessly. Beam inwardly. No longer outnumbered. No longer alone. Mom and Dad lean back in, trying to peek at the nightmare my *sisters* have sent me to Florida to inflict.

I pull the box toward me, hiding the EZ setup pictures on the label from their view. Ideally I would have had the whole system set up, tested, and working perfectly while they took a nap so I could do my own uncomplicated demonstration. But the twins refused to take a nap earlier and I'm running out of time. I give it another try . . .

"I know how upsetting this is, Mom and Dad," I say in my most soothing, compassion-filled voice. "Why don't you both lie down for a little bit and I'll set it up and we can see how it works?"

"We don't want to lie down!" they announce, eyes wide open, glaring at the Box.

"You usually take a nap in the afternoon," I answer. "Go ahead and I'll—"

"WE DO NOT NEED A NAP!!" they announce more forcefully, eyes flashing at me now.

"How about a snack?" I say, gesturing out of the room. "Sit on the porch with a snack while—"

"NO SNACKS! NO NAPS!"

The twins are turning on me. I wish my sisters were here. I wish they were here instead of me. I need them to navigate this moment. To convince the parents who so proudly still take care of us that they should wear baby monitors around their necks to keep them safe. It was all so logical until I was sitting in the middle of it, and now I can't stand it. I don't want Mom and Dad to be old enough to need emergency call buttons. I don't want to be the one to tell them they're too fragile to walk down the hall, take a bath, or go to bed without wearing a help device around their necks. I don't want them to feel humiliated.

I hate that my sisters didn't have more stamina so one of them would be here instead of me. How am I even related to such light-weights? For once in their lives, couldn't one of them have been bossier than I was so they would have to be here doing this??!

Now I'm back on the nice solid ground of sibling resentment. It emboldens me to open the box. "My *sisters* think you need this!" I say pleadingly. "They won't speak to me if I don't at least convince you to give it a try!" I see Mom and Dad soften, their eyes fill with compassion. They've refereed thousands of sister conflicts. They know I'm stuck in the middle and they want to do anything they can to fix it for me.

I pull the base unit from the box and place it on the counter. They stare. They want to do anything they can to fix it for me—except this.

"DON'T PUT THAT BIG THING IN THE MIDDLE OF

THE KITCHEN COUNTER FOR ALL THE WORLD TO SEE!" they protest.

I unplug their phone from the wall . . .

"DON'T UNPLUG OUR PHONE! WE WON'T BE ABLE TO MAKE CALLS!"

I plug the base unit into the phone jack in the wall . . .

"DON'T PLUG THAT IN THERE! THAT'S WHERE OUR PHONE PLUGS IN!"

I plug the landline into the base unit . . .

"DON'T PLUG OUR PHONE INTO THAT BOX! PEOPLE WILL HEAR ALL OUR CONVERSATIONS!"

I push the button on the base unit to test the connection. A voice comes over the box's speaker: *"Hello. This is the monitoring center. Are you ready to . . ."*

Pandemonium ensues. Mom and Dad are on their feet, pointing at the box in alarm: "SOMEONE'S LISTENING! THERE'S A STRANGER LISTENING THROUGH THAT BOX! GET HER OUT OF HERE! UNPLUG THAT THING AND GET IT OUT OF OUR HOUSE!"

How much worse could this possibly get, I think. And so . . . I reach into the shipping package, remove the call button pendants that go with the system, and place one around each parent's neck.

Much worse, it turns out. It could get much worse.

"I AM NOT WEARING SOME OLD-PERSON CALL BUTTON!"

"I DON'T WANT SOMEONE LISTENING TO ME THROUGH MY SHIRT!"

"GET THIS OFF ME GET THIS OFF ME GET THIS OFF ME!!"

In their effort to pull the pendants off, one or both parents accidentally push the call button, which calls the monitoring station, and in seconds the voice is coming out of the box on their kitchen counter again.

"*Hello. This is the monitoring center. We received an emergency call at . . .*"

"THE STRANGER'S BACK!" Mom and Dad yell. "GET HER OUT OF OUR KITCHEN! WE ARE NOT WEARING THESE NECKLACES! WE DO NOT WANT THAT LADY IN OUR KITCHEN!"

Pendants are flung on the table. Dad yanks the monitoring box cord out of the wall. Mom grabs the box and tries to stuff it back in the shipping package.

I wait for the chaos to stop, the twins to sit, and blood pressures to stabilize.

It takes a while, but when it finally feels safe, I start all over in a nice calm voice. "Millions of people have this system, Mom and Dad," I say. "It could be a great comfort to you! With the pendants on, you can press the button to get help any time you need it. If you fall and can't press the button, it will sense you've fallen and will send help!"

For a second, I think they're silent because they actually are comforted. And then we're off again . . .

"THE BUTTON KNOWS WHAT I'M DOING? I'M NOT WEARING A BUTTON THAT WATCHES EVERYTHING I'M DOING!"

"No, no!" I say. "It only knows if you've *fallen*! If you can't get up or are unconscious, it calls the paramedics!"

They stop and stare.

"If we're unconscious, how will the paramedics get in?" they ask.

"We'll have a lockbox outside your house with a key in it," I answer.

"WHAT?? NO! WE ARE *NOT* LEAVING A KEY OUTSIDE FOR STRANGERS TO COME WALTZING IN! IF THERE'S AN EMERGENCY, WE'LL DIAL 911 AND LET THE PARA-MEDICS IN OURSELVES!!"

"How will you dial 911 if you're unconscious?" I ask, my benevolent caregiver patience wearing thin.

They look at me as if I'm the illogical one.

"We'll dial 911 before we become unconscious!" Dad exclaims. "Honestly, honey! You worry too much!"

I try to regroup. Meanwhile Mom gets up, turns the front burner of the stove on high without putting a pan of anything on it, and walks into the next room looking for something or other. I turn to Dad to point out the fire hazard Mom just created, but Dad's leaning forward in his chair to pick up packing material that dropped when I opened the shipping box and is on the verge of losing his balance and toppling on his head. I scan the room like I used to for my toddler—like a "What's Wrong with This Picture?" puzzle—and see danger everywhere. Throw rugs with the edges curled up. Pointy table corners. Open staircase. Heavy things on upper shelves. Sharp knives way too close to the edge of the counter. A stack of old magazines on the floor exactly where someone could slide on it.

The twins are both on their feet now, going about their business. Defiant. Determined. Oblivious to all the potential disasters that are so clear to me. The qualities that have kept them so full of life, curiosity, and independence are the same ones that drive my sisters and me insane with worry. But so far no one's tripped, slipped, fallen, broken a neck, cracked a skull, poked out an eye, or gotten scalded, stabbed, choked, or electrocuted. They've done an amazing job of taking care of our family, themselves, and each other without my sisters and me hovering.

I know I need to take a big breath and a little step backward. As much as my sisters and I want to protect them, the best thing we can do to help Mom and Dad stay strong and capable is to let them continue being Mom and Dad. As horrible as we'd feel if something happened when we weren't guarding against every possible accident, we need to let them be in charge of how and where they live while they're still so able.

And so I resist the urge to run in front of Dad with pillows in case he falls. I don't hover over Mom each time she goes near an appliance. When they see me relax a little, I feel them relax. When I quit trying to be the boss, they take over, helping me do what I came to do. As soon as I stop trying to parent them, they resume being the parents helping me. Amazingly, by the time they're ready to take a nap, they agree to keep the monitoring system call box on the kitchen counter "for now." Mom shoves it behind the toaster "where no one can see it" with a dish towel over it "so no one can see *us*!" . . . but it's there. They also agree to keep their emergency call button pendants. Mom's keeping hers in her sweater drawer, Dad's keeping his on a hook in his closet with his neckties. "We'll run and get them if we have an emergency!" he says, giving me a little hug. "So you never have to worry!"

This is not at all what I expected when I came on this mission. This day, which was plotted as a way for my sisters and me to take care of Mom and Dad, has become, instead, a way for Mom and Dad to take care of my sisters and me. They're not letting the emergency call system stay in the house because they think it will make them more safe.

They're letting it stay here because it will make *us* feel more safe. They understand the comfort we'll have knowing they have a way to call for help, even if the call buttons are buried in their drawers and closets. This is Mom and Dad at their finest, tucking their girls in at night, making sure we have less worry and much better dreams.

I watch them walk back down the hall to their bedroom. Dad still without shoes, socks, knee braces, or his cane. Mom still in slippery slippers, this time balancing a pitcher of bedside water on top of three library books. But they're okay. I smile because I *will* have better dreams tonight.

I pull out my phone. There's a long line of text messages waiting from both sisters:

> How'd it go? . . . Are you okay? . . . I'm
> so sorry for what I said! . . . I feel terrible
> that you're there by yourself! . . . Please
> let me know what happened! . . . You're
> the best!

I sit at the table. Feel a big wave a relief. All is forgiven. My sisters and I will recover from this, just as we've recovered from many things before. We have to. We have lots still ahead of us and are going to need each other.

I need my sisters now. Need to unload this day and everything I newly understand. Need to pour my heart out to them, tell them how important they are to me. I pick up my phone and smile. Then I type the three special little words that say it all:

"IT'S *YOUR* TURN."

16.

DIARY OF A BUBBLE WRAP SCRAP

Saturday, 10:30 a.m.: In a bold act of defiance, I march out to the trash bin and throw away a piece of used, unrecyclable Bubble Wrap. Mother would be mortified.

Pride surges. I march back in the house. I've taken a stand for my new commitment to uncluttered living. Rejected Mother's Way.

10:35 a.m.: Shame takes over. It was a perfectly good piece of Bubble Wrap. Could be used a hundred more times. I march back out to the trash and rescue the scrap from the bin.

10:37 a.m.: Defiance kicks back in. I march the Bubble Wrap back out.

10:39 a.m.: Shame takes over. I march the Bubble Wrap back in.

10:41 a.m.: Defiance. Bubble Wrap out.

10:43 a.m.: Shame. Bubble Wrap in.

10:45 a.m.: I stand in the kitchen, Bubble Wrap clenched in my hand. Worse. A lifetime of birthdays, Christmases, and Mother's Days is also clenched in that hand. Mom has never thrown out anything with *wrap* in the name. Not Saran Wrap, not Reynolds Wrap. Not, heaven forbid, anything having to do with gift wrap.

"Oh, the wrapping paper is so beautiful!" Mom exclaims every time a gift is opened. "Here! Let's carefully peel the tape so the paper doesn't tear! . . . Wait! I can flatten that out and fold it to use next year! . . . Don't wad up the tissue paper! I'll save it for another gift! . . . Wait! Save the ribbon! . . . Save the bow! . . . Save the box! . . . Save the gift bag! . . . DO NOT THROW OUT THE BUBBLE WRAP!!"

After we open gifts on Christmas morning, everyone in the family has a little pile of presents in front of them. Mom—looking as delighted as anyone in the room—has a pile of rescued gift wrap, tissue paper, ribbons, bows, boxes, gift bags, and Bubble Wrap in front of her.

10:48 a.m.: I pry my fingers open, drop the scrap of Bubble Wrap on the counter, grab my car keys, and drive to the store, where I buy a $9 plastic storage bin in which to store used scraps of Bubble Wrap. Pride surges. I've found a way to take charge of my own life without being haunted by visions of Mom on Christmas morning.

11:15 a.m.: Shame takes the wheel. Mother would be horrified that I've spent $9 on a plastic storage bin when I have perfectly good used cardboard boxes at home. I turn the car, drive to another store to look for a better price. Buy a different plastic storage bin for $6.89. Reduce the guilt by $2.11.

11:45 a.m.: Am almost home when I remember the 20 percent off coupons I have for a different store. Drive there and, since I'm saving so much, buy two storage bins. Why not commit to a real system? I think: one bin for used Bubble Wrap, one for used gift wrap.

I can almost feel Mom's pride, which makes me equal parts happy that I'm pleasing her and irritated that I'm succumbing to her.

12:25 p.m.: Take a detour to a different branch of the same 20 percent off store to see if they happen to have the bins I just bought only both with purple lids, since the last store had only one purple lid and one green lid, and as long as I'm investing in a system, everything should match. I spend most of the drive trying to decide if Mom's winning because I'm being frugal while buying systems to save scraps of everything, or if I'm winning because I'm developing my own system, which is superior to her system.

12:45 p.m.: This branch has one with a purple lid, but it's a different brand, so the purple probably won't match, and the bins will surely be unstackable. It's way too much effort to run out to the car in the parking lot to do a color and stackability check of what I already own, so I buy four new bins with the extra coupons I have in my purse—one bin with the potentially unmatching purple lid, two with orange lids, in case the purple's all wrong, and one with a blue lid—thinking I could also expand the system to include a bin for flattened used tissue paper, in which case I could keep one purple, one orange, and one blue and go with a splash-of-color storage tub theme. I no longer feel Mom's pride. Now I feel her inner conflict. Part of her would cheer my ingenuity and stamina; part of her would lecture me about all the silly, unnecessary expense.

1:17 p.m.: Drive back to store number one. Now that I might be committing to a three-bin system, I need to make sure there isn't something better that I didn't consider on my first pass. Store number one, in fact, has a plastic *drawer* system, which I didn't look at before, which could be used not only for Bubble Wrap scraps and pre-used gift wrap, but rescued tissue paper and recycled bows. I buy the drawer system in two different heights and depths because I don't remember the dimensions of my cabinet space at home and certainly don't want to waste time driving home and measuring. I channel more inner turmoil from Mom. She'd be mortified by all the charges, except that she's also a world-class shopper and can get into the joy of the hunt as much as anyone. She *taught* me to keep shopping when the shopping's done. She'd be ill, but thrilled about all the possibilities stuffed in my car.

2:00 p.m.: I sit at the kitchen counter and calculate: I spent $97.89 on plastic storage systems today. This includes one $17.99 set of stacking drawers, which I'm keeping, and $79.90 in drawers, bins, and multicolored lids, which are filling the back seat and trunk of my car and will need to be returned.

I pick up the scrap of used Bubble Wrap that started it all, put it in the top drawer of the new $17.99 drawer set to which I'm committing, and sit back to admire it. The manufacturer's label with its UPS code is stuck right on the front of the drawer and ruins the whole pristine look. I try to peel it off, but only part of the top layer of the label comes off. I try to scrape the rest off with my fingernails. I take the Bubble Wrap out, hold the drawer under hot water, scrub the label with dish soap, scouring powder, and a Brillo pad. I work at it with a knife, Formula 409, and nail polish remover. Now there's a big scratched patch where I've been scrubbing, clawing, and scraping, still covered with a thin, sticky film of glue.

I march into my home office and miraculously find a pack of large self-stick labels. I stick one on the front of the plastic drawer to cover the whole scratched, sticky area, and write *Bubble Wrap* in Sharpie.

The words aren't centered on the label. Again I hear Mom's voice. This time she's admonishing me with "Anything worth doing is worth doing well." As irritating as it is to still need to please her, I still need to please her.

I peel off the part of the label that will come off. Cover with a new label and, more carefully this time, write *Bubble Nrap.* The W looks like an N, so I write a new label. And then another new one and then . . .

4:30 p.m.: I decide the label should be made on the computer. Four failed printing attempts later—including one in which the sticky part of a whole sheet of labels gets welded to the roller thing inside my printer and I have to spend another hour with the online troubleshooting guide learning how to unstick it—I have a label. It's 7:00 p.m. I have achieved one label on one plastic storage drawer: *Buble Wrap.*

Misspelled. I quit.

One Bubble Wrap scrap used up my whole day, and by the time I'm done driving back to all the stores and standing in customer service lines to return all the storage system versions I don't want, it will have used up my whole weekend. It will use even more time next month as the credit card statements come in, and all those charges and credits have to be reconciled with my new stack of receipts. A month-long drama, launched by the classic primal urge to please Mom, respect Mom, and emulate Mom, all while figuring out how to be my own unique person, which I know is Mom's deepest wish. Honoring and rejecting, synchronizing and separating. Wound through every minute of my life. Mom's impact as unbreakable as if it were wrapped in its own perfectly good little piece of Bubble Wrap.

I can picture Mom now, three thousand miles away in a different time zone, tossing in her sleep. I can almost see her wrestle awake, stare at the ceiling, and ask that sweet ancient insane middle-of-the-night Mom question:

"Do you suppose she ever thinks of me?"

17.

I'M FLUNKING RETIREMENT

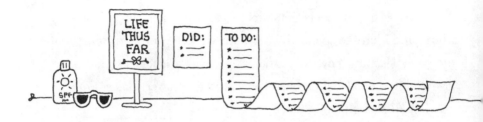

The interrogations started the day after my comic strip ended, the first day in thirty-four years that *Cathy* hadn't been in the newspaper. The cashier at the corner market where I'd been stopping for a decade glanced up from her register and hit me with the first brutal question:

"What are you up to these days?" she asked.

She'd apparently missed the previous two months of moving multimedia tributes leading up to my strip's finale, so I answered proudly, speaking the words for the very first time:

"I retired!" I said.

"Retired . . ." she repeated kind of wistfully as she rang me up. "So what are you up to now?"

"Ha-ha," I answered, shaking my head. "I'm taking a break!"

"Nice. Doing what?" she asked—just nonchalantly enough that it made me think she might not know what I'd been doing for the last three decades. I'd said hello to her for ten years, but she and I had never really talked.

"Well . . ." I began, pulling a newspaper from the stand next to the counter, allowing myself to beam just a bit while also trying to speak with great grace and humility, "I just finished a rather successful career." I opened the paper to the comic page and pointed to the space where *Cathy* had always been in the *Los Angeles Times,* now filled by someone else's strip. "I wrote and drew a comic strip that ran right there for thirty-four years!" I explained. "My name was in the paper every day right there!"

My words hit before the feeling did, like how it is when you slam your hand in a door and only experience the pain seconds after the fact. Until that moment, the reality of ending the strip hadn't really occurred to me. I stared at the page. Someone else was in my spot. After all this time, there was no trace of me on the comic page at all. I peered at where my strip used to be, verified how bad it felt to not see my characters and name there. It was as though I'd disappeared completely overnight. Like looking at the world after someone dies, I thought. The shock that life just rolls on, with other people to fill up the spaces.

The cashier glanced at the paper with a patient cashier smile, then continued to make change for the carton of milk I'd come in to buy. The end-of-life decisions that had taken up my entire last year and a half roared through me in seconds:

How I agonized over the decision for months without telling anyone . . .

How I finally called the editor who took a chance on my work thirty-four years ago and told him I couldn't do it anymore . . .

How I was racked with guilt that I was abandoning everyone—the incredible company full of people who'd supported my work, the wonderful newspaper editors who'd bought my work, the cherished readers who depended on my work . . .

How I could have made another choice, could have let the newspapers run reruns . . . could have kept my work alive and in print for years . . .

How I didn't. I chose to pull the plug. Cut off life support on a perfectly healthy creation. This was no accidental death. This was . . .

Another customer had approached the counter and was asking about canned tomatoes. I had to quickly, surreally, rally past grief and the concept that I'd needlessly murdered my namesake—rally and deliver my own obituary to the cashier before she lost interest in me. Make sure that on this first day the strip wasn't in the paper, that at least this woman who'd asked about my life, at least she'd know I'd had a good one.

"I had a big life," I began from my pulpit right there in front of the checkout counter, "internationally beloved, iconic charac—"

But the cashier had already finished my sale and was walking away from the counter to help the tomato lady find what she needed.

That's how my retirement started. It's gone downhill from there.

The questions are relentless and ruthless:

"What are you up to these days?" friends ask.

"I'm helping my daughter and parents!" I answer. Selfless and honorable.

"But what are you *doing*?" they persist. Selfless and honorable are never enough.

"That's what I'm doing! I'm a full-time mom and daughter!"

"Your daughter's in school all day and your parents live three thousand miles away. What do you *do*?"

The questions are tough. The competition's brutal.

My generation ruined retirement. All those dynamic, driven innovators and superachievers who did so many universe-changing, society-transforming, consciousness-elevating, expectation-smashing things. They ruined retirement. Nobody gets to get old anymore. Nobody gets to quit. My peer group is producing absolutely no plump, elderly ladies in floral housedresses and tidy poufs of white hair. No sweet, sleepy husbands in suspenders and slippers napping under the sports page in the hammock. No one's sitting in a La-Z-Boy in the afternoon with a basket of mending and *The Price Is Right*.

The oldies in my generation are hotter than the youngies. Full heads of super-conditioned, tousled layers of black, blond, brunette, or chestnut hair . . . bright, beaming, line-free faces . . . flat abs and awesome rears in fluorescent workout spandex. Grandpas zooming past on cyclocross bikes, grandmas rocking aviator shades. A lust for adventure flashing from dazzling smiles—smiles full of the perfect white teeth of the perfect young people formerly seen only in toothpaste ads.

No one retires. They reinvent. Repurpose. Rediscover passions and pursue an even more meaningful chapter two. The exuberant magazine articles full of testimonials make me sick. The commercials full of old people acting like young people made me sicker. The real-life humans are even worse.

What Susan did in that first October of my retirement: reenrolled in college at age sixty-eight to pursue her long-lost dream of becoming a pediatric nurse.

What I did that first October: looked for my glasses and yelled at my child for handing a history paper in late and not rinsing out her cereal bowl.

What Ruth did in November: bought a set of power tools, restored an empty warehouse space, and opened an art studio for underprivileged teens.

What I did in November: tried to remember why I walked into the kitchen. Argued long distance with Mom about how long thawed chicken lasts in the refrigerator.

Even my exhausted peers who say, "When our jobs are over, we just want to travel!" don't mean they just want to travel. Members of my generation don't fly anywhere to lie down on a beach. They go on spiritual quests to thatched-roof bungalows in remote islands . . . language-immersion cooking schools . . . survival treks . . . healing, plein air painting retreats. Travel has purpose—to explore, educate, challenge, give back, grow. Even people who want to "just let go" let go on chakra-balancing, mindfulness-training, restorative yoga, and core-crunching cruises. No one ever just goes someplace and lies down.

I do not want to look or act old, but I would like to be *expected* to look and act old so I can look and act young by comparison. There's none of that now.

When I was doing the comic strip, my daughter used to say I had fifteen good minutes a week: one tiny, relaxed chunk of time that started right after I drove the week of finished art for the strips to FedEx and ended fifteen minutes later when I began panicking about the next week's strips. I was never totally present for anything or anyone if I had a strip deadline looming. When I quit, it was because I suddenly had three even worse deadlines looming. Each one felt a lot more urgent than the ones for the comic strip. Together they made me insane with panic that I was running out of time for everything all at once.

My daughter was starting her last year of high school.

My parents were getting close to age ninety.

I was hitting a "milestone" birthday.

If I didn't stop the strip then, I thought . . . when? I'd never have another chance to be a full-time mom while my child was living at home and in school. I'd never get these last years with my parents back. Never create anything else if I didn't liberate myself from the weekly FedEx hurls.

I thought retirement would offer a little relief, but every year since, the deadlines have closed in more. My "milestone" age graced me with perspective, but also the wrenching self-awareness that I'm almost next in line to not be here anymore. I'm right in the middle of this precious place between my child and my parents— grateful for every second I have with them—but acutely aware that everyone's time is running out, including mine, for anything else.

They call it the "sandwich generation," but it seems much more squashed than that. More like the "panini generation." I feel absolutely flattened some days by the pressure to be everything to every-one, including myself. And the people around me don't relent.

"What are you up to these days?" friends ask.

"I'm pursuing various creative projects!" I decide to answer. Arty and mysterious.

"What projects?" they persist. Arty and mysterious are never enough.

"Um. Well . . . I can't discuss them yet," I reply slyly.

"How are all the projects you can't discuss going?" they ask the next fifteen times I talk to them, and then I have to quit returning their calls because they know too much. Know I probably haven't started anything yet.

"What are you up to these days?" a brand-new friend asks.

"I'm organizing my entire house so I can have a nice clear space in which to launch the next fabulous phase of my life!" I answer. Optimistic and respectable.

"How far have you gotten?" she persists. Optimistic and respectable are never enough.

We don't speak again.

"What are you up to these days?" a different new friend asks.

"I spend my days wandering around trying to remember passwords, arguing with myself about exercising, feeding myself, and printing return labels to Amazon," I answer. Honest and brave.

"Oh," she answers. And that's that. No time, anyway, for new friends right now.

Even if people didn't keep asking what I'm doing, my generation's expectations and impatience are embedded in my DNA. Untapped potential hangs over me like a giant pair of unused running shoes. It feels as if everything leading up to right now was just getting me ready for what I could *really* do . . . and that now, when I finally have the life experience and confidence to start, I'm almost out of time. *I'm out of time and I didn't even start yet!*

That's how retirement feels. *I'm out of time and I didn't even start yet.*

I can't stand all those efficient members of my peer group who are managing to care for children and parents *and* reinvent themselves while I end so many days with nothing crossed out except things like "take vitamins."

I can't look at the brilliant, articulate, inspiring woman on TV who's promoting the third bestseller she wrote in the five years it took me to write the first two sentences of this book. I hate that if I ever even finish *this one thing*, it will have old-lady-ness attached to it, like "She finally got that book she talked about done by her hundredth birthday!"

I hate that my generation ruined retirement. Why can't we just sit in nice plastic lawn chairs in the backyard like Grandma used to? I shut my eyes and picture my un-stressed-out grandma. I see young me, full of dreams, twirling around in the yard in front of her. I see the great big glorious jumble of everything I wanted to do and be, which, until recently, *I THOUGHT I STILL HAD PLENTY OF TIME TO FIGURE OUT!* Dreams too big to even speak of now, I think, opening my eyes. Too embarrassing to admit I still hold such great big young dreams at such an old age.

I hear the front door slam and the sound of my daughter, who just arrived home from visiting friends, tromping toward her room.

"I can't take the pressure!" comes the oh-so-familiar college freshman wail.

"Everyone keeps asking what I'm doing with my life and I don't know, okay?? I thought I had plenty of time to figure it out! Why can't everyone quit asking about my future plans??!"

I sigh, walk down the hall, and tap on her bedroom door.

"YOU DON'T KNOW WHAT IT'S LIKE, MOM!" she cries from inside her room. *"YOU DON'T KNOW WHAT IT'S LIKE TO BE UNDER SO MUCH PRESSURE TO DO SOMETHING WITH YOUR LIFE!"*

"Yes I do, baby," I whisper from the other side of everything. "Honestly, I do."

18.

THIS IS YOUR BRAIN ON
SWEET POTATO CHIPS

The first twenty-six beta-carotene-rich chips are because that's the serving size.

The second twenty-six chips are a reward for being attentive to serving size.

The next twenty-six chips are because I cheated on the last twenty-six and ate fourteen broken pieces while I was counting out the twenty-six chips and I did not try to piece them together to make them count as any of the twenty-six allowed chips.

The next fifty-seven chips are punishment.

The next ten are to knock myself unconscious so I'll quit eating chips.

The next time I'm in a store and buy a bag of sweet potato chips, it will be to prove to myself that I've grown and changed since the last bag of chips and that I'm mature enough to restrain myself.

We crave snacks.

We hunger for victory.

19.

DON'T TELL A WOMAN
TO JUST WEAR JEANS

Y ou'd have more room in the closet if you got rid of some of those jeans," my husband at the time casually noted long ago. One of the many loving, insightful observations he made that sealed his doom.

"I can't get rid of any of the jeans! They don't fit!" I remember answering, giving him a chance to redeem himself. Inviting the hug of compassion that any female friend would know was appropriate.

He only stared. Stared and asked, "You can't get rid of jeans that don't fit?" as if I were the one not making any sense.

At that point in our marriage, I knew it was pointless to try defending my position. It wouldn't make him understand or like me one speck more. It might even make him view *me* as a doomed spouse and put him in the emotionally self-righteous lead.

"There are only ex-husbands. There are never ex-jeans!" That's what I'd say if he were here today. Hah.

But he's not here. I am standing alone in front of the same closet. A closet that's all mine now. I take a good look and sigh.

I'd have more room in the closet if I got rid of some of these jeans, I think.

The e-vite that made me face the closet this morning arrived one hour ago. A classic example of the deterioration of social graces for which the twenty-first century will surely be known. Invitations used to be delivered by the U.S. Post Office at least two weeks before an event. The pretty *You're Invited!* card could be stuck on the re-frigerator door—right between us and the food—a tangible re-minder of the good choices we hoped to make if we wanted to get into what we hoped to get into on party day.

Today's invitation popped up on my iPhone email while I was brushing my teeth after my second heart-healthy, 310-calorie bowl of breakfast granola this morning. The party's in two days. The perky, unbelievably cruel directive reads: "Just wear jeans!" Which is why I'm standing here at 9:00 a.m., in fiber-filled pj's, facing what was nowhere on the list to deal with for the foreseeable future: the jeans section of my closet.

There it is. My denim diary. My great big blue stack of heartache and hope. Fat jeans, medium jeans, skinny jeans, really skinny jeans, jeans that fit for fifteen seconds before breakfast after the stomach flu on a low-humidity day in 1987—the ones I still think of as my "real size." Jeans I saved to remind myself how big I used to be. Jeans I saved to remind myself how little I used to be. Jeans I could never, ever get rid of because of the victories they represent, the defeats I need to remember, the pain I'd feel if I ever had to spend money buying some of those sizes again. Jeans covering the entire span of human potential.

I try on just enough pairs to confirm what I already suspect: I have jeans covering the entire span of everything but me. Twelve pairs of jeans. Not one pair that has anything to do with the version of myself that needs to "just wear jeans" in forty-eight hours.

It isn't as though the issue hasn't come up lately. Ninety-nine percent of the blouses, tank tops, jackets, sweaters, wraps, and sweat shirts in my closet were bought because they'd be "perfect with jeans." When none of the jeans fit, the whole wardrobe is useless. The jeans control everything. I stare at the lifeless stack. Of course I don't *have* to wear jeans to the party. I could wear the long skirt or stretchy workout pants that have been making it possible for me to leave the house lately. But every woman knows that would be to admit defeat. That would be letting the blue jeans win.

An hour later I march into the last place on earth a woman my age should go to buy blue jeans: a blue jean store. I'm unfazed by the 5,000 pairs of jeans lining the walls and stacked on the tables, which have intimidated me in the past. Not put off by the youth culture into which I have just stepped or the screaming music that surely is cranked up so loud so it will drown out the wails of parents when their children lead them to the cash register to pay $90 for faded-out pants with holes in them. Music that mostly keeps people my age out.

Not today.

Blue jeans belong to people my age, and I've come to claim what's rightly mine. My generation made blue jeans cool. We made jeans essential. We were the founding mothers and fathers of the universe in which jeans now roam freely—the original laid-back, kicked-back, rebel-against-restrictions, "just wear jeans" people. I flash back to college, to the transformation I watched on the Diag of the University of Michigan, the place every student crossed and gathered every day. It was my freshman year—the year 12,000 U of M coeds ditched the nice preppy college skirts and button-down blouses our moms had just spent the summer buying, ironing, and packing. We ditched them and changed into jeans. Changed into different people. Changed into people who could say NO to all kinds of things, including skirts, blouses, underwear, and irons.

Jeans were the uniform of awakening. They helped free the voices of some of us who had no idea we had anything to say. Even a shy girl from Midland, Michigan, who had never, ever rebelled against anything. Even if I still obeyed all the rules, even if I only actually watched the whole revolution from the side, jeans connected me to something beyond the safe bubble in which I grew up. They were the opposite of prim skirts. Jeans were loose and comfortable; they literally felt like women's minds started to feel—less restricted, free to challenge rules, question norms, rebel against roles.

Jeans leveled the playing field. Men and women wore the exact same ones. And because we did, jeans were honest. They didn't send mixed messages, hurt, or make us feel bad about ourselves. Everyone had one pair of basically the same brand, style, and fit, two pairs at the most. It was unthinkable that there would be a different look or that anyone would ever outgrow the ones they already owned. Our jeans were made of denim that gently softened and shaped to the people who wore them, never insulted anyone by springing back to their original brand-new state. Faded denim was earned, not bought. Those sweet, forgiving, naturally faded pants. Those glory days of life before memory fibers.

I sold my Econ 101 textbook back to the bookstore in my third week to buy my first pair. I bought jeans and flunked Econ. The jeans seemed way more relevant.

"Can I help you find something?"

I'm startled back to the present. I turn to face the salesperson standing next to me. She's eighteen, I'm guessing, the exact age I was when I got my first pair of loose, liberating, life-changing college jeans.

The jeans she's wearing are shredded stretch denim, sort of like a half-body girdle with holes. Peeking out of the hole on her right thigh is a tattoo of what might be the Little Mermaid. Hot pink jewels form a cute, sparkly peace sign next to her crotch. Her shrink-wrapped denim ankles are planted in peekaboo, half-unlaced construction worker boots with four-inch heels. She looks free, but it's unclear from what.

How on earth did we get from me to her?

How is it that as soon as unisex jeans went out of favor and companies started designing "women's cut" versions, jeans became something many women couldn't fit into? What happened to all those dreams on the Diag that turned my generation's uniform of emancipation into this salesperson's saucy denim girdle? How did the pants that leveled the playing field become another cause for tears in the dressing room or in front of closet mirrors? How did my generation let jeans, which were the definition of happy clothes, turn into something stacked up in our own closets that don't even fit *us*?? I need answers. I need accountability.

"Um . . . *hello*?? Are you looking for something?" the salesperson repeats.

"I need some jeans," I answer. Understatement of the century.

"What size?" she asks. Insane question of the century.

No turning back now. I'm full of granola and indignation. Absolutely no reason to not be 100 percent honest about my size.

"I wear a size 8, 32, 14, 10, 6, or a 0," I announce. "In some stores I'm a 000. Some manufacturers make their 10's fit like 4's, which might make me a 16. Some make their 12's fit like 6's, which would make me 9. However, a dozen different size 9's can fit completely differently even if I'm having a 'perfect size 9 day.' In some jeans, I'm a 2. Once I was a 34. I might be a 7."

"Awesome," she says. She kind of peeks around me, glances at my butt, grabs three pairs off a stack, and hands them to me. I look down at them in my hand without even unfolding them.

"Do you have any jeans with zippers longer than two inches?"

"No."

"Well then, never mind." I hand the jeans back and move on.

$$\vartheta\text{---}\mathscr{X}\text{---}\vartheta$$

If the e-vite had said "just wear a swimsuit," it would have been only slightly worse, I think while entering the next store, which has music and clothes more appropriate for my age. At least a swimsuit is a swimsuit. At least a different swimsuit isn't required for every different occasion. Women's jeans don't only have to fit the body, they have to fit the event. Did the invitation's instruction to "just wear jeans" mean elegant jeans? Dressy jeans? Casual jeans? Earthy jeans? Straight leg? Boot cut? Flare? High rise? Cropped? Skinny crop? Baggy crop? Tomgirl? Boyfriend? Dressy dark denim? Casual dark denim? Super-casual, baggy fit, distressed denim with fancy pumps? Stone-washed shredded denim with stiletto sandals? Super-thin, non-stretchy smooth denim with ankle booties? Faded denim leggings with flats?

Maybe because I'm a driven member of the Blue Jean Generation, I have the will and stamina to persevere. I've watched my daughter give up in tears after trying on the first ten or fifteen pairs. But I march on . . . through this store . . . this mall . . . through another mall . . . through other department stores . . . specialty stores . . . shops for mature women . . . many, many, many dressing rooms . . .

And finally . . . after what feels like a thousand failed tries . . . I pull on some jeans that sort of feel as if they could belong on me. As if they might actually fit. I squint into the mirror in disbelief. I twist and peer at myself from every angle. Do they actually fit my body, or do they merely fit how desperate I am to go home and put on sweat pants? Am I so beaten down that I'll take anything? Have I looked at myself in so many pairs of bad jeans today that I'm incapable of seeing what's wrong with this picture, or is there nothing wrong? The zipper zips . . . the button buttons . . . nothing hurts . . . They might be okay, I think. They might even be good. I stand back from the mirror. Sort of casual, sort of dressy—a bold statement of ambiguity that's a perfect match for the contradictory feelings I have when I peek at the price tag and see that I'll be paying $145 for them.

I feel good enough that I open the door to the dressing room and let the salesperson see them on me. Good enough that I ask her to help me find pieces to complete the look for my upcoming party. We choose an arty tunic that hits mid-thigh and lovely suede boots that come to the top of my calf, so only seven vertical inches of denim are actually visible on either leg. It's summer in Los Angeles, but in a city that both reveres edgy fashion and prays for rain, a woman wearing boots on a hundred-degree July day can be seen as totally hip or totally hopeful, not necessarily one who's trying to cover anything.

I drive home exhausted and conflicted, but also triumphant. I put my new jeans on top of the stack in my closet. I'll never get rid of them, even if the day comes when they're too big or too small. I step back to admire what I've accomplished. All the blouses, tank tops, jackets, sweaters, wraps, and sweat shirts make sense again. All the things I've pledged to sort and unload suddenly have purpose and possibility because they're "perfect with jeans" and I own jeans that fit. Jeans that will not only get me to the party in two days, but give me a great big respite from sorting out the rest of my closet for a long time to come.

I feel a familiar little rush of freshman year. Feel a little bit liberated.

Once again, my blue jeans have set me free.

FIVE MORE REASONS
I DIDN'T EXERCISE TODAY

1. I'm afraid I'll look silly.

2. I'm afraid I'll look weak.

3. I'm afraid I'll look old.

4. I'm afraid I'll look as if I need to exercise.

5. I'm afraid I'll quit.

20.

THE ORGANIZER

A silent cheer to myself as the cab pulls up to my parents' house in Florida. "I'm going in!" It's 9:00 p.m., Sunday night. Mom and Dad have been asking me to help them reorganize and pitch, and I'm happy to do it. One full week of sorting linen closets, kitchen cupboards, and bathroom cabinets! Setting up systems for bills and correspondence! Braving storage boxes full of ancient travel guides and souvenirs! Separating true keepsakes from "why on earth are we still keeping these?" I'll work ten hours a day, if that's what it takes! I'm marching in as the adult—with energy, focus, and the cool, clear, decision-making skills it's possible to have when it's someone's mess besides mine.

"Welcome, sweetie!" Mom and Dad greet me at the door with beaming smiles and warm hugs. "We're so happy you're here!"

"Me too," I say. "I have big plans for this visit!"

"Us too!" Mom answers as I pull my suitcase in the door. "Our dear friends Kirsten and Gene are stopping over for breakfast tomorrow. They can't wait to see you! Then Dad made reservations at the cute seafood place you love for lunch, and there's a wonderful new tropical plant exhibit we want to take you to before dinner!"

"But I came to help!" I interject.

"Oh, and thank heavens for that. We need your help!" Dad says.

"So much to do here!" Mom echoes.

"Okay then," I say, "Tuesday! First thing Tuesday, I'll—"

"Mom has both of you signed up for a stretch class Tuesday," Dad interrupts, "and there's a ball game on TV we can watch in the afternoon!"

I've been here three minutes. Two days are already gone. "Okay," I say with all my adultness. "Starting Wednesday, I'm tackling all those projects you've said you wanted to do!"

Mom pulls the calendar off the wall. "Dad has a periodontist appointment we were hoping you could take him to Wednesday morning," she notes, "and then we have matinee tickets for the tango troupe that's in town!"

"Thursday?" I try weakly.

"Thursday, Friday, and Saturday are pretty full. Then Sunday's church and lunch afterward, and then you'll have to pack to fly back on Monday!" Mom wraps her arms around me in a hug. "Your whole visit will be over!"

"But I came to help!" I try.

"Oh, and thank heavens for that. We need your help!" Dad says, joining the hug from the other side.

"So much to do here!" Mom echoes, squeezing more tightly. I'm an actual human panini now. Me and my big agenda squashed between layers of parents. Now I'll not only need to reorganize their whole house, I'll need to do it in between all the activities they so sweetly planned. Somehow stuff my agenda into their agenda. I wiggle out of the middle. "I love you, Mom and Dad," I say, "but we should get to bed. Big day tomorrow!"

Big, big day, I think, pulling my suitcase to the guest room. But I'm up to the job. I know how to operate in Mom Mode. I did it for my child, I can do it for my parents. Break tasks into tiny goals that I can achieve while they do complicated things like put on socks and shoes. Make use of every second of their naptimes! And most important . . . wake up two hours before they do!

Day 1: 5:00 a.m.

I quietly lift one piece of paper off one stack on the kitchen counter when . . .

"Sweetie! Why are you up so early?!" Mom asks, walking into the kitchen.

I drop the papers, startled, and turn my back to the counter to face her.

"Why are *you* up so early?" I ask.

"I wanted to make sure I set the coffeemaker on auto," she says.

"It's on, Mom. See the little red button? It's all set! Go back to bed!" I say, trying to shoo her out.

"Why are *you* up so early?" she asks again, more awake this time.

"I . . . um . . . just thought I'd straighten things up a little in here," I answer.

"What things?" Mom asks, suddenly looking very wide awake.

"Why are you two up so early?" Dad asks, marching into the kitchen.

"She's straightening things up on the counter!" Mom announces.

"What things?" Dad asks, his wide-awake eyes scanning the countertop.

"Just a few . . . Why are *you* up so early, Dad?" I ask, more than a little frustrated at having been caught in the act of trying to help.

"We like everything on the counter right where it is," Dad says.

"It's five in the morning! Let's talk later! Go back to bed!" I say.

"We can't go back to bed unless you go back to bed so we'll know you aren't trying to straighten anything up!" Mom says.

"Fine! We're all wide awake now!" I say. "I was simply going to pull your bills out of this pile by your phone and make folders for them in your office."

"We always keep our bills on the counter," Mom says firmly.

"I thought I could at least toss out the junk mail that's in the same pile," I suggest.

"We need to open all those before we toss them because the mail carrier went to all the trouble to deliver them," Dad answers.

"Also we reuse the envelopes," Mom adds.

"How about if I just get rid of old newspapers?" I ask, picking up a small stack.

"No! Those might have articles we might need to clip for people!"

"How about a used sticky note??" I ask, picking one off the counter and holding it in the air. "Can I throw out one used sticky note with a grocery list from last Thanksgiving?!"

"No! I wrote the Holecs' new address on the back of that!" Mom says, plucking it from my hand.

"You use the backs of sticky notes??"

"You *don't* use the backs of sticky notes??"

I raise a mangled piece of wire in the air. *"Here!"* I say. *"One stretched-out paper clip! Can we get rid of one stretched-out paperclip??"*

Mom and Dad stare at me as though I've lost my mind, which I sort of have at 5:15 a.m.

"Don't be silly, honey," Dad says. "We keep the stretched-out ones in case we need something really tiny to poke a hole in something."

"I can't do this without coffee," I say, walking to the machine to push the on button.

"No!" Mom rushes to stop me. "It's all set for auto! See the little red light? We have to wait for the auto start!"

This launches a ten-minute search for the coffeemaker manual so I can prove it's okay to override the auto button . . . which launches a discussion of how happy I'd be to set up a nice organized file of appliance manuals . . . which launches a review of how much they prefer their system of keeping appliance manuals in random drawers throughout the house . . . which launches absolutely nothing that was on my list for Day 1.

Day 2: Naptime

"How long do you think you'll be sleeping?" I ask Mom as she and Dad head to their room for a late morning rest.

"No more than an hour," Mom answers. "You should take a nap, too!"

"Great idea!" I say.

I wait for the sound of their door to close, then spring into action. I bolt down the hall to their tiny, packed home office, the area they've said is most overwhelming to them . . . calculate what's needed to do a complete overhaul . . . rush to the office supply store . . . zoom through it with my list . . . rush back with $500 of pristine new file folders, pens, letter trays, a file cabinet, matching wastebaskets, and a bookshelf to assemble . . . stagger to the front door with the first load from the trunk of the car when . . .

"I thought you were taking a nap!" Dad says, standing in the open front door.

"Um . . . I just ran out to . . ." I begin.

"What happened to your nap?" Mom asks, appearing next to Dad.

"I wanted to get started on your office and . . . what happened to *your* naps?" I ask.

"What's wrong with our office?" Mom asks.

"I hope you didn't buy anything new!" Dad says, peering suspiciously at the bags in my arms. "We want to get *rid* of stuff!"

"The last thing we need is more stuff!" Mom chimes.

"I picked up a few things that will *help* you get rid of stuff! You just need some new systems, new supplies, and places to put things," I offer, trying to not sag under the weight of the bags in my arms.

"No new supplies! We have all kinds of supplies!" Mom says.

"We have too many things!" Dad echoes. "The last thing we need is more places to put things!"

"Okay then," I huff, exasperated. "I'll take all this back. Is that what you want? Do you want me to turn around and return everything I just bought to help you do what you've said you needed done??"

"Heavens no, sweetie," Mom says. "It's time for lunch and then you have the ball game with Dad!"

"Returning things can be tomorrow's project!" Dad says.

Day 3: Stolen Moments

Mom's busy in the kitchen, cleaning lettuce leaves one by one, with the care of a surgeon. Dad's busy studying The Weather Channel to see if he should be worrying about any family members in other states before we leave for his periodontist appointment. I tiptoe into their bathroom with the haul from last night's secret 9:00 p.m. run to Target: shelf paper, pretty organizer baskets, a new shower curtain, and a new bath mat when . . .

"What's all that?" Mom and Dad are suddenly both in the doorway of the bathroom staring at me, my Target bags, and the squirt bottle of all-purpose cleaner in my hand.

"I just thought I'd freshen up your bathroom a little!" I say in my best happy, helpful, trying-to-not-sound-agitated voice. "You've had the same shower curtain for forty years!"

"We like our shower curtain!" Mom states.

"And your bath mat—" I begin.

"We love our bath mat!" Dad states.

"I could at least get rid of some of the things in the cabinets you don't need and organize the things you do need in nice, pretty baskets," I try.

"We might need all the old things! We don't need pretty baskets!" they counter.

I give up.

I stuff it all back in the Target bags, stand up, and face them.

"I came here to help!" I say. "You said you *wanted* help. You said every room in your house needed a total overhaul, and I came to do it!"

"Thank you, sweetie! We're so grateful for your help!" Mom says, giving me a hug.

"There's so much to do here!" Dad says, hugging me from the other side.

"But you won't let me do anything!" I answer from the middle of the sandwich.

"Of course we will, sweetie! You can do anything! Anything at all!" they both say, squeezing me tight. "Just don't move anything, change anything, throw anything out, put anything in a different spot, or spend any money!"

Days 4-7

Ditto.

Day 8: Goodbyes

Something always happens the morning I leave Mom and Dad's house. It happens for my sisters when they leave, too. No matter how long the visit was—even if it felt way too long—it's always suddenly way too short. We start missing one another while we're still standing in the same room. In the last hour of the visit, everyone tries to say and do every single thing that didn't get said or done in the days or weeks we were there. Everyone feels a great big need to give and forgive.

My sisters and I become more patient, thoughtful listeners. Dad makes piles of movies we never got to, books and magazines he thinks we might like. He checks and rechecks the flight schedule, The Weather Channel, road delays, and his wallet, to make sure he has a twenty-dollar bill to tuck in our hands. Mom cuts up little Baggies full of apple slices, carrots, sandwiches, chicken legs, nuts, and cookies—as if, since we won't let her help pack our bags anymore, she can at least pack our stomachs. If they could, I think Mom and Dad would hop into our suitcases themselves.

Because it's the morning I'm leaving, I spent longer than usual reading the paper with Dad and listening to his stories. I'm down to thirty minutes before my cab arrives, racing through the house to finish packing, when I hear Mom's voice coming from the dining room.

"I'd love it if you could help me organize my stationery situation!" she calls.

I stop in my tracks and go back down the hall to where she sits at the table. "*Now*, Mom??" I ask, my arms loaded with things I still need to pack. "The cab will be here in half an hour!"

"You're so good at making systems for things!" she says, gesturing to the piles of paper on the dining room table she must have pulled from all sorts of drawers and shelves while I was reading the paper with Dad this morning. Fifty years of random types of notepaper, envelopes, greeting cards, stickers, and stamps. There's no need to remind Mom that I've been here for a week and this is exactly the kind of project I wanted to spend days tackling for her. I chuckle at the impossibleness. At Mom's perfect timing.

This is her goodbye gift—as heartfelt as the chunk of coffee cake I saw her slip into my carry-on bag earlier. Mom knows I came on this trip to help, and she wants to help me help her before I go. She wants me to leave with the gift of having something checked off my list. And now I need to help her help me help her.

"Great idea, Mom!" I say. "Let's see how far we can get!"

In the few minutes we have left, we admire Mom's pretty notepaper . . . laugh as we read through some of her greeting card collection . . . start organizing her stash of rinsed-out plastic bags and flattened twist ties to use should we ever get a system started . . .

And then, way too soon, the cab honks, and suddenly my suitcase and I are at the door.

"If only you were staying another week to help us deal with all our messes!" Mom sighs and gives me a hug. "We'll tackle it all on the next visit!" Dad announces, joining Mom from the other side. A farewell sandwich. Way too much emotion in the middle of this one for me to say much except "I'd better come back soon."

And that's how we left it. I'm on the plane back to California now. Everything—including the plan to go through everything some other time—is completely intact. When I come back again, everything will be exactly where it was before. Bills stacked with junk mail and old newspapers on the kitchen counter next to the phone. Office full of old files in ancient folders. Linen cabinets stuffed with history we never even opened. Untouched boxes of recipes, family pictures, and souvenir circus programs. Bathroom cabinet full of expired first-aid products, gift soap too pretty to use, vitamins no one takes anymore, lotions no one's ever opened. In Mom and Dad's house, relationships last forever. Nothing is ever wasted or discarded; everything has a purpose and another chance. No one ever divorces a shower curtain or breaks up with a bath mat. When you belong to Mom and Dad, you have a home forever.

I smile at 30,000 feet somewhere over Kansas. There's something very comforting about knowing it will all be there when I get back. Something a little bit wonderful about having accomplished absolutely nothing on this visit.

21.

LOVE STORIES

I should have known it would never last the first time I watched him load a dishwasher. The way he put big dirty pans in on top of fragile glasses . . . stuck bowls in between plates instead of lining bowls and plates up in their own rows like a normal person, so only six items fit in an area that should hold twenty. He put "top rack dishwasher safe" items on the bottom rack. Had long spatulas sticking way up out of the silverware tray without thinking they could block the thing that spins around and squirts water, and that if the spinning thing were blocked, the motor could overheat, the dishwasher could catch on fire, and the house could burn down.

I rushed into marriage way too young. That was one problem. I was only forty-seven years old. Only forty-five when I met and started dating him. There were red flags everywhere before we'd even had date number three. I should have run for my life. But I was way too in love for my feet to think about moving, and apparently the brain is willing to overlook a casserole dish caked with dried enchilada sauce being stuffed into an already full load when the heart is smitten.

I didn't have the maturity or self-confidence to call him out on issues like dishwasher loading . . . or how he'd open a box of crackers by grabbing it and trying to rip the top off instead of following the clearly printed instructions, so for the whole life of the box, partly shredded cardboard flaps would just stick straight up from the top instead of closing properly, and the crackers wouldn't stay crunchy. I knew nothing about confrontation or conflict resolution.

I had studied all the "Understanding the Male Brain" books and had written about relationships myself for years, but had zero experience living under the same roof with a male brain. The only person I'd ever lived with was my daughter, who was four years old when I met my husband, five when we got married. People used to joke that it would ruin my comic strip if I ever got happily married, but the reality of a man in the house was so much more material-rich than anything I could dream up that being married added a lot to my work. I waited seven years after my wedding to have the characters get married in the comic strip, hoping that enough time had passed so that no one, including my husband, would think I was writing about us. I also waited because I'd promised my faithful single readers that Cathy would never abandon them for "the other side," and I felt massively guilty about going back on my word. It finally became impossible to write about going on a date when it had been so many years since I'd been on one.

Besides no practical experience, by the time I met the man I married, I had a 9,000-item list of requirements. Some he mowed down on date number one, with sky-blue eyes and a sense of humor that made me laugh so hard, I cried. The other 8,967, I figured I could fix. I had lots of experience with erasers. The beauty of writing and drawing about relationships on paper is that I could make up the lines for both people, and I'd been doing that for a long time. I could erase the whole other person if I wanted. Or scribble the other person out with permanent ink. Or wad the other person up. Or shred the person into minuscule pieces that I would purposely throw in the trash, not the recycling bin, so even the teensy scraps of him wouldn't have a chance of being re-formed into something useful. Absolutely no earth-friendly file folders made from the gentlemen I shredded during my comic-strip-creating days.

That part was possibly also my fault. My ex-husband mentioned it twenty or thirty times in our couple's therapy sessions one through five—that I was a little bit too used to controlling the conversation by writing all the words for both sides to actually *be* in a conversation with a live person. I planned many things to say in response to him for session number six, but we never got to that session—partly because my husband was also planning what he'd say in response to what he thought I'd say in response to what he'd said. Both of us were writers and took upcoming therapy appointments as assignments, not so much to delve into the heart of our problems, but to see who could better script the dialogue for the next meeting.

By the end of session number five, it was clear that we'd turned the whole thing into a creative competition, each person trying to win the session. Of course we both wanted to win the therapist's sympathy, but even more, we wanted to see which one of us could make the therapist laugh the most. Entertaining though it was to try to outwit each other with an audience, it wasn't really worth the $250 per fifty-minute session. Much more cost-effective to break up, we decided.

I don't mean to make it sound as if it didn't matter, because it mattered a lot. My husband and I felt unbelievably blessed to have met when we did. We were a miracle for each other—he with a young son and me with a young daughter. Our children fell as in love with each other as he and I did, and it seemed as if we had all the pieces to start a beautiful new phase of life that neither of us ever imagined we'd have. We shared the exact same dream of making our sweet blended family work and of the long, long future we'd all have together.

There was profound sadness when we finally admitted we'd failed, and many, many tears that weren't the laughing ones. But what was best about us as a couple resurfaced when we were breaking up—it was there at the end just like it had been in the beginning, even with the 8,967 things I never got fixed. Even while we separated, my ex-husband made me laugh until I cried. We had so much fun planning our divorce, we almost could have fallen back in love and started all over again.

ϑ—♡♡♡♡—ϑ

Everyone has love stories—ones that worked, ones that didn't, ones that never made it past the imagination. This time of life makes them all come to mind. It isn't possible to reflect on where the years went, what happened, how we wound up living where we live, and which people we'll call family for the rest of our days without thinking about our love stories. About all those choices. All those things that happened or didn't happen, starting in the fifth grade, or maybe even before, when it first occurred to us that we kind of liked some-one. That very first second it mattered to us if the other person liked us back.

Some of us were single for a really, really long time. Some of it was on purpose.

The world had just opened up with possibilities for women that went way beyond being housewives when I was in my prime dating years, and I fell in love with idea of launching my own life and career before I got involved with someone. I loved the thrilling freedom and power of having a job, driving to an office, and supporting my-self. I loved living by myself, in an apartment I found and set up on my own, every single decision discussed only with my dog. But I was a young woman in my twenties, and I also loved the idea of falling in love with a person . . .

The easy answer was to go out only with people who were as unready to get involved as I was. Much less risky to date someone who promised a doomed future than someone who might threaten the solitary life I loved and worked so hard to earn. But in a short amount of time, all my independence and empowerment only seemed to increase how vulnerable I was to relationships that wound up making me insecure and needy. I couldn't stand it when someone I decided I loved didn't love me back, even though that was the whole attraction in the first place. I couldn't resist the challenge of trying to get the wrong person to change his mind.

This is all a lot more clear now than it was then. At the time, it created a totally contradictory bubble that was my happy and not so happy world—simultaneously loving my life exactly as it was and longing for a life I didn't have. A push and pull that ultimately launched my comic strip and provided a lot of what I wrote about for many years. The heart versus the brain. I was always a little bit irritated by how often the wrong one won. Also a little frustrated by the unnecessary grief I inflicted on myself. But then, I wouldn't trade one second of the incredible life I got to have that grew out of all that.

Some of us were lucky enough to have a dear friend through the worst of our dating years. A person so special she not only propped us up through all the drama then but is still close enough that she can give some perspective now. I have a friend like that. She just met me for coffee and is sitting across the table from me with a fat-free latte and a plate of cinnamon rolls.

We were soulmates during years of singleness. Codependent support systems full of mutually bad advice throughout our twenties and thirties. She's the only person I know who consistently made even worse dating choices than I did—the one woman I leaned on to advise me on mine. We were each other's totally incompetent relationship coaches. When everyone else we knew was sick of hearing about "him," we were there for each other. Champions of false hope. Defenders of each doomed obsession. We both finally got married at ages most would consider a little later than normal. We both raised daughters. Both got unmarried.

And now we're both compelled to look back and do the same kind of reflecting—trying to organize all the little pieces of life that got us up to right now. Our daughters are close to the same age she and I were when we became friends. We both wonder what possible founts of wisdom and dating advice we can be for our girls after the choices we made. After all those what-were-we-thinking years.

We've been doing a binge-review of relationship blunders for an hour . . .

All those brain cells given over to Mr. Wrong.

All those hundreds of dollars spent on beautiful shoes to make a man who never once looked at our feet fall in love with us.

All those thousands of hours shopping for what to wear on the rest of us.

All those weeks waiting for the phone to ring.

All those makeovers, that frantic primping.

All that time spent translating every little syllable into a possible expression of the love he surely felt but never learned to express.

All those pounds gained in revenge for his not being who we pretended he was.

All those big, humiliating ideas . . .

Yes! You should write a poem and tuck it under his windshield wiper while his car is parked at another girl's house!

Yes! You should knock on his door on New Year's Eve because he was probably planning to propose at midnight, but just got too scared to call and invite you out!

Could my dear friend and I have been worse for each other?

Yes, we decide, on latte number two and cinnamon roll number three. Yes, we could have been and were. It wasn't only that we helped each other rationalize relationships that weren't good for us, it's that we did it during years in which there were so many wonderful, positive new champions of a different way to be. Women cheering women on to assert ourselves, believe in ourselves, and demand more for ourselves in every part of life.

It was way more complicated then than it seems now. There was so much inspiring, uplifting new talk about self-respect and having it all, but hardly any examples at the time of women who were able to do it. Most of us had grown up in houses where the men were in charge, watching TV shows like *Father Knows Best*. The men we dated grew up in those houses and watched those TV shows, too. They had the same mom and dad role models. It was hard enough for a young woman back then to figure out what to wear on a date, let alone figure out how to create a totally different reality in her relationships. Hard enough to find a guy to go out with, let alone one who was open to being dethroned and reprogrammed. Men and women were still arguing about things like "whether a man should give a woman permission to have a job." Women were excited by the new world other women were talking and writing about, but without real-life proof, it was hard to believe it was possible to try for a loving, equality-based relationship with someone who would support our dreams, not try to stifle them.

I remember carrying magazine articles about how to have more enlightened relationships in my purse and restudying them in the ladies' room in the middle of dinner dates. I remember feeling filled with support and knowing exactly what to say until I sat back down at the table. I remember that not that many boys wanted a second date with a feminist.

It's a little bit painful for my friend and me to see our daughters and remember who we were when we were their age. The very best years of our lives—when we were young and pretty and bursting with hope, innocence, and optimism. When love should have been welcomed, not feared. When we had so much to give and so often gave it to the wrong people. It helps to play it back with someone who was there. It's a tribute to the power of female friendship that my friend and I are still speaking to each other. We look at each other now and shake our heads—for all the bad choices we helped each other make, for all those dreams and delusions we supported.

"I hate you," I say, laughing warmly, toasting my friend with what's left of my latte.

"I hate you more." She laughs just as warmly, toasting me back.

"At least we're done now, aren't we?" I ask. "We're safely on the other side."

"Oh, yes!" she answers. "Thank heavens those years are behind us. We survived. It's a whole different world for our girls. Things are complicated for them, but they won't have an entire society to transform while they try to date. They'll be fine. I'm so happy and relieved I can be done with love."

"Me too," I say. "I've had a wonderful life, but I feel as if I'm finally back to who I am. My own home, my dog, my daughter. I'm grateful I had love in my life, but I'm thrilled to be done with it now."

"One hundred percent done!" she echoes.

"So done!" I echo her echo.

We hug, promise to not let so much time pass before we see each other next, and pay the check.

We're just about to reach the door of the restaurant to leave when a man steps in front of us. Handsome. Sky-blue eyes. He smiles and opens the door with a Prince Charming sweep of his arm. My friend thanks him with an involuntary middle school giggle. I'm mortified to feel myself blush.

We are so done with love. Love, on the other hand, will apparently never quite be finished with us.

22.

THE DAY I WASHED MY FACE WITH BATH SOAP

ell me about your skin care regimen!" the department store cosmetician cooed, admiring my young, innocent skin and welcoming me into the Club. This was decades ago, back when I had young, innocent skin and, as salespeople quickly gleaned, a young, innocent charge card in my purse to match.

"What do you use to wash your face?" she asked eagerly, inviting confidence and sisterhood.

"Soap!" I answered proudly, encouraged by her warm reception.

"Soap??" She leaned in, seeming riveted.

"Yes!" I replied, thrilled that I knew the answer to the first question on the very first day I was brave enough to approach the department store cosmetics counter. "Yes! I *always* wash my face with soap!"

"*Bath soap??*" She gasped.

I didn't know what I'd done wrong, only that I was apparently no longer in the Club. I remember being hit with an overpowering blast of perfume as all the other cosmeticians in the department whipped their heads around to stare, sending all their over-the-top scents in my direction. I suddenly reeked of Wrong Answer. I turned all the colors of blush in my cosmetician's display. I felt very unproud.

We don't wash our faces with soap, I learned. We cleanse with a gentle, non-detergent facial cleanser. The cleanser is to be preceded by a hypoallergenic makeup and environmental toxin remover . . . then a mild exfoliating scrub . . . *then* the cleanser . . . then toner, serum, targeted fillers, and plumpers . . . and *then* we can start the complex moisturizing system, a different product for each dry or oily zone.

It took $235 to buy my way back into the cosmetician's favor. Just to get to a clean face. Just to achieve the blank facade upon which I could, if I ever got a raise or was willing to skip a rent payment or two, begin to build my look.

It took two showers to lose the aroma of failure when I got home.

It took decades to lose the mental residue of being scolded for not knowing how to be a girl.

Who knows why we finally snap, but it finally happened. Today. 6:30 a.m. Cup of coffee number two. I rise up from the newspaper at the kitchen table. Stomp down the hall in my pajamas. Fling open the bathroom door. Power-glare at my morning face in the mirror. I grab a bar of soap from the plastic dish on the edge of the tub. Lean over the sink and for the first time in many years . . .

Wash my face with bath soap!

HAH.

I step back from the sink. No beauty alarms are blaring. I peek out the bathroom door. No police standing in the hall. I look in the mirror. No flaking, cracking, blotching, or any of the other signs of skin damage I was warned would occur if soap ever touched my face. I can't believe it. My mind reels with rebellion.

What other naughty things can I do?

I reach under the sink, pull out an economy-size container of cheap discount store body lotion, squirt out a big blob, and *use it to moisturize my face.* I peek out the bathroom door again. Still no police. Hah.

The next hour is a beautiful blur of defiance.

I pull my hair into a ponytail without worrying that there are no cute casual wisps framing my face! . . . I pour cereal in a bowl without measuring three fourths of a cup! . . . Add berries without counting them! . . . Make new coffee with *whole milk and real sugar*!

I'm giddy with anarchy. What's next? Lashes without mascara? Lips without gloss? Thighs without Spanx? Chocolate without guilt? Thank-you notes without apologies? White bread? Without fake butter? Outdoors without shoes? HAH!

I run out of my house in my pajamas and stand barefoot right in the middle of the yard. I lift my unsunscreened face to the early morning sun for a full two seconds.

I like being a woman. I like rules, structure, and tips. I want to fit into the Club, or at least be somewhere on the edge of the Club. But the thousands of dollars I've spent on skin care trying to preserve a youthful look and my decades of obedience to the rules of womanhood were never quite as rejuvenating as this.

I wiggle my bare toes in the grass and make a pledge to myself, to the part of me that got lost at the cosmetics counter that first day years ago. From now on, I promise to take fewer steps trying to achieve a "dewy face" and to take a lot more steps that lead to the happiness I'm standing on right now: dewy feet.

23.

IT TOOK A VILLAGE

Stray socks on the kitchen counter . . . sweat shirts draped over the back of the couch . . . shoes, tights, and school papers dropped in a path down the hall . . .

I follow the trail of my daughter into her bedroom. I take a deep breath of the last nineteen years: Love Spell body mist mixed with the memory of dried finger paint. Saucy tank tops and SpongeBob SquarePants pj's spilling out of open drawers. A jumble of little girl fantasies and big girl dreams: Magic wands and miniskirts. Strapless bra on a Tinker Bell blanket. Fishnet tights hanging from *101 Dalmatians* hooks. Tangled necklaces. Mangled power cords. A desk covered with everything but a place to do schoolwork. A heap of T-shirts and tiny teen dresses on the floor of the open closet.

I allow myself a wistful moment to take it in, to imagine how I'll miss it when my daughter packs it all up and moves back to college after her break. The emptiness. The unbelievable, unbearable emptiness of her being gone.

I only allow myself a moment because she left two days ago.

This isn't everything she's about to take. This is what's still here after she already took everything. As though a whole civilization of teenage girls had to evacuate with no time to grab their belongings. That's how it looks in this room. Except she had lots of time to grab things. We had to buy an extra suitcase for all she grabbed. This is what's *left*.

"You forgot this top!" I said, lifting a cute almost-new one from her laundry basket after she finished packing her last suitcase the night before she went back to school.

"I hate that top," she scoffed.

"You loved it when you begged me to buy it for you! What about these leggings?" I asked, picking a pair out of the pile on the floor. "This cute jacket??"

"Mom, you told me to pack and I packed!!" she whined.

"But you're leaving behind so many cute things!" I implored, gesturing to the room. "So many perfect school clothes!"

"No one wears school clothes to college!" she argued.

"Excuse me??" I asked, exhausted and spent—literally spent, after a week of Target, mall, and drugstore runs.

"NO ONE WEARS SCHOOL CLOTHES TO COLLEGE!!" she snapped.

Scoffed. Whined. Argued. *Snapped.* After everythi— But never mind . . .

I sit on my daughter's bed and sigh. I take another deep breath of her room. I try to find my happy-mom place between how sad I am that she's gone and how glad I am that she left.

I need my village. My support system. I need Bob, a dear friend who's been part of our family forever and has helped me through so many transitions.

"Teenagers get obnoxious so we won't miss them so much! It's their gift to us," I say to comfort myself, but also to comfort Bob, who surely felt as hurt as I did when he heard what my daughter said. Yes, Bob's right here too and was also here that night. He witnessed the whole thing. He actually looks more wounded than I felt because our dog ate half of his rubber nose and one of his plastic eyes the day my daughter brought him home from the fair when she was three. I pick him up from the other side of the bed: Bob, the stuffed rabbit. Our dog never cared about ears, so Bob heard everything that ever went on in this room, even all kinds of things it's probably best he never shared.

"Teenagers also get obnoxious so *they* won't miss *us* so much," I say to formerly identical twin polar bear cubs, Meg and Peg, from the Los Angeles Zoo gift shop, who also watched the mother-daughter packing drama. Peg was the victim of a grape Slurpee accident when my daughter was five. Sad for Peg, but we decided permanently purple fur was a good thing. It helped us talk about not feeling bad when you feel different. Also, we agreed it made Peg a more patient listener because we quit calling her by her sister's name half the time.

I pick up Mary, the stuffed golden retriever puppy my daughter carried everywhere for years. A being so crucial to everyone's sanity that when we realized Mary had been left at a hotel at Legoland AFTER we'd driven three hours home, I called an emergency babysitter to put my girl to bed, got back in the car, and drove three hours back to the hotel to rescue her—then three more hours back home. "She wanted you with her at college," I say tenderly to Mary, holding her up, "but she needed room in her suitcase for two hundred dollars' worth of hair products. None of us can take this personally." I give her a kiss on what our real-life dog left of her nose.

When they say "It takes a village," I'm pretty sure they mean a village of humans, but I'm also pretty sure people lean on whoever's available. My family lived far away in different time zones . . . Friends were busy with their own lives . . . The Internet didn't exist yet . . . I was single . . . and was too busy, proud, and clueless to ask for or even know I needed help when I did.

This was my village a lot of the time, especially in the beginning. I scan the mostly half-blind, de-nosed, partly hairless, matted menagerie piled on the bed, lining the bookshelves, and plopped in a corner of the room—stuffed dogs, bears, cats, birds, and one beloved tiger with a satin ribbon around her neck on which a faded *Hayley* is written in wobbly first-grade printing. Some members of the village are still half dressed in costumes, as if my daughter outgrew them right in the middle of a game. I know all their names and histories better than I know those of many of the people in my life. They know more about my daughter and me than anyone on earth. They saw it all, from the very beginning.

The elders of the village—the stuffed animals who were here when I brought my daughter home from the hospital—saw how my precious new baby snuggled so trustingly in my clueless new-mom arms that first night. They saw how completely overwhelmed I was by how instantly she accepted me as her mother. How surreal it was for me to sit with her in the rocking chair I never imagined would be in my single-person home . . . to feel her relax into sleep as I fed her. They saw me gaze at her tiny perfect face, gently rock her, and lovingly sing her very first lullaby.

They saw how she woke up screaming the second I started singing.

Every single time I started singing. They saw how, by the end of night two and forty-eight hours of no sleep, I admitted that my voice might be the problem, staggered to the other room, and brought back a tape player and a stack of professionally recorded lullabies I'd been given as baby gifts. They saw how I silently mouthed the words as my baby was lulled to sleep by the audiotapes, the satisfaction I got from pretending Dionne Warwick's voice was coming out of my mouth.

My village is a nonjudgmental group. None of them ever felt the need to mention how some version of what happened that night, three days into motherhood, got repeated thousands of times throughout the nineteen years that followed: my learning to understand and appreciate who my daughter is, to respect her opinion, to give her what she needs, all the while trying to hang on to some little shred of how I planned for things to go . . .

All those beautiful stroller walks we started, with me joyfully pushing her as I introduced her to the trees, birds, and flowers . . . that ended with me carrying her home wailing because, I finally accepted, I had the one baby on earth who hated being in a stroller.

All the mingle 'n' jingle groups, the tiny tots dance classes, the sing-along sessions, the junior gyms, the wee ones soccer leagues, the art for little people places we joined and abandoned because she refused to mingle, jingle, dance, sing, tumble, play soccer, do art . . . or, basically, leave my lap.

All the fantasies of meeting friends for leisurely Sunday brunches, my darling daughter in a booster seat by my side . . . that for reasons I don't need to recount, turned into many, many carry-out containers of pancakes we ate at home in our own kitchen by ourselves.

Even all my dreams of teaching her to eat a proper breakfast at home at the table with nice manners . . . how they deteriorated into her on all fours on the kitchen floor lapping cereal and milk out of a bowl with her tongue during a long phase in which she had "turned into a cat" . . . And how, when visiting friends saw her and were horrified by how I'd caved in to my child's whims, I put a bowl on the floor next to hers and ate my cereal there on all fours too, meowing like the mother cat I needed at that moment to be.

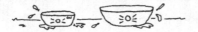

My daughter and I bonded deeply right from the start over all the things we discovered that we loved together—dogs, the park, playing dress-up, painting on the porch, baking, reading books, inventing stories, building castles out of blocks, sand, and cardboard boxes.

But we bonded just as deeply, or even more so, over things that seemed to come easily to others that were hard for her and then so hard for me. We were a team. Defiant survivors of her early childhood—playgroups she didn't fit into, a school system not set up for how she could learn, activities where she felt lost or left out . . . testing, tutors . . . all those horrible looks from other mothers whose children didn't melt down at the mall, bite the dentist, or have humiliating full-blown panic attacks every time they boarded an airplane. We got through all that . . . hauled her through the academics . . . then the nightmare of middle school girls, then the nightmare of high school boys . . .

I went into motherhood planning to be a serene, self-assured role model of accomplishment, sharing the strategies and tips that helped me be successful. A fount of wisdom. That's what I planned.

My child wanted none of it.

Stories of my accomplishments only made my daughter, who struggled to do some of the most basic things, feel worse about herself. Tales of how good old-fashioned hard work easily led to me getting great grades and a wonderful career made her want to quit. She worked harder than lots of kids, and nothing came easily. My wisdom demoralized her. My perky tips made her angry.

My daughter wanted confessions. She wanted to hear about my failures, fears, embarrassments—the worse, the better. The more humiliating, the more reassuring.

Did you ever wear your shoes on the wrong foot?

Did you ever get called on in class and start crying in front of everyone?

Did you ever spell your own name wrong?

Did you ever sit down for lunch and have all the other girls get up and leave?

Did you ever spill a whole drink in your lap?

Things like that. Stories of how I froze with fear and couldn't speak to the cute boy on the playground gave her hope. Stories of how I chatted with Johnny Carson on *The Tonight Show* did not.

I knew the power of commiseration from writing the comic strip for so long, but I wasn't expecting it from motherhood. Also, the comic strip put a comfortable distance between me, the person, and her, the character in the newspaper. My daughter only wanted the me part. Specifics. Names and dates. Photos, if possible. *How bad did you look? . . . Who really saw you and what did they really say?* The more details I shared of times I'd blown it in life, the more inspired she seemed to be to try. The more open I was about when I'd been afraid and weak, the braver and stronger she got. The more honest I was with her, the more honest she was with me.

Drawing all those lines in the comic strip was nothing, it turned out, compared to the many, many lines I had to draw as a mom—between helping too much and helping too little . . . between being too strict and too lenient . . . between being the strong, all-knowing parent and being a friend sitting on the floor, confessing all the things I *didn't* know.

I didn't exactly have to make up stories of my shortcomings.

One of the great things I attempted as a mom was to get married to a man with a young son when my daughter was five years old, so she could grow up with a dad and a brother. One of the great things I didn't do was figure out how to make my marriage and blended family work. By our tenth anniversary, my husband and I finally accepted the fact that everyone would live more happily ever after if we weren't all under the same roof.

Along the way, my daughter got to see plenty of examples of her imperfect mom in action. It helped a lot that we had a track record of talking and being able to laugh about the blunders. That also helped all four of us leave our family with wonderful memories of the things that did work when we were together. I came away with an ex-husband who's still a best friend and a stepson I adore. My daughter has a dad who loves her dearly and a stepbrother who will always be a big, important part of her life.

My eyes land on a picture of the two of them on her dresser across the room. They're in the elementary school sandbox, arms wrapped around each other, both heads tilted back, howling at some shared, private sister-brother joke. I'm filled with love. Then filled with love's first cousin, guilt. What I could have, should have, done differently . . . how I didn't make this family that started so sweetly last . . .

I wrench myself out of past remorse back to the here and now, but guilt comes along for the ride. The heaps of belongings on the dresser next to the joyful sister-brother picture . . . the jumble of stuff on the floor . . . Every bit of every pile that my daughter left for me to clean up in this room represents some failing of me as a mom. I helped my child learn to try and laugh, but I did not teach her how to fold, iron, organize, or put things away.

Guilt expands and multiplies before I can stop it. I also didn't teach her to budget, cook, or play the piano. She doesn't know how to garden, clean the oven, sew, change a tire, roller-skate, build a wagon, tie a Girl Scout knot, fold a fitted sheet, do group sports or ballroom dance. *She does not have an appreciation for art, music, or literature or understand the divisions of Congress or how to knit or write in cursive and it's all my fault. . . .*

I reach across the bed for Carly, an especially dear, de-nosed, de-eyed, matted-furred, half-costumed stuffed puppy. "It's all on my list every time she comes home from college, Carly," I say, hugging her. "Part of the problem, you think? She comes home with all sorts of newfound confidence, and I greet her with the List."

I turn to the rest of my stuffed-animal village and try to put what I know we're all feeling into words. "Our girl's trying to figure out who she is without us, just like we are without her," I finally say. "Every goodbye's a little bit harder because it's one closer to when it will be time to really let go. She comes home needing to try out her new independence and gets belligerent because I don't appreciate the new upgraded version of her. I insult her by greeting her with the

List, but I don't mean to. I'm just panicked that I only have a short break to teach her everything I didn't teach her in life until now. Scared that I didn't do enough and that I'm out of time.

"But there's the middle of the visit too, when we both let down our defenses, when we relax, have fun, and are in love with each other. When we're back to who we are. The team. When we can laugh like best friends at all that's behind and still ahead of us. Back to being more than I ever dreamed a mom and daughter could be, when Dionne and I sang her that first lullaby."

I stand up and beam at my village. "We did it," I tell them. "We raised a young woman who's sweet, sensitive, hardworking, and doesn't bite dentists anymore. She has ambition, values, and a sense of humor. We got her launched. We gave her a family. She made it to college. She can scoff, whine, argue, snap, and try all sorts of other things to demonstrate how much she no longer needs us, and we'll still be here. Hearts wide open. We will love her exactly as much, and we will never doubt how much she loves us back."

I smile at the piles of the last nineteen years she left all over her room. I smile at the unlikelihood that my empty nest will ever actually be empty. At the impossibility of my ever giving away these dear stuffed animals like people suggest, or packing them up in plastic storage boxes where they won't be able to breathe.

"We did it!" I say to my village. I turn off the light, walk out of the room, and close my daughter's bedroom door behind me.

"We did it!"

I lean back on the closed door for a moment, suddenly full of something I've never let myself feel. I think about my mother. About all the mothers. Every mom on earth has her own challenges that no one else will ever really know. Every mom has dreams, tries her best, carries so much inside, finds her way, loses it, starts all over again and again and again. Every mom deserves this moment, I think— what I'm feeling right now. I shut my eyes and whisper it to myself:

"**I** did it."

Tears come from nowhere.

I say it again anyway, right through the tears. I open my eyes and say it right out loud:

"*I did it.*"

24.

THE ITSY-BITSY, TEENY-WEENY
TORTURE CHAMBER

L ook! This one might be cute!"

WHAT?? I snap to attention and stare. Stare in disbelief at what my right hand just plucked off the rack: a swimsuit.

A *SWIMSUIT.*

Are you kidding?? I think to myself. *After all we've been through?? Are you out of your mind?? . . . No! Wait . . . I AM your mind! Put that back immediately!* I scold.

I order my left hand to snatch the suit away from my right hand, but my left hand disobeys and grabs the same suit in a different color off the rack.

"It might be even cuter in this color!"

WHAT? What is wrong with you, hands?? . . . And feet! Why aren't you running for the exit?? . . . Legs?? Seriously? You, of all body parts!! Move!

Take us out of here!!! Get me away from this place! I am not spending one more second of my life in the swimwear department!!! I don't need or want a suit! I will never be anywhere where swimming could happen, and even if I were, I WOULD JUMP INTO THE POOL FULLY CLOTHED BEFORE I'D SUBJECT MYSELF TO THE EGO-OBLITERATING HEARTACHE OF TRYING ON SWIMSUITS AGAIN!

I love everything about the glorious female spirit. I love women's ability to rise from the rubble, to restore, forgive, inspire, believe, dream, support, honor, care, create—to have hope where hope seems impossible. I love every single thing about the glorious female spirit except how it can lead me into the dressing room of the swimwear department like it just did. Over all my objections. One little bit of unfailing female faith rose up and overcame all memory of what happened the hundreds of times I've tried on swimsuits before. Hope dragged me—along with eleven more suits it made me pick up on the way—into the dreaded room again with *"Maybe one of these will fit! Maybe one of these will look nice on me!"*

There seems to be only one salesperson in the three-story Macy's where I shop, so no one cares that I brought in an armload of suits, instead of the store limit of six per room. I'm happy not to have a salesperson nearby today. Extremely happy to not worry that anyone might pop her head in the door for a peek at how everything's fitting. There's no place women need the compassion of other women more than in the dressing room of the swimwear department, but no place on earth where most women would prefer to be all alone. So many tears shed in these little rooms, not an ounce of water weight ever lost. I do a quick scan of every corner, checking for cameras to make sure the room isn't being monitored by security personnel; that all those employees who aren't on the floor aren't gathered in the surveillance room watching me try on swimsuits.

Then again . . . what if they are? I stand taller and look in the mirror. I stare straight into the defiant pride of the twenty-first-century female and everything women exactly like me can finally claim for ourselves. The freedom not to be judged, restricted, or have to hide. We reject the unnatural and unattainable image of the scrawny supermodel! We joyfully celebrate all shapes and sizes, proud of every beautiful natural robust curve of the female form! Body-shaming is over! We will never again allow ourselves to be defined by our weight, measurements, or someone else's version of "beauty." *We are done with all that!*

I triumphantly hold up the first suit that I'll try on the beautiful natural curves of my own body. Apparently no one shared the news about how wonderful we all feel about ourselves with the swimwear manufacturer, because the giant tag reads: *"Look 10 pounds lighter in 10 seconds!"*

I pull a few more suits from the pile and check out their giant tags:

"Appear sleeker and slimmer in seconds!"

"Miracle fibers have three times the control power of spandex to mold, hold, cinch, shape, lift, and reposition!"

"Guaranteed to enhance the bust! Elongate the torso! Flatten the tummy! Sculpt the waist! Minimize the thighs, hips, and rear!"

I haven't gotten a swimsuit anywhere near my body, but so much has been revealed: all the contradictory messages with which women live all the time.

"SWIMWEAR FOR EVERY BODY TYPE!" on the cover of one magazine . . .

"HERE'S KIM IN A BIKINI SIX WEEKS AFTER GIVING BIRTH TO TWINS!" on another.

"CELEBRATE OUR LOVELY MATURING SHAPES!" on one . . .

"JOAN LOOKS HOTTER THAN EVER IN A BIKINI AT AGE 65!" on another.

"LOVE YOURSELF AT ANY SIZE!" . . . followed by . . . "LOSE FIFTEEN POUNDS IN A MONTH!"

If we're so fantastic as is, why are there a thousand messages every day encouraging us to make parts of ourselves disappear—everything from our fine lines to our fine thighs—with "REDUCE! SHRINK! MINIMIZE! DIMINISH! DECREASE! TRIM! LOSE!"

I sigh like women always do. Rally like women always will. Try to take all my confidence, competence, pride, and perfectly toned self-respect and squash it into this season's offerings. After all we've already been through in these dinky fluorescent-bulb-lit rooms, how far have we come? I'm curious.

I begin with a tankini, a long tank-style top paired with a modified bikini bottom—a beautiful concept that looks darling on the hanger. The answer to many of our prayers. The designer thought of everything—except the fact that a woman who wants to wear a long top because she's more comfortable *not* displaying the beautiful natural curves of her midriff would also be more comfortable if what's covering the curves weren't skintight, turning said midriff into a shimmery teal-blue sausage roll, every little ripple hugged and accentuated by the clingy fabric. Also, the designer made the tankini top three inches too short. No doubt wanted to give the confident twenty-first-century women a chance to flash a little skin . . . but the three inches of what's between the bottom elastic of the tank top and the top elastic of the bikini bottom are honestly not anything even the most empowered among us needs or wants to flash. Tankini number one is ripped off and flung on the stool in the corner.

Tankinis number two through six have the same irreconcilable sausage-roll issue, but add the bonus problem of all having some version of a plunging neckline, with varying degrees of padded, push-up, or molded cups, requiring a cleavage display some don't want to make for all sorts of reasons. Women who are proudly cleavage-free, with lovely sleek A+ cup chests, have a whole different problem. They either can't wear 99 percent of these suits or else have to make peace with wearing some version of a fake front at the pool and beach. The whole issue of needing to embellish, diminish, or rearrange the most womanly part of a woman's body seems way at odds with the whole lovely point of a woman feeling good about herself as she is.

I take a break from swimsuit tops and decide to refresh my spirits with some of the many new options for the lower half. I'm thrilled to see, as I hold some up, that we no longer need to be victimized by someone's archaic, insulting, misogynistic concept of what a woman's lower half might require.

More bad news.

The new bikini bottoms are very similar to the old bikini bottoms. Some are slightly more generous in cut, but all are out of the question for reasons I proudly choose not to enumerate.

The new skirted bottoms are rejected almost as quickly. They're either so balloony they look as if they belong on Grandma or are so tiny they reveal all the reasons I wanted to wear a skirt without covering anything I wanted the skirt to cover.

The new boy-cut swim bottoms are just cruel. Instead of being fun baggy female versions of fun baggy swim trunks for men, they're made of skintight stretch material and are cut like mini bike shorts, so they grip the largest part of the top of a woman's thighs like tourniquets. After all the fashion magazines I've studied over the years, I assume the thinking was that "Baggy wouldn't be sexy!" just as I assume, looking at the price tag, that our version costs three times as much as the men's version because the company wanted to help us celebrate that "We're worth it!"

I try one of the body-contouring one-piece swimsuits that say they will do all that enhancing, flattening, sculpting, and minimizing. As promised, it squashes, constricts, reshapes, and relocates flesh. I peer into the mirror. I can't really feel good about me because the part of me molded by the suit no longer resembles me. The parts of me sticking out from the suit—my arms, legs, and top of my torso—look much worse than me at my worst because all that extra everything had to go someplace. It's also hard to appreciate this version of myself because my internal organs and ribs are being crushed by the crisscross panels of girdle-grade spandex, and I'm about to pass out from lack of oxygen and blood flow. I was feeling way better about me, no matter what I looked like, when I could breathe and had a pulse.

I pry the suit off and try on a nice non-constricting full-coverage tank. It actually feels as if it might fit, but I rip it off before even looking in the mirror because I glance at the tag and see that it's two sizes bigger than the size I usually wear. I'm not about to contaminate my closet with anything that has that number on it. In case women don't already feel bad enough trying on swimwear, we usually have to go "up" a size to get anything remotely close to fitting. An almost incomprehensible lack of compassion and empathy from the women's swimwear industry, which of all industries should be tuned in to how women feel. I've already resigned myself to the reality that I have to go up one size. But buy a suit *two* sizes bigger than my size? Never. I feel a special joy flinging that one onto the "out" pile.

I slip on a cover-up someone left in the dressing room and take a moment for all my vital signs to return to normal. I should be offended to my core by all the suits, I think. But I'm a woman, and even offended, my core is still full of compassion. I consider the impossible challenge of designing something that satisfies the sensibilities, shapes, and sizes of billions of women. Women want and deserve to have fun swimsuits that let us be free to play and enjoy the outdoors and water. Women want to look pretty and appealing. We want to look as if we're part of the culture—that we fit in, literally, to what other people wear. We don't want to look like our grandmothers in swimwear, but we also don't want to reveal things we don't want to reveal. I imagine the incredibly difficult job swimwear designers have. My heart goes out to them.

When I'm feeling rested and refreshed, I try on suit number eleven: the monokini. My heart ceases to go out. I'm staring at myself in a one-piece with waist-high leg holes and peekaboo openings in the tummy, sides, and back where all the womanhood that isn't squashed by the uber-spandex boinks out in every "I no longer feel good about me" way possible. Nobody should have created this swimsuit. Ever. I tear it off. Whoever thought of this one should be fired and jailed. Or worse, be forced to wear one himself.

And then, just because it's there . . . and just because I *AM* totally worth it and deserve a little levity . . . I move into what is the grand finale of almost all my swimwear shopping episodes: I try on a bikini. The skimpier, the better. I'm *not* trying on a bikini because I hope to find one that fits. I'm not trying it on for punishment. Quite the opposite. At this point in the shopping, I'm lured strictly by the thrill of sport, curiosity, and humor. Pure spectator fascination. How bad CAN I look? How insane ARE the swimwear companies? Possibly 1 percent of the female population looks good in a bikini, and yet these tiny two-pieces are always 90 percent of what's offered. Do women's swimsuit designers ever look at any actual women? In one of their suits? Do they ever look at an actual woman looking at *herself* in one of their suits? I get the bikini off the hanger . . . figure out all the tiny straps of the top and get it situated on my situation . . . wriggle into the teeny-weeny bottom with the itsy-bitsy ties . . . then turn to face the mirror with wide-open eyes.

The bikini does not disappoint.

Why is it, I wonder, changing back into clothes as fast as possible, that the more power women have gained, the skimpier swimwear has gotten? Great-Grandma, in the 1800s, had zero say over anything. Swimwear covered her from the neck to the ankles. Grandma, in the 1920s, got the right to vote and got swimwear that exposed her knees and calves for the first time. Mom, in the 1940s, had the responsibility of helping keep the whole country functioning while the men went to war. Swimsuits bared her thighs. My generation, in the 1970s, marched in the streets, loud and proud, for the passage of the Equal Rights Amendment. Swimsuits revealed our belly buttons. My daughter's generation is empowered in every single area of life. Swimsuits display it all. They make the most powerful generation of women in the world the most naked.

And now, in a great big reduction of logic, the sexy suits that are the symbol of women's right to be seen and heard wind up silencing a lot of women who try to wear them because we're no longer supposed to admit we might not be totally happy with our beautiful shapes. Now we need to squash ourselves into the swimsuits and squash our feelings in there, too. We have the world's blessing to reveal *everything* except insecurities. Show *everything* except that we might be a little bit self-conscious about all those womanly curves. The wonderful new freedom to love myself exactly as I am makes me feel lonelier and a little bit worse because I'm not supposed to admit it when I don't.

I used to write that all women have two main figure problem areas—the top half of our bodies and the bottom half of our bodies. But a lot has changed. A lot of us really do feel pretty good about ourselves a lot more of the time. We really aren't tormented by the images of "perfect" bodies like we used to be. Our main figure problem areas now are places like the swimwear department, where we have to face all those contradictions in the mirror. Where it's us all alone, staring at our reflection and trying to figure out how to wrap all those mixed messages around our lovely selves and be part of the contemporary world without feeling strangled or defeated.

I'm completely dressed and mostly recovered. Just in case anyone's still watching from the surveillance room, I've hung all the swimsuits back on their little plastic hangers. I'm proud of myself for facing the swimwear department today, but even more proud that I can finally declare I'm done with this place. I am never going to change swimwear. I refuse to conform to what it continues to expect of me and I see absolutely no reason to ever subject myself to it again.

I stride out of the swimwear department with my head held high. I'm striding right past the evening wear department, which is next to swimwear, when I'm stopped in my tracks. I watch, stunned, as my right hand plucks a sequined black stretch-velvet floor-length mermaid gown off the rack. From someplace deep within I hear:

"Look! This one might be cute!"

25.

THE DAY I DIVORCED MY PURSE

We need to talk, Purse.

"I don't love you anymore. If I'm totally honest, I've fantasized about dumping you for years. I've only kept hanging on because I wasn't brave enough to try going solo.

"I got my first version of you when I was three years old and started practicing to be a woman. Pink and plastic, with a ladybug stuck on the front. Everyone said it made me so grown up and I started believing I was incomplete without you. By the time I was a teenager, I couldn't leave the house if you weren't on my arm.

"But I've changed, Purse. Everything's moving and shifting in my life, and honestly, you're just weighing me down. It isn't only that I feel obligated to take you everywhere, but that you need so much attention when we get home. You were perfect in the beginning, but now you're aggravating and disorganized. You hide things from me. I spend half my life trying to get to the bottom of what's going on inside you. I resent how panicked I still am if I don't know where you are.

"It isn't *you*. I'm not leaving you for a bigger purse or a more attractive purse. I'm not interested in starting over. I'm divorcing the whole category. I want to walk out into the world unencumbered for once. Just myself. Zero baggage.

"Watch me do it! I'm taking the phone, driver's license, and credit card you make such a big production of carrying . . . taking them away from you and tucking them into my back pocket. And now I'm walking out the front door! Just like that! I'm leaving you on the kitchen counter! I'm slamming the door behind me and walking toward my car without you!

"Look out the window if you can, Purse! Look at my un-weighed-down arms stretch out for the first time! Look at my liberated hands and fingers wiggle, my shoulders relax! I'm free for the first time since I was three years old! Look at me twirl on the walkway! I can't believe I've missed this wonderful feeling my whole life!

"Now that I see how easy it was to walk away, I can't believe how much I dislike you! I resent how much of my life I wasted thinking we always had to be together!

"Now that you're locked inside the house and I'm standing here by the car . . . now that I'm looking down the street and imagining the whole, glorious, unburdened, liberated life I have ahead of me . . .

"Now . . . now . . . now . . . now . . .

"Now what I really hate, Purse, is that somewhere deep down inside, you have my car and house keys."

26.

STOP TRYING TO UPGRADE
YOUR MOTHER

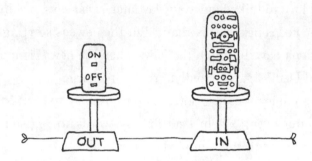

ad calls from the living room. "It's time for the news!"

"On my way!" Mom answers, scurrying in from the kitchen, as she does every single day at 6:26 p.m.

I stand in front of my parents' chairs, facing them, my back to the TV, and beam. I have no big plans to organize or overhaul on this visit. No car trunk full of supplies to try to transform their home. But I did think of one thing I could add to their lives that could really make a difference.

"You're blocking the TV, sweetie!" Mom says, waving urgently toward the chair next to her. "Have a seat!"

Mom and Dad are doing wonderfully well on their own, but I

want to make these years the very best they can be. It's hard to watch them be diminished even a little by all the parts of themselves and the world that don't work the way they used to. I can't stand the loss of control I know they feel, and I want to help.

"Sit!" they order me. "It's time for the news!"

I don't sit. My moment has arrived.

"Ta-da!" I say, pulling a remote from behind my back. "While you two were at the eye doctor this morning, I had TiVo installed!"

"We'd love to talk about your day later," Dad says, picking up the remote he keeps next to his chair. "But the news is starting!"

"You don't have to watch the news when the news is on anymore, Mom and Dad!" I say excitedly. "You're in charge!"

Dad's too busy pressing buttons on his remote to hear. Mom's too busy leaning over to help Dad for my words to register. "Something's wrong with this thing!" Dad laments.

"You have a new remote now!" I say, holding up the one in my hand. "Your old one is finished! Your new one has different buttons that will change your life!"

Mom and Dad stop. Their eyes flash from their old remote to me. They look stunned, as if I were the nightly news anchor and have just announced a hostile invasion of their living room. As though my words—*new remote, old one is finished, different buttons*—were little bombs I dropped on their world, not the happy, empowering surprise I intended.

"Look! With this . . ." I start.

"No time for talking!" Dad interrupts, shaking his head vigorously and poking at the buttons on his remote. "Let's get the news on before we miss the whole show!"

I put the entire room on pause and mute for a minute so I can think.

Have I just barreled into my parents' world with yet another brilliant invention that will ruin their lives? Me? Their self-proclaimed protector?

Surely this is different.

This isn't like the day the simple sewing machine that was Mom's pride and joy finally broke and got replaced with a new one that was so complicated she quit sewing.

This isn't like when Dad's perfect one-button camera became obsolete and was replaced with the new "user-friendly" one that was so hard to use he never wanted to take pictures anymore.

This isn't like the computer that replaced their nice reliable typewriter and ruined everything. Ruined self-expression. Ruined letter writing. Ruined expense keeping. Ruined list making. Ruined filing. Ruined nice-looking envelopes. Ruined ever being able to find anything.

Is it?

I've seen Superman wrestle a blister pack of printer ink cartridges to the ground to pry it open, only to have the printer flash a "cartridge not installed properly" screen. I've watched my gentle Mom beat her little fists on her new high-efficiency washer because "It keeps trying to wash my clothes with no water! It won't let me put in enough soap! It locks the lid with no warning!" I've seen them huddle together trying to get a human on the phone or find a troubleshooting guide online. I've seen the next generation of everything from cars to can openers make them feel less competent and less connected to the world. As if enough, at age ninety, isn't already slipping away without their permission.

I can't stand how valiantly they've tried to change with the times and how often they feel frustrated by modern life. I've promised myself I wouldn't allow one more thing in this house that could make them feel inadequate in any way. I didn't just do it. Did I? No! I got them TiVo because it will *give* them control, not take it away! It will put power in their hands!

I look at the new remote in my hand. At all those new buttons. I look at Mom and Dad . . .

They sit quietly. Stoically. They gave up on the remote they were trying to make work, as well as all hope of watching the news tonight, several minutes ago and have simply been watching me. Their initial stunned look has settled into the gentle, world-weary gaze of the Greatest Generation. Full of patience, resilience, tolerance, and an unbelievable willingness to try to be grateful for improvements they wish someone wasn't trying to inflict upon them.

The Gracious Generation. That's what they are. I forge ahead, determined to prove that *this* unwanted improvement will be different. I un-pause and un-mute myself, raise the new TiVo remote in the air, and play the highlights of my presentation.

"You're not missing the news, Mom and Dad!" I say in my most enthusiastic voice. "It's being recorded right now by TiVo, without a videotape! You can watch the news anytime you want!

"You can start watching the news from the beginning even if the news is half over in real time!

"You can watch in real time, but if you need to leave the room for a few minutes, you can hit pause and then resume watching without missing one second!

"You can skip past the commercials! You never have to watch an irritating ad again!

"You can record all those great PBS shows you circle in the paper that don't come on until nine, when it's too late to start watching anything!"

Even as the words leave my mouth, I'm thinking this sounds worse. Worse than their incomprehensible new microwave. Worse than their new twenty-five-function blender. TiVo won't only be tricky to learn. It will destroy some of the things they can still count on to give structure and purpose to their days. Printed TV schedules. Clocks. Calendars. The reason to be a certain place at a certain time. Things that ground them in a kind of security that's already just a faint memory to my generation—an emotional safety net of a regular, predictable order of life that my daughter's generation will never know.

Mom and Dad gaze at me sweetly anyway as I explain the thing I've brought that will ruin all of that. The wonderful new invention that will help make the precious rhythm of life obsolete.

"Well! Thank you!" Mom says, getting up, smiling politely. "What a lovely gift. We'll have to study it."

Dad gets up too, gives me a hug, and whispers in my ear, "So thoughtful, sweetie, but she gets a little confused by new things. After this nice gift, maybe we should stop trying to upgrade your mother."

"But . . ." I say as they walk out of the room. I click the TV on and cue up the recording of the nightly news. "But . . . look, Mom and Dad!" I call to them. "The news is on! The exact same news that was on at six-thirty is on now! Your new TiVo saved it! Don't you want to watch?"

I don't have to hear their answer to know it. Know it and suddenly agree with it. I look at my watch. It's 7:08 at Mom and Dad's house in Florida.

I click the TV off. It isn't time for the news.

27.

ODE TO EYELINER

Thank heavens for makeup, that's all I can think, staring at my un-made-up reflection in my bathroom mirror back in Los Angeles. I've aged a little, but I don't have to succumb to *this*. Absolutely no reason to resign myself to the stoic, au naturel look for tonight's dinner party. I've earned the right to use a little magic to look as fabulous on the outside as I am on the inside.

I smile, pulling out my tray of tricks and laying it on the counter. I know exactly how to perk up these faded eyes, lips, and skin with a few minutes of eyeliner, mascara, foundation, blush, and lipstick.

I lean into the magnified makeup mirror to start.

I recoil.

Recoil at the 10× magnification of truth that stares back: I already have on eyeliner, mascara, foundation, blush, and lipstick. I put it on an hour ago. Not only is the old lady in the mirror *me in full makeup*, but the old lady completely forgot she already did her whole beauty routine.

"SHOULDN'T YOU BE GETTING READY?!" I yell out the bathroom door, directing my frustration toward the den so my voice can be heard over the Golf Channel. Not the one in my house. The Golf Channel in my house was disconnected the same day the man who used to be planted in front of it also disconnected and moved to a den in a different part of town. My yell is in general to all men in all dens all over the universe. I yell to be heard over all Golf Channels and every single smug male voice that calls back:

"I'll jump in the shower when you're five minutes from being ready!"

What it must be like to be male and have your face look the same every single time you look in the mirror?

To have no dinner-party version of your face to create.

No work version.

No Saturday-morning version.

No Saturday-night version.

No lunch version.

No beach version.

No wedding version.

No breakup version.

No holiday version.

No five-pound evening bag full of versions to get you through a two-hour date.

I remember watching a young woman in the ladies' room of a restaurant, frantically redoing her face. So insecure, she apparently couldn't stand for her date to see her with un-touched-up eyeliner. As though he'd want to marry her if she got the mascara just right. Oblivious to the fact that he might actually be more attracted to her if she'd stayed at the table so he could eat his twenty-six-dollar entrée while it was warm.

I pity her.

Then I remember that the young woman was me.

"SHOULDN'T YOU BE GETTING READY YET??!!" I yell out the bathroom door again at all the invisible men.

What must it be like to be male and leave the house without—as my mom's archaic generation calls it—"putting on your face"? The injustice makes me crazy, but not crazy enough to go to tonight's dinner party without putting on my face.

I apply another layer of makeup over the faded one I forgot I put on an hour ago. Carefully. Too little makeup, and I look dead. Too much and I look desperate to *not* look dead, which my daughter has pointed out is even worse.

I stand back from the 10× magnification mirror. Happy. Restored. I look like myself again.

I walk into my Golf-Channel-free den and take a moment to sink into a my man-free love seat before I leave for tonight's event. I feel good about myself. I feel good about all of womanhood—about the ridiculous conformities and contradictions with which we make peace. About the fact that even with the thousands of extra hours we spend preparing to walk out the door, we still go so far and accomplish so much. I celebrate the grace and beauty our extra efforts add to the world.

My dog—ever in sync with my emotions—charges toward my happy aura, bounds onto my lap, and joyfully licks my contented, confident face. Licks the last fifteen minutes of eyeliner, mascara, foundation, blush, and lipstick right off.

I'm ready for so many, many things in life. Leaving the house for a dinner party tonight, not so much.

28.

WHAT KIND OF FRIEND HAS NO
WI-FI IN THE POWDER ROOM?

Hi, Cathy! Nice to see you!"

"Nice to see you, *too!*" I bubble.

We hug. Kiss cheeks. Hell begins.

Neighbor? Teacher? Sister of the hostess? Marcia? Fran?

"How's your daughter liking freshman year?" she asks. I have no idea who this woman is, and she remembers that my child started college this year.

"And how are those darling dogs?" she adds. She remembers everything.

"First I want to hear about *yours!*" I lean in, deflecting it back to her. "How are *yours* doing?"

"My what?" she asks.

I lean back out. *Dogs? Cats? Children? Tropical fish?*

"Your little ones!" I say.

"Oh, they're not so little anymore!" She laughs.

I hate this woman. She's giving me nothing. Either we've had such a connection prior to this that it doesn't occur to her I don't know who she is, or she knows that I don't know and this is how she amuses herself at dinner parties.

"What are they up to this summer?" I forge on, digging for clues.

"Jack just wants to sleep all day and Ricky still lives to play ball!" she says, shaking her head with a smile.

In the olden days, I could assume that Jack and Ricky were human children. Now they could be cat children, dog children, gerbil children . . .

"And Suzy just learned to say 'Hello!'" she chirps.

Or parrot children.

I'm saved by the hostess who walks past with "Time to move to the dining room, Cathy and Paula!"

Paula! I spin toward the dining room. "Nice talking with you, PAULA!" I say.

I probably spun a little too quickly, but I need to get away from Paula before I'm found out. Before Paula, who knows everything about me, knows who I am.

I stop at the edge of the beautifully set table.

There are place cards. Right next to *Cathy* is *Paula*. I'll be spending the evening next to this woman and have been completely out of conversation since I told her how nice it was to see her.

I excuse myself to the powder room. Not to hide. Not to cry. At least those pitiful days are over. I excuse myself to the powder room so I can Google Paula. Search her on Facebook. Search her on the hostess's Facebook. Search emails. Search . . . nothing. There's no Internet in here. Up in the corner of my phone where all the happy connectivity indicators are, the dreaded "No service." I wave the phone around the room, high over the toilet, in the cabinet under the sink. Zilch. There are a dozen backup bars of soap in this bathroom. Zero bars of the Internet. I feel ill. Very ill. *What kind of friend has no Wi-Fi in the powder room???*

Someone's jiggling the handle. "Just a moment!" I answer. I flush the toilet and run the water so the jiggler will at least think I've done what I was supposed to be doing in here. I return to the table. No choice now but to be completely truthful. I sit, gather my courage, and turn to Paula.

"Sorry I was detained," I say. "I felt ill in the powder room."

Stroke of genius. Paula scooches her chair away from me and my potential flu germs and strikes up a conversation with the person on her right. I breathe a grateful sigh of relief and peek at the woman on my left, someone I've definitely never seen before. I bow my head and silently give thanks for the food and for the blessing of having a chance to redeem myself. I turn to the new woman and smile.

"Hi," I say. "My name's Cathy."

"I know that!" She bubbles. "Great to *see* you! How's your daughter liking freshman year?"

Neighbor? Teacher? Sister of the hostess? Marcia? Fran?

Her water glass is blocking my view of the place card with her name, and even if it weren't, it wouldn't include a synopsis of our shared history that I could read without her noticing.

I hate this age.

29.

IN DEFENSE OF MY 2,000TH TRIP TO THE MALL

Eleven years. That's how long I've been driving a skirt around in the trunk of my car trying to find a top to match it.

"It goes with everything!" That's what the salesperson declared all those years ago when I bought it. "That skirt goes with absolutely everything!"

It goes with absolutely everything except anything that's been created yet. I know because I've tried it all. Sweaters are too long, too short, too bulky, or too clingy. Blouses are too tailored, too sporty, or too frilly. Jackets are too jacket-y. The lovely muted tones of the skirt's beautiful print match nothing. The skirt has logged 500,000 frequent-trier miles in the trunk of my car . . . in malls all over town . . . and in the air. It's gone on trips with me, even once on vacation to Paris—one eighth of the precious space in my suitcase given over to the skirt and the hope that the country of France might provide what malls in nine American zip codes didn't.

Women in our family don't give up. Not on people. Not on causes. Certainly not on a sort-of-casual-sort-of-dressy-softly-flowing-unbelievably-flattering-go-anywhere-midcalf-length skirt that would be stunning with flats, boots, or heels—if only I had a top to match.

Just yesterday my mother brought it up on the phone, as if she were checking in on a grandchild: "How's the search for a top to go with that skirt coming along?"

My sister mentioned it last week: "I found a sweater that almost would have worked for the skirt."

Complete strangers volunteer ideas when they see me holding the skirt up to racks of tops in a store: "I saw something that might work with that in the next department! Want me to show you the one I mean?"

Matchmakers. Explorers. Seekers. Most women love joining another woman's hunt. We're all at the mall on some kind of mission—a quest to find something to go with something . . . or make sense of something . . . or rekindle something . . . or dream something . . . or discover something . . . or share something . . . or get perspective on something . . . or take a break from something . . . or . . . something.

"Shopping isn't about shopping!" I tried to explain years ago to my husband at the time. "We're looking for a lot of things besides clothes when we go to the mall. Even if we're technically looking at clothes, we're searching for all sorts of bigger, more important things. Life things."

My husband, who once ordered thirty-five pairs of identical socks online so he wouldn't have to walk into an actual store, stared at me.

"Women assemble the pieces of life!" I forged on, determined to get credit for my part in sustaining the universe. "That's why there are pretty flowerpots in front windows, framed pictures on mantels, and children eating heart-shaped waffles at breakfast tables!"

My husband, who once bought a swimsuit at an airport newsstand on our way to Hawaii because he forgot to pack anything for the beach, rolled his eyes.

I rolled mine right back at him.

"We turn houses into homes, people into families, clothes into outfits . . . We make things whole!"

With that, I picked up my purse and headed for the door.

"As long as you're going shopping," he called after me, "grab me a pack of underwear and a couple new pairs of jeans!"

Just as well, I thought back then and still think now. How much do we really need our loved ones to know? What possible end would it serve for a life partner to understand me well enough to ask follow-up questions—like why so many of the beautiful outfits I work so hard to assemble never get to leave my closet because they're "too nice to wear"? Clothes I put on only for special public appearances—like going to the dentist—and then rip off and rehang as soon as I get home, so I can get back into happy sweat pants and a baggy sweat shirt.

I can ask my mother the questions, since she's the one who trained me.

"You've owned that blouse for fifty-six years, Mom," I say. "Why do you take it off the second you come home from the grocery store?"

"Oh, this is much too nice to wear in the house! I might get something on it!" she answers.

"Is it dry clean only?" I ask.

"Heavens, no," she answers. "Everything I own can be tossed in the wash!"

"Then why do you worry about getting something on it?"

"It's too nice! I'd feel too dressed up!" Mom declares. "I wouldn't feel like myself! I can't go around the house not feeling like myself!"

No need to ask Mom why it's okay to not feel like herself when she sees other people, since the identical respect for beautiful un-wearable clothes is embedded in my genes. The "too nice to wear" category is only the start. Women in our family have all sorts of other clothes we also don't wear for all sorts of other reasons:

Clothes we don't wear because they don't fit.

Clothes we don't wear because they need a button resewn or hem fixed and we can't stand to pay someone else to do it when it would be so easy to do it ourselves, and then we never get around to doing it.

Clothes we don't wear because we don't feel like ironing.

Clothes we don't wear because we don't like them anymore, but we can't get rid of because they were bought on sale.

Clothes we don't wear that still have the price tags attached that we waited too long to return, and now can't stand to give away because they're brand-new.

Clothes we don't wear because they were never our style, but we can't pass them on to anyone because they were a gift and we're afraid whoever we give them to might run into the person who gave them to us.

Clothes we don't wear but will never part with because of "The Time Mom Gave Away the Lavender Sweater." How many times have the women in our family relived that one: the tragedy of Mom's beautiful lavender sweater that went with nothing, which she finally surrendered to Goodwill. Mom owned it for four decades without ever finding the right thing to wear it with. She finally let it go. ONE DAY LATER, a dress the exact odd color of the sweater—a dress that was wearable only if it had a matching sweater because it was sleeveless—came into her life. The dress she'd searched for for decades was here. The sweater was gone. Mom marched back to Goodwill with her new lavender dress and demanded that they go through thousands of donations to find the matching sweater—not to get it back for herself, but so she could give the recipient of the sweater the dress too, and spare another woman the endless search Mom had endured. There's a special memorial section of almost-wearable clothes in my closet that's devoted to lessons learned from the Lavender Sweater Incident.

Plus . . . there's unwearable body-hugging holiday wear, the un-worn workout wear . . . tops that promised to make someone love me . . . pants I've hung on to decades after it was over . . .

And yet, even with so many unworn clothes at home, sometimes I go to the mall just to be with people who think I need even more clothes. I like to try on new versions of myself. For a few minutes or a few hours, surrounded by all those pretty things so neatly ironed and hung up on matching hangers, I can pretend I'm not a person with a closet full of chaos at home. One small purchase of anything new—a two-dollar pair of socks, a four-dollar scarf; anything—can change how I feel about everything. There's something magical about taking something that isn't a problem yet home to meet the rest of my life.

When my daughter was young and I was exhausted from work and motherhood by Friday evening, I would sometimes park her with a babysitter at home, drive to the mall, and just stand there in the middle of it all. Looking for nothing, wanting nothing except to be in a place where the "MO-O-OM!" I kept hearing wasn't directed at me. Where I could watch another mother haul a shrieking toddler out of the Disney Store . . . or see another woman take the same pair of pants in four different sizes into a dressing room because she had no idea what size she was after the week she'd just had. Lots of times, the best thing I brought home from the mall was one sentence: "I'm not the only one."

Online shopping is joyful instant gratification, but trips to the mall are almost always about something else. Especially now, when everyone I know is in the middle of some huge overhaul of stuff. People packing up their kids' childhoods so they can turn their bedrooms into tidy home offices; moving parents from large homes to little assisted-living spaces; friends downsizing their own big lives into condos. Everyone I know is trying to get rid of stuff. Trying to remember who we were before we had all the stuff. To discover who we might be without all the stuff. Who we could be if we had room for different stuff.

At this time of life, when the urge to unload is so strong, when every single thing we could ever need can be ordered on an iPad without getting out of bed, the mall is, strangely, even more comforting. I can only assume it's because there's all sorts of stuff there besides the stuff.

"What do you DO there for so long??" my husband used to ask.

"How could it take FOUR HOURS to shop?? When I *have* to go to the mall, I'm in and out of there in four *minutes!* What could you possibly do there for FOUR HOURS??"

I kiss my new guy—my dog, who never asks questions like that—goodbye, walk to the car, pop open the trunk, and lift out a tattered shopping bag. The bag containing the Skirt. The skirt I've been driving around for eleven years. I pull the skirt from the bag and hold it up to myself in the driveway. I admire the lovely muted tones of the unmatchable fabric. I note the softly flowing lines that would be so flattering if the skirt were ever on my body instead of stuffed in a shopping bag in my trunk.

I think fondly of the years I've wasted trying to create a future for us. I remember Paris. How my sister, who took that vacation with me, eagerly spent three days of our five-day trip searching for a top to match my skirt. How we spent so much time shopping for the top, we had to do the entire Louvre in fifteen minutes. How we bought a book in the Louvre gift shop and wept together on the long flight home looking at all the pictures of the artistic masterpieces we missed seeing because of our futile obsession with finding something to go with my skirt. I remember how we toasted each other with our sixth little bag of airline pretzels and vowed that if we had it to do all over again, we would do the exact same thing.

I think of my mother's supreme patience at the mall when I was young, as I tore through personalities, trying on every possible version of being a girl, snapping at Mom because she kept insisting I looked nice, not like the dork I saw in the mirror.

I think of my supreme patience when I do the same thing with my daughter.

I think of Dad's supreme patience, the endless hours he spent waiting outside stores for three sisters and a mom to shop when I was growing up. He didn't like the mall but loved to be with us so much, he usually wanted to come along. I have a perfect mental picture of him, sitting on a bench outside a store with a transistor radio to his ear, trying to tune in the World Series that he was missing while my sister tried on hour after hour of homecoming dresses.

I get in the car, put the shopping bag on the passenger seat, and head for what must be my 2,000th trip to the mall. I'll be irritated by the parking lot, the noise, the people who refuse to rush, and the people who refuse to slow down. I'll hurry past the fast-food court, the perfume ladies, and the sunglass kiosk so I won't be tempted. I'll seek revenge on companies that quit making the basics I could finally buy without thinking by finding other companies to whom I can pledge allegiance. I'll get to feel a little bit arrogant, a little bit humbled. I'll practice not being intimidated by people selling clothes I can't—and don't even want to—afford.

I'll look for familiar faces of women who must feel just like I do. A tired smile as we pass on the escalator, a beaming one in Shoes. The commiseration of strangers. Women shopping for a little rest from the rest of their lives. A spark of hope. Something new to introduce to the closet. Camaraderie. Connection. Moral support. Reinvention. Restoration. Possibility. Validation. Hope. Tests of willpower. The triumph of a great deal. The trying on of fantasies. The search for something to go with something . . . or make sense of something . . . or rekindle something . . . or dream something . . . or discover something . . . or share something . . . or get perspective on something . . . or take a break from something . . . or . . . something.

Something to make me feel a little bit different—even if all it makes me feel after an hour or so is really happy to leave the mall and go back home.

That's what I'm going shopping for today. I glance at the bag on the passenger seat. Maybe today I'll even find a top to match the skirt.

30.

MY MEANINGLESS MIDLIFE SIX-MINUTE FLING

hy? I crinkle up the words, furious that I let myself be vulnerable again. Flatten them back out, search for what else they could possibly mean. How could I let myself get involved again? I'm too old for this. I crinkle the words back up. I can't believe I committed so freely and completely before I knew the facts.

The *Nutrition Facts.*

I flatten the words back out. There they are, plain as day:

Calories: 250. Servings per container: 5.

I stare at the empty Almond 'n' Fruit Granola Crunch bag in my hand. *Anyone* would assume this contained one small healthy snack, not five. I feel betrayed to my core. I've just accidentally said yes to almost as many calories as I should eat in a whole day. Betrayed and all alone.

It gets worse almost immediately.

I'm not alone. I feel the granola clusters start to expand inside me. Feel the dried cranberries and apricot pieces doubling and tripling in size in my stomach. The fiber-rich almonds are dividing and multiplying, dividing and multiplying. By tomorrow I'll need to wear baggy smock tops and jeans with elasticized front panels.

I look down in dismay. My bump is already starting to show. One innocent six-minute fling and I'm pregnant with Almond 'n' Fruit Granola Crunch. I try to steel myself for a great big stint of unplanned motherhood. Brace for the repercussions of this one irresponsible episode.

It gets worse almost immediately.

My eyes land on a display of garbanzo beans and I realize I'm still in the grocery store. I'm only in aisle two of a fifteen-aisle market, a fraction of the way through my grocery shopping. I've finished the relationship, am carrying an Almond 'n' Fruit Granola Crunch love child, and haven't even paid for the snack bag yet.

How appropriate, I think ruefully, that almonds were involved in what just happened to me. Now, when I feel so strong and unseducible. Almonds keep sneaking up from every direction. Was their impact not bad enough before? Almonds used to appear only in little gift bags at two of life's most emotionally loaded events: bridal and baby showers. Pastel-colored, candy-coated Jordan almonds—symbols of another woman's superior life choices. Party snacks that scream:

"She's getting married and you aren't!"

"She's having a baby and you aren't!"

How many beautiful showers did I leave and immediately eat my 1,500-calorie souvenir gift bag of Jordan almonds before I even got to the first stop sign on the way home? How many pounds of self-pity have almonds already added to my life? Perfect, I think, patting today's Almond 'n' Fruit Granola Crunch baby bump. Perfect, somehow, that almonds did this to me now, when I'm so solidly committed to making smart choices. As if there weren't enough lessons in humility at this age.

At best, almonds are part of the required regimen of a new heart-healthy food plan . . . but I've proven way too many times what happens when I try to eat the "recommended" amount. At worst, almonds have slipped into the new heart-healthy naughtiness snack industry, in which so much bad-for-me weight is gained on good-for-me food. Pinto bean and flax chips. Goji berry brittle. Quinoa crackers. Spinach açai smoothies. Food I don't even like but commit to in abundance because of the antioxidant-rich, nutrient-dense, immune-system-boosting ingredients.

I've worn the unfairness all over me. There are millions of options for the food that goes in the mouth. Still only one option for the type of weight produced once it's swallowed. Shouldn't baked organic beet chip fat look more attractive than Cheetos fat? Shouldn't a box of gluten-free, fruit-juice-sweetened carob cookies produce healthier-looking pounds than Reese's Peanut Butter Cups? Shouldn't too many sprouted ancient grain muffins look hotter in yoga pants than too many red velvet cupcakes? Shouldn't Almond 'n' Fruit Granola Crunch not count *at all* because it's so healthy? Unanswerable questions in this unimaginable time when we can somehow be so bad while we're being so good.

I must appear a little confused . . . or maybe I've just been standing in one spot too long, because a passing stock boy asks if I need help finding something.

"No, thank you," I reply, holding my head high and my stomach in. I turn my cart toward the front of the store and gesture with the flattened bag in my hand. "Best that I just move to the checkout line and pay. I have a growing family and everyone will be getting hungry for supper soon."

31.

FOUR KINDERGARTEN MOMS
AND A BOTTLE OF PINOT GRIGIO

I told my mother it wasn't safe for her to drive anymore and I took her keys away!"

The happy chatter at our dinner table stops abruptly. The other two friends and I stare with disbelief at the one who just spoke.

"You took your mother's keys away??" the friend on my left asks incredulously.

"Keys and driver's license!" the first friend proclaims proudly.

"Just like that??" the one on my right asks, shaking her head.

"Oh, there was unhappiness, but I told her I love her and wanted her to be safe," friend number one says with a shrug and raises her Pinot Grigio in a toast to herself.

We were kindergarten moms together. Bonds don't go any deeper than that. We perched like nervous mama birds on teeny chairs at the kindergarten orientation open house a lifetime ago, when the children we sent off to college last fall were all five years old. Perched there with knees folded up halfway to our chins, bending us into almost fetal positions, which couldn't have been more perfect for exactly how we felt. We did our bravest half-smiles while our eyes flicked from face to face, searching for signs of anxiety that matched our own: red-rimmed eyes, tooth mark dents in lower lips, heartache written in lines of dissolved mascara down cheeks. Brows stiff as we prayed this would be the right school, the right teacher, the right friends. Hands clutching the information sheets that were passed out, as though hanging on for dear life to a list of school supplies would somehow keep our babies closer.

We found one another that day, fourteen years ago, the four women having dinner together right now. We all wore the exact same mismatched combination of hope and terror to the kindergarten orientation open house. Four first-time panicked moms feeling equally unready for the next step.

The kindergarten at our elementary school was its own cute separate one-room building, painted red and white on the outside, like an old-fashioned schoolhouse. It even had a steeple with a big brass school bell on the roof. An unbelievably sweet and innocent oasis in an otherwise ego-packed, traffic-jammed suburb of Los Angeles.

Not that that helped. The sweetness of the place might even have made it more jarringly cruel when the teacher said it was "Time to say goodbye!" ten minutes into the first day of school. She patiently watched us do the opposite of the "firm and cheerful!" goodbyes she'd coached us to do . . . and then came to the tiny tables where we sat wrapped around our little ones and, one by one, helped peel apart the weeping mother/child teams who couldn't do it on their own. I remember looking at her as if she were a crazy woman and clutching my daughter even more closely when she got near. Did my daughter have a harder time saying goodbye than the other children because I had a harder time saying goodbye? Of course she did. Did I care? I did not. I couldn't believe anyone actually expected me to leave.

When the teacher finally got us out the door, I stood outside the kindergarten building with the Panicked Ones and pressed my face along with theirs against the big picture window, searching for a glimpse of my girl. On day two of school, the teacher covered the picture window with construction-paper pictures the children made the day before. On day three, we climbed on benches, stood on tip-toe, and peered into the high transom window above the window she'd covered. On day four, the principal was summoned to remove us, the custodian took away the benches, and we were shamed into going home or to our offices. Most of us. There was a rumor that one mom sat in her car in the school parking lot for the entire year so she would never be more than fifty yards away from her child. It wasn't me. That was my big kindergarten triumph. The mom camped out in the school parking lot wasn't me.

Pinot Grigio and Pellegrino are passed around the table, dinners served. We're still reeling from the announcement that one of us got keys away from her mother and are in interrogation mode:

"How did you get her to do what you wanted??"

"How did you know she was ready??"

"How did you avoid the meltdown mine had when I barely broached the subject??"

We asked these exact same questions when our children were five. And here we are again. We were first-time parents to little children; now we're first-time parents to aging parents. And exactly as unprepared for the next step as we were then. Only now there are no information handouts, no irritating teacher telling us "it's time," no parenting-the-parent classes. Not that we would listen to advice. When our kids were in kindergarten, none of us wanted input from the experienced moms in the class who were on child number two or three. Even though they'd been through exactly what we were going through, they had NO idea what we were going through. Our kids were different.

"My daughter can't carry her own backpack. Her arms are too little!"

"She can't use her words. She's too shy!"

"She can't sit still. Her imagination is too special!"

"She can't sing along. She has a hypersensitivity to sound!"

Mom after mom, making pitiful excuse after pitiful . . .

Okay, fine. Those examples were all me. But we all wrestled with our own challenges. Of all the moms, Beth and I were probably the most independent women and the worst at letting go. I remember hearing another mother mutter that she couldn't believe such self-sufficient women were raising such clingy daughters. Our girls screamed the loudest and longest when we took them to school and flung themselves back on us the most desperately when we picked them up.

A couple of weeks into kindergarten, instead of rushing out of the room into our arms, our daughters marched out confidently holding hands, declared that they'd decided to be sisters, and asked us to leave so they could stay longer to play. Beth and I sobbed some more, but wrapped ourselves around each other this time, not our girls. We were useless helping our daughters take the next step. They took it on their own and showed us how it was done.

We could use some leadership lessons now. All the kindergarten moms at this table could. We're right back at zero. Perched on pretty restaurant chairs this time with a great big load of the exact same fears as well as brand-new ones. As hard as it was to watch our little ones grow up, it's even harder to watch our parents go the other direction, to have all the developmental milestones go backward. Absolutely no clapping, cheering, and making videos when our aging parents move into the next stage. Mom and Dad could run, now they can walk. Then it's a slower walk. Then a slower, wobbly walk. Then a walk with walker. Then . . .

My eyes flick from face to face searching for signs of anxiety that match my own. No one bites her lower lip now for fear of chipping expensive dental work . . . we've converted to waterproof mascara . . . brows are stiff for possibly different reasons . . . and my friends are sharing other kinds of unrelatable success stories . . .

"A woman in my office just moved her mom across the country into an independent living community a mile from her house," the friend on my left offers with a sigh. "That's like getting a spot in a neighborhood preschool!"

"My yoga teacher got her dad into a place that has levels of care so he can transition to a different area as his needs change," the friend on my right says. "Like getting into a preschool that goes all the way through twelfth grade. Her dad will be safe forever. Her dad is IN!"

"I know someone who just did it, too," the third friend adds. "Moved both parents into a senior care condo. She said they've made friends, do all the group activities, have their own spots in the dining room, are regaining confidence and mobility . . . It's like a Montessori senior living center!"

The bottles make another round; wine to three of us, sparkling water to the fourth. We all reject guidance now, just like we did when our children were little, for pretty much the same reason: Ours are different.

"My mom and dad can't move! They're too attached to their home!"

"They can't eat in a group dining room! They love cooking and cleaning up!"

"They can't join organized activities! They hate activities!"

"They can't be with a bunch of old people! They don't think they're old!"

Okay, fine. All my examples again. But I know my friends all have their own challenges with their parents, just like we all had with our children. We're all trying to navigate between helping too much and not enough. We know the day Mom and Dad accept that they're too old to do some things will be the same excruciating day they'll actually be too old to do those things.

By the end of her second glass of wine, the friend with the car keys doesn't look triumphant anymore. "It was the worst day of my life," she says, retelling her story with tears spilling over this time. "I only made it sound easy because I want to remember it differently than it happened. I didn't ask for Mom's keys. She handed them to me because she said she got too scared to drive. She couldn't even get her driver's license out of her wallet by herself. I had to help, and then I hugged her like I did my son when he was little. It was just like when I had to help him move to the next stage. He was so afraid of feeling himself changing, just like my mom. I had to help them both let go of who they'd been."

If we didn't learn enough humility in kindergarten, we're learning it now. Little pieces of the people we love keep going away, and we're powerless to stop it. Superman couldn't remember how to tie his necktie last Easter . . . Mom got appointment dates mixed up . . . Jacket zippers are becoming impossible . . . Every little task takes longer, more details need to be repeated. More and more, our parents will need us to figure out what to do and when to do it to help keep them safe.

Four kindergarten moms fourteen years later. We raise our glasses and toast how far we've come. We toast the hope, faith, and senses of humor we've helped one another keep, the wonderful little people we somehow raised. We toast the long, humbling, challenging road ahead and how much easier it will be for all of us because of the deep connections we made with each other from our tiny perches at the kindergarten open house all those years ago.

And then we toast the day we hope is years from now—when the children we've protected for so long will have the strength to help us do what we're trying to do for our parents. What for now we're perfectly able to do for ourselves: One by one, three of us take our car keys out of our purses and hand them to Beth, our designated driver. No one's leaving this restaurant without a safe ride home.

For now, we know that besides our children, besides our parents, we're also the guardians of ourselves. We have to be. The work of the kindergarten moms is far from done.

FIVE ALL-NEW REASONS
I DIDN'T EXERCISE TODAY

1. I have to find a new gym where no one knows me.

2. My yoga pants make my rear look big.

3. I don't want to blow my knees out.

4. I'm not happy with my socks.

5. I have to start on a Monday or it doesn't count.

32.

JOYFULLY PREPARING FOR THE CELEBRATION OF DEATH

On February 5, my sisters and I gathered for our mother's birthday to witness the signing of the "Do Not Resuscitate" form.

Not for her. That's another story. She signed the DNR form for her computer.

"If this contraption starts to die one more time, that's IT!" our mother declared. Our mother, the kindest woman on earth, the patient, loving, selfless saint who never gave up on anyone, who could breathe hope and health into anything. *"I'M PULLING THE PLUG!"* she yelled, eyes flashing, directly into her computer's screen.

"AND I'M HELPING YOU DO IT!" Dad announced. Our gentle,

compassionate dad, who rescues worms on the sidewalk and puts them back in the grass, who got up every three hours to feed an injured baby squirrel we found, who's always been willing to go anywhere, do anything to help something survive. Dad was over it. We watched him sign the DNR for his laptop a few months earlier. Dad was ready for the end. Dad was almost looking forward to the day he could haul the lifeless electronics out to the curb.

We have all suffered too much.

The emergency trips to the Genius Bar, only to be told the fault was with our parents, not the equipment . . .

The long line of specialists we found to make house calls who got everything going again until the moment their techie vans pulled out the driveway . . .

The community college computer classes Mom's taken over and over . . .

The instruction books Dad's studied like a flight manual . . .

The desperate long-distance middle-of-the-night calls to my sisters and me: "I was trying to find Mollie Alstott's address and I clicked the little gizmo on the right and then everything disappeared! It all went blank!" . . .

The hours and hours my sisters and I have spent trying to coach from across the country: "Just double-click on the contacts icon on the bottom . . . No! Mom! . . . the one with the little picture of the . . . What? You did *what*?? Now you need to drag it down from . . . What?? *I don't know where your cursor is! I'm in California! Can't someone in Florida find your cursor???*"

The user-friendly replacement computers we've bought our parents caused even more suffering. Everything about them was just different enough that the skills Mom and Dad had finally perfected were useless. The new, updated machines made them feel even more inept than the old, outdated ones.

Mom and Dad have friends who Skype with relatives in Europe every week. It makes them feel ashamed. They have friends who share photo libraries as easily as sharing popcorn. It makes them feel incompetent. Their grandchildren could do more on their computers when they were two years old than Mom and Dad can do at age ninety. It makes them feel like ninety-year-olds.

And so my sisters and I gathered around Mom's desk as a special gift for her birthday. We laid the official DNR form in front of her, just as we had for Dad's computer a few months before. We witnessed the signing of the form. We pledged that none of us would disobey either of their wishes and try to do anything to revive any electronics ever again if they started failing.

Mom and Dad looked so relieved.

"We hope our computers will croak together," my kind, loving mother said.

"When one starts going, we might need to give the other one a little assist," my gentle, compassionate father agreed.

"When it's over, I will write the obituary," Mom added. "On a nice piece of pretty notepaper with a ballpoint pen."

"And I will put a stamp on Mother's envelope, drive it to the post office, and hand it to a U.S. Postal Worker to put in the day's outgoing mail so it can be delivered to the newspaper!" Dad cemented the deal.

"And then . . ."—Mom smiled and Dad smiled back—"then things can finally get back to normal around here."

33.

LEFT AT THE ALTAR

At last. I was ready to take the vows again. Finally open to the kind of healthy, wonderful relationship I'd seen so many others have. I was done blaming past failures on everything and everyone. Ready to embrace a new life and devote myself to making it work.

Preparations were done. Announcements were made to family and friends. The moment came. The person officiating the commitment ceremony looked down at her papers, then back up at me with an approving nod, and spoke the two words that abruptly ended it all: "Bone health."

o o o

I'm standing, stunned, in the private enrollment office at the gym in my brand-new $320 workout outfit. I feel like a bride left at the altar. A bride in overpriced, unreturnable spandex. A bride in equally unreturnable custom-insole support sneakers and pristine new wedding-white socks. I came here to commit to a future with the fabulous hot body I finally believe I deserve. I did not come here to commit to a future with bone health. My officiant, dressed in a mini magenta fitness onesie with *TRAINER* across the chest—the person I just let *weigh and measure* me—makes a little checkmark, hands me the Goals page from her clipboard, and bops out of the room.

I clutch the paper like a bridal bouquet. Silently repeat the words, just as any crushed bride standing at the altar would repeat any two-word relationship ender: "It's over." "Another woman." "I'm sorry."

"Bone health."

This is *not* what I came here for today.

I came to the gym ready to say "I do!" to the sexy, sleek-muscled, flat-stomached, tight-reared, shapely armed, lean-legged body the universe has been telling me was out there for me my whole life. I want *that*! I'm finally ready to do everything it takes to get *that*! I did not spend $320 on wedding spandex and matching orthopedic sneakers for bone health!

The trainer bops back in.

"Bone health is a fine goal," I say as politely as possible, "but what about . . ."

"Cardiovascular integrity! Of course!" she interrupts, plucks the Goals page from my hand, snaps it back on her clipboard, and checks another little box.

"Well, yes, but what about . . ." I continue.

"Joint mobility!" she proclaims and makes another checkmark.

"Well, yes. But . . ."

That other thing! I think to myself. *The sexy, sleek-muscled, flat-stomached, tight-reared, shapely armed, lean-legged body thing that you promise everyone else! THAT thing!"*

"Of course!" She nods knowingly as if she heard every word. "Goes without saying!"

I smile, straighten, pull my wedding spandex down over my rear, and wait to hear the words I came hear.

"You'll also gain improved digestive function!" she pronounces.

Joining a new gym at my age is the exact equivalent of joining a dating site at my age and realizing my "ideal life mate" is eighty-nine years old. I can't look at my twenty-two-year-old trainer and argue that I'm ready to commit to a hot, lean, sexy new body any more than I could walk into a juice bar and announce that I'm ready to commit to a hot, handsome thirty-five-year-old hunk. I'm too old. Too old to ever look like the babe in the poster on the wall of the gym, no matter how many hours in a row I work out. Finally old enough to have the confidence and willpower to commit to the body I want and deserve, and am too old to achieve it.

Of course I'll get stronger by joining a gym again. Of course it's all good for me. But it's demoralizing when all the improvements for my age bracket are for the interior, not the exterior. No one talks about the radiant young skin I could have anymore. They offer to "repair skin damage at the subepidermal level." The woman in the commercial doesn't pat her tummy to flash the killer abs that I too could have. She pats to tell me that I too could increase the probiotic culture count in my intestines. All those 10,000 steps I'm supposed to take every day? Not for slimmer hips, just "increased blood flow to the brain to help slow memory loss." And now not a peep about the sexy, svelte muscles I could get by joining this gym. Only that weight training will increase my bone health and do all those other inner things that will help me stay an old lady longer.

I'm tired of spending all my time and money on the inner me! I silently protest. *I want results on the outside! Visible young-person outer results, not old-lady inner results!!*

My trainer either doesn't notice my angst or is dismissing it as commitment jitters. Or she's simply been too busy getting the vows and an extremely one-sided prenup ready for me to sign. Pages of waivers saying the gym isn't responsible for any amount of pain or unhappiness I might experience in the relationship. Clauses declaring I agree to keep paying every month, even if I want out. Gym alimony. I take one more good look at my Goals page. It's like a bad arranged marriage. Was there something better out there for me?

Standing at the altar in wedding spandex.

Do I really want to go home and start all over? Do I want to take a chance that the next experience could be even worse? That the next trainer at the next gym might assess me and declare my fitness goal to be "increased bladder control"?

And so I sign the vows. As a symbol of my commitment, I get a little plastic bar code to wear on my key ring that will be scanned to identify me when I come in. I slip it on the ring, right next to the little plastic bar code from the grocery store loyalty club. A perfect wedding set: grocery store and gym.

I leave with my vows and prenup stuffed in my purse. I hold the key ring up as I walk toward my car, hoping someone will notice my new bar code sparkle in the sun.

Is the need to belong to something so strong that I'm proud of pledging myself to a future with anything? . . . Or is part of me actually still young enough to secretly believe I'll turn this relationship into what I came here dreaming it could be, in spite of what everyone says? Do I really think I can trample all logic, science, and reality? Resemble anything close to the hot, toned babe in the poster one day?

Yes, I do.

I DO!

Standing on the sidewalk in wedding spandex, I feel a flush of endorphins create blushing bride cheeks. Now, *this* is a commitment I want to own. I will sprint past the limits! Lift all those expectations! Stomp all over what others believe is possible.

Good thing, I think, unlocking the car with another flash of my bar-code wedding set . . . Good thing I'm going to have nice strong bones.

34.

SEDUCTION 101

"Can I send a text or is it better to wait so I seem mysterious and aloof?"

"How soon can I answer a text without appearing too eager?"

"If I text and don't get a text back, can I text again or will that ruin everything?"

"Are emojis out of the question at my age?"

Three hundred years of relationship experience between us, and my friends and I are clueless. We huddle together on Joan's back porch, exactly how we used to huddle with our girlfriends in the corners of the gyms at all our middle school and high school dances.

Full of questions and fruit punch. Except these days, since contact is now possible 24/7, there's no relief. Not one second in which there isn't the chance that a special someone might want to connect with us. Not one moment when there isn't some clever, crazy way of reaching out that we think of in the middle of the night but *should not consider doing.*

"I could fly there and show up at his door bringing breakfast for a surprise visit!"

"I could write a love song, film myself singing it, and post it on YouTube!"

"I could bribe someone to get me access to her Facebook page!"

Three hundred years of experience between us and we're not ready for this. We're not delusional single women. Not searching for love. Not trying to date. We're much more desperate than that:

We're Mothers of College Freshmen.

One nervous, clueless mom after another, trying to tutor each other through the required mom course—Seduction 101: How to Entice Your Kid to Make Contact. Late nights spent trading notes on how to lure our children back to us before we explode with worry. Comparing frantic mom quizzes, hoping someone will know the answers: *Where is she? What could he be doing? Who's she with? Why haven't I heard from him?* We live with phones strapped to our waists, stuffed in pockets, bras, and purses. Ready for the miracle of any little tweet, text, bing, peep—anything—coming from any of them that would reassure us our child is okay.

They will never call home just to chat. We learned how futile a dream that one is during heartbreaking College Freshman Mom Month Number One. They won't call at all, won't answer if we call, won't listen to or respond to voice mails. Voice is over. The spoken word is out. It wouldn't matter anyway. We're apparently not sup-posed to reach out at all. We liberated their generation from the archaic "boys have to make the first move" law only to have them turn the new freedom against us. Now "children away at college have to make the first move." Moms can only make little flirty ges-tures from the sidelines and hope we intrigue our children enough that they'll text back and tell us they're still alive.

What I wanted to say to my daughter this morning:

Are you okay? Are your classes okay? Are you safe? Are you scared? Are you stressed? Are you lost? Are you eating? Is that special TempurPedic pillow that cost more than my first mattress helping you fall asleep? I miss you, my precious baby! I love you more than life itself!!

Instead, I texted a photo of our dog chewing a hole in the sofa cush-ion with the caption "thx 2 u, this tastes like choclt!" that took me forty-five minutes to carefully compose. Must pretend I'm not desper-ate to hear from her. Must not seem needy. Must not appear that I like her too much or she'll run the other way.

It would be one thing if my daughter were a carefree spirit who had operated on her own throughout high school and gradually pre-pared me for the big post-graduation Mom Dump. But until several months ago, she couldn't sustain life for fifteen minutes without ask-ing for help.

"MOM! There's a spider!"

"MOM! My ponytail's lumpy!"

"MOM! I can only find one flip-flop!"

"MOM! The clicker doesn't work!"

I'd heard "MOM!" every six seconds since she learned to speak. I was panic-stricken that I was sending her to college with a complete lack of life skills. And now not a word. Worse than not a word.

When she graduated from high school, I graduated from Beloved Creator and Keeper of Life to Wrong Person. If she sees my name on the caller ID, I'm the Wrong Person calling. Should she ever answer the phone, it will be with her "Hello Wrong Person" voice.

She even clicked the little button on her phone so it no longer shows on my phone whether or not she's read my text message. It says my message was *delivered*, but doesn't say *read*, so now I can't tell if she's standing there looking at my Wrong Person text and rolling her eyes or if she's too busy doing something I don't want to think about her doing and hasn't even read it. I've shared everything in her life since the day she came home from the hospital and now I'm suddenly, completely, left out of everything.

My back-porch girlfriends and I promised to be there for one another as our children went off in all directions this fall, to share the agonizing process of launching and letting go. The giant tangle of pride, panic, and a hundred other things we never imagined. We trade tips, confessions, worst moments, best guesses. We never thought we'd be having conversations like this. When we sent them off with our hopes, dreams, and $700 smartphones that instantaneously link them to the entire universe, we never dreamed it would be quite so tricky to stay touch.

"Does 'luv u 2' mean my son loves me or needs me to pay his Hulu bill?"

"Does 'k talk latr' mean later today? This week? She'll call? I can call??"

"Has anyone else stooped to scrutinizing the cell phone bill to see who she IS talking to for all those minutes??"

I try to imagine how my parents survived when my older sister and I left for college, long before cell phones. There was one pay phone per floor in my dorm, and a lineup every Sunday night to make a three-minute call home. Sometimes I didn't even bother getting in line, and I know my sister didn't either. *I'll just call next week*, I'd think, and go do whatever I thought was more fun. I never once thought what I now know with every cell in my being—that Mom and Dad planted themselves on kitchen stools in front of the wall phone immediately after church every single Sunday morning and stayed there until midnight, hoping the phone would ring. Dad probably brought a pillow to the kitchen some nights and rested his head on it on the counter right under the phone, just in case one of our calls still came.

I remember their anxious, eager voices when we finally talked. It was long distance and expensive, but three minutes every week or so was all they had. By the end of my freshman year, the cute, wide-eyed, preppy students who arrived at the University of Michigan in September turned into long-haired, ratty-jeaned, authority-rejecting, society-overthrowing, war-protesting rebels. Still, Mom and Dad had no way to call and see if my sister or I were okay, or even if we still resembled ourselves. All they could do was grip each other's hand, squint at the film footage on the nightly news, and pray they didn't recognize either of their girls in front of any burning administration buildings.

My daughter and I have unlimited talk and text on our cell phones. Our phones are always with us. We could talk twenty-four hours a day. We could be on FaceTime—talk and *see* each other twenty-four hours a day—and it wouldn't cost one penny more. We could, but we don't. Somehow the fact that constant communication is possible makes us be in touch even less.

My back-porch friends and I are mourning it all—the unthinkable grief we caused our parents, the unbelievable grief our children are causing us, the unimaginable challenge of trying to get through Seduction 101. We're passing another round of tissues when one woman raises the cheerful concept that our children's lack of communication is a sign of healthy, age-appropriate individuation and boundary setting, and that we should celebrate how magnificently our kids are coping on their own. We wrap the woman's cookie in a napkin, put her fruit punch in a to-go cup, and ask her to leave. The rest of us resume commiserating . . .

And then it happens. A phone rings. All five remaining friends—none of whom ever changed our identical default iPhone ringtones for fear we might miss a call while we were messing with the settings—lunge for pockets, bras, and purses. Six frantic seconds and then . . . It's mine! I run inside to finally have the moment I've been dreaming of with my beautiful little freshman.

"Hello??!!" I answer.

"Hi, sweetie!" I hear.

It isn't my beautiful freshman. It's my mom. The mom *I* haven't called in more than a week. The one who's been sitting in her kitchen across the country wondering how to call *me* in a way that wouldn't be intrusive.

"I found a great recipe for using up extra fruit!" Mom says.

Mom, who still rehearses things to say that won't make her sound clingy. Who knew I needed to hear her voice, even if she also knew she would probably be the Wrong Person today.

"Should I pop it in the mail for you?" she adds warmly.

Mom's nonthreatening verbal "tweet." A lifetime of love in under 280 characters.

"Thanks, Mom. That would be great," I answer. I feel her knowing smile through the phone, warming and reassuring me from the inside out. She and Dad made it through my college years and still always find ways to stay connected when I don't. I don't feel quite as clueless as I did before. I'm part of the circle—parent, child, parent, child. I feel Mom connect the ends and wrap it around me like a hug.

And now I know with all my heart that if I just wait another twenty or thirty years, I'll hear my girl say exactly what I say next:

"I'm glad you called, Mom. You're exactly who I want to talk to right now."

35.

THE LAST CHAMPIONS
OF PHOTO ALBUM GUILT

hotos. I need to discuss this situation before I explode.

My parents' generation doesn't think about it any-more. Their boxes of unorganized pictures will simply be bequeathed to the next in line.

My daughter's generation doesn't need to think about it. Their pictures are shared or deleted instantly or stored for them automatically in the cloud.

My generation doesn't want to think about it. It's too huge and hopeless. My friends leave the room when I bring it up. Nobody wants to be my photo-problem friend. The thought of our billions of beloved pictures—unorganized, un-albumed, unprinted, unedited, unlabeled, un-downloaded, and unbacked up in various abandoned systems, stranded on various devices all over the house—makes everyone a little bit sick. The images that mean the most make us a lot sick. We know they're there . . . someplace. Waiting . . .

I would leave the room myself when I bring it up, except I can't find the door to get away from myself. Especially not in the middle of the night, which is when my brain always wants to start the conversation.

3:00 a.m. Photo album agony hour. Eyes wide open.

My days are full of all sorts of other goals at this transitional time of life—a healthy, normal urge to get perspective on the past, throw out what doesn't matter, and treasure what does. Cleaning closets and bathroom cabinets. Nice, satisfying jobs I could theoretically begin and complete in a matter of hours.

At 3:00 a.m., when absolutely nothing can be done, I think of all those pictures.

No generation before or after will have the photo problem that people of my generation have. Another burden we silently carry because no one can stand to think about it, let alone discuss it. When our mothers raised children, one roll of twelve- or twenty-four-exposure film lasted a year. They had only two dozen prints *per year* to manage. When our children raise children, every moment of their little lives will be automatically archived on multiple smart devices. They'll have even less to manage.

My generation? *So* much to manage. We were the last generation of the film years, when it was suddenly possible to shoot hundreds of pictures per event, not per lifetime. Thirty-six-exposure rolls of film, thirty-minute photo processors on every corner. Hundreds and hundreds of prints and negatives, with no way to keep track of them all. My photo situation was completely out of control by the time my daughter was six hours old.

My generation was the last of that era, producing more boxes of unorganized prints and negatives than any people in history . . . AND we were the first generation of the digital years. Pioneers who could suddenly shoot *thousands* of pictures per event, before there was an easy system for downloading or storing. Pioneers who didn't read the instruction books, so the first 4,500 pictures many of us took say they were shot on 00/00/00. Thousands and thousands of pictures taken in the early days of digital. Some saved on current computers, some on old obsolete computers, some printed, some transferred to now-unreadable CDs, some never even downloaded. Some of life's most special moments on tiny unlabeled, un-downloaded memory cards tossed in random drawers throughout the house for "safekeeping." My child's sixteenth birthday is there somewhere, possibly mixed in with the paper clips and rubber bands in the kitchen junk drawer. Who knows? I didn't take the one second necessary to even write a date on the memory card. Each time I proudly thought: "I'll never forget what's on *this* one!" as I tossed it in the drawer.

I know my friends have photo situations waking them up in the night just like I do. I know women in my same phase of life share an overwhelming urge to sort and organize everything *right now*. And I know what's driving this: a deep maternal calling to put our family's life in order.

Women have always been the sentimental historians, saving little pieces of this and that, re-creating and preserving events with the pictures we frame on the walls, the scrapbooks we give to loved ones, the stories that can be told and handed down through the albums we make. We're the glue guns of the family. Keeping it all intact. Providing the comfort and security of seeing an order to the past. We do it for ourselves, to make sense of things. We do it for our children, to help them know who they are. We do it for friends, to show them how much we care. We do it for the people who will come after us so they'll know we existed, so we can inspire them from the other side about the importance of family, the need to stay connected to each other.

But we haven't done it yet.

How could we? Our shoeboxes, storage tubs, Ziploc bags, and random envelopes of predigital prints and negatives, along with the unbacked-up hard drives and un-downloaded, unreadable memory cards full of digital pictures, are overwhelming. Overwhelming and buried all over the house. No one will make sense of any of it or put it all into pretty albums or beautiful scrapbooks if we don't. No one will ever even know the pictures exist if we don't find them. We're the end of the line. The guardians of the biggest, most impossible collection of unorganized photos in the history of the universe.

We're the last champions of photo album guilt.

There.

I shut my eyes, feeling self-righteous and proud, at least, of how well I've fully expressed the enormity of my generation's burden . . . when I'm suddenly jolted by two words:

IMAGE DEGRADATION!

A 6.0 on the Panic Scale. Followed almost immediately by two wrenching aftershocks:

FORMAT OBSOLESCENCE!

UNRETRIEVABLE FILES!

Eyes wide open again. I instantly, horribly, remember that my lifetime of precious memories are not only unorganized, un-albumed, unprinted, unedited, unlabeled, un-downloaded and unbacked up . . .

but are all *disappearing*. Photos are fading. Nonarchival album pages are eating away at the few beloved images I actually got into albums. Memory cards are deteriorating. DVD backups are warping. Backup drives are becoming outdated and inaccessible. Every single way that pictures are saved is becoming obsolete and everything needs to be resaved a new way.

AND IF IT'S HIDEOUS TO THINK OF ALL THE PICTURES, WHAT ABOUT THE 50,000 HOURS OF TREASURED FAMILY VIDEOS THAT ARE ROTTING IN THE CLOSET???

And that's that.

I pull the covers over my head to protect myself from whatever I think of next. There's so much to put in order at this time of life. So much to do and redo.

I squeeze my eyes shut. I will myself to imagine that I've dealt with the photo situation. I force myself to visualize neat piles of pictures in chronological order. I visualize boxes of heirloom photos scanned and digitized so they'll never fade or warp. I see a happy picture of an updated backup system. Then a shot of a backup to the backup. An online family archive. Grandchildren poring over the meticulously labeled family history I've left.

I fill my mind with these happy pictures. I make mental pages of the mental pictures. I put them in a lineup of pretty mental albums. Label them in gold nonfading acid-free archival-quality mental Sharpie.

Finally I sink back into my pillow and flip through my future. It's all so beautiful and peaceful, I think as I drift back to sleep . . . It's all so possible . . . At least until I wake up.

36.

PRINCE CHARMING

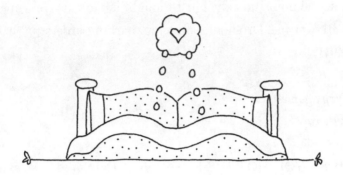

I wake up first and will myself to stay completely still.

I listen to him breathing next to me. I think of his kind face, how he smiles in his sleep. I think what a miracle he is, how my life changed forever the day we fell in love.

I think without moving one cell. If I even peek through almost closed eyelashes he'll wake up. If he wakes up, he'll want to do all sorts of things I don't want to do at six in the morning.

His breathing changed. He *is* awake . . . but he's not sure I'm awake. I feel his loving eyes, searching for any sign of life, feel him straining to hear me move. The extreme connectedness I cherish in the evening, so utterly unwanted at 6:00 a.m.

I try to beam a silent message across the pillows: *Leave me alone! Let me wake up at my own pace for once!* My breathing is so shallow,

I'm barely conscious. I consider holding my breath until I pass out rather than letting him win the morning again. No part of me is relaxed anymore, but at least I'm not doing what he wants to do.

I beam another silent message: *Can't you get up without me?! Just get up and walk away!*

And that's that. *Walk* is definitely a word he can hear even if I just think it, and unfortunately, I just thought it. He's up. He's an animal. Paws all over me! Drooling, pouncing, barking orders:

"Walk!"

"Food!"

"Tuggy game!"

"Belly rub!"

"Ball!"

"MUST YOU DO THIS EVERY MORNING??!" I snap at him.

He forgives me for being grumpy.

"MUST YOU SLOBBER ALL OVER ME??!"

He forgives me for being ungrateful.

"MUST YOU BE SO FORGIVING??!"

He forgives me for being insane.

"MUST YOU BE A DOG??!"

He grins his goofy grin, and this day, like every one of the thousands of days we've been together, he forgives me for being human.

37.

UNEXPIRED LOVE

"GOOD UNTIL NOSY DAUGHTER READS LABEL"

Your mayonnaise expired in 2016," I say as cheerfully as possible, considering this will be my last meal on earth and the woman about to murder me is my mother.

"I should have expired in 2016, too!" Mom chirps back. "And here I am!"

Here she is, lovingly preparing the nice lunch that will poison me during another quick trip I've made to Florida. She plops an extra-big scoop of the mayonnaise into a bowl full of chopped hard-boiled eggs.

"Um . . . did you get new eggs or are those the ones that have been in there?" I ask as politely as I can.

"Why would I get new eggs when I had all these to use up?" she answers matter-of-factly.

"Because those eggs expired in July and it's September now," I say.

"Eggs never go bad!" Mother announces, a slight edge to her voice.

"Well, actually, Mom . . . "

She sighs, plants one hand on her hip, and shoves a container of mustard toward me. "Here! Want to reject my mustard while you're at it?"

I check the label. "This says it expired in 2011."

Mom's eyes flash, arms stretch outward. "I should have expired in 2011, too! And here I am!"

It's hard to argue with a healthy ninety-year-old.

No time, anyway. She's plucked an ancient-looking little jar of allspice from a shelf full of other ancient-looking little jars, and is tapping it on the counter to un-congeal the contents so she can sprinkle some into her bowl of old mustard, mayonnaise, and eggs.

I hold out my hand.

"Oh, for heaven's sake," she grumbles, shaking her head and handing me the jar. "Spices last forever."

Forever or—I squint—according to the blurry, faded allspice label, until March 7, 1998.

There's no time to discuss this, either. Mom's sticking a plastic food storage container full of frozen soup into the microwave.

"What . . . are . . . you . . . doing . . . Mom??" I stammer.

"Heating up some nice soup to have with our egg salad!"

"You can't microwave food in plastic! The toxins in the plastic get activated and contaminate the food!"

Mother's glaring now. "I've never tasted any toxins!"

"This isn't even BPA-free!" I continue, opening the microwave and grabbing the frozen tub. "It's old plastic, Mom! Expired plastic! And the soup . . ."—the freezer frost has cleared enough to make out a faint *Christmas, '92* written in Sharpie on the top—"the soup is from—"

"It's been *FROZEN!*"

Mom, the most joyful human I ever met, the most sweet-spirited, even-tempered, open-minded, easygoing, gracious, benevolent, happy person I know, isn't any of that anymore. Mom is ticked.

"Here!" She smacks a frozen baguette on the counter. *"Bread!* Are we allowed to eat *bread?!"*

"I'm sorry, Mom," I say, picking up the frozen loaf and cradling it, feeling suddenly terrible for ruining the nice lunch she'd planned. I flash-forward, as I often do in this wrenching time of life, to when Mom won't be here. When I would give anything to eat one more of Mom's beautiful expired-ingredient meals with her. When I will be standing here sobbing in Mom's mom-less, ancient-food-less kitchen, filled with remorse for having spent one second of our precious last time together criticizing anything she does.

"Of course we can eat bread, Mom!" I say. "Yes! Let's eat bread!!"

"Don't bother looking for an expiration date."

My eyes dart up from the bag they might have been scanning while I was thinking about how sad I'll be. "I'm not looking for an expiration date!"

"Why did you put on reading glasses to look at a loaf of bread?"

"Um . . ."

"Doesn't matter," she says matter-of-factly. "You won't find an expiration date. I always repackage bread in one of the nice long plastic bags in which they deliver our newspapers!"

I quit cradling. Stare at my mother. She lifts the baguette from my hands.

"The bread is on the *inside* of the bag!" she announces. "Perfectly clean! The ground only touches the *outside* of the bag!"

My nineteen-year-old daughter won't eat a cherry tomato that was picked five seconds ago from a pot on our back porch if it has one fleck of brown on it. My ninety-year-old mom joyfully uses last month's lettuce, last year's cheese, and anything put in the freezer in the last century, wrapped in anything reusable from anywhere.

"Expiration dates are a big scam," Mom announces with the moral authority of someone who survived the Great Depression, World War II, and the invention, death, and reincarnation of the Twinkie. "They want you to throw out perfectly good food and spend money on new food!"

With that, she plants a nice big scoop of expired egg salad on each of our plates. She pulls the vintage baguette out of the used newspaper bag, slices it on her salmonella-infused wooden cutting board from 1952, and carefully lays two pieces of bread on an ancient, carcinogen-emitting plastic plate in the microwave to warm. Gets out a chunk of butter still partially in the shape of a chicken from last Easter. Sticks the now partly thawed tub of frozen Christmas '92 soup back in the freezer for when I'm not here to comment.

Mom's graceful ninety-year-old hands have made thousands of meals with 100 percent unexpired love and patience. I see her amazing spirit, which has risen above a lifetime of disappointments and disagreements with grace and humor, carry on. So much was taken from Mom's generation. Choices, chances, opinions, power. She's at least always had this: Her Kitchen, her helm, where she's always gotten to be the boss. I think of everything she's made happen here—the babies she raised, the crises she solved, the impossibly disconnected egos she magically blended and baked into one deeply devoted family. I think of all her education, dreams, and talents channeled through that gracious spirit, played out by those graceful hands, working her Mom Miracles in the kitchen, and of how far she came to get here.

Mom was born in a tiny log house with a woodburning stove, no plumbing, and no refrigerator in a remote village in Slovakia. Also no trash cans, because nothing was ever thrown out. They raised all the food they ate, stored brined meat in outdoor sheds, cabbage and potatoes in frozen holes in the ground. They speak a language called Rusyn in that region which, even though Mom has no trace of an accent, can still roll off her tongue like a beautiful, exotic song.

When she was three years old, Mom came to the United States on a steamship with her terrified mother. When I used to travel with my three-year-old daughter, I brought two carry-ons stuffed with toys and games to entertain her for a two-hour flight. Mom says she remembers seeing a ball of aluminum foil sparkling in the sun on the ship deck, and that that's what she played with all the way across the Atlantic Ocean. My grandfather had been working in Cleveland's steel mills to bring them over. My grandmother was twenty-three. She left her homeland with toddler Mom and never went back.

My grandmother never saw her own mother again. Never even got to talk to her. The only way to communicate was letters, but neither she nor her mother could read or write, even in their own language, so it was up to other people to write for them. Everything my grandmother and her mother said to each other for the rest of their lives was written down for them by their husbands. No pictures. No phones. Just letters that went by boat. Months and months between letters. Oceans between hearts.

Mom told me once, "I finally taught my mother how to write her name so she didn't have to put an X when she needed to sign something."

I am one generation away from that.

My mother grew up in an immigrant community in Cleveland,

learned to speak English in the first grade, and loved to write. A high school teacher thought she was so gifted, she worked to get Mom a scholarship to Kent State University. Mom was not just the only one in her family to go to college; it was considered disrespectful in their tight community for a girl to leave her household duties to go on to higher education. She graduated from Kent with a BA in journalism, dreaming of a writing career.

Mom still glows when she talks about her first job, as a copywriter for Rike's Department Store in Dayton, Ohio—how she loved going to the bustling office, loved the challenge of deadlines and the thrill of seeing her words in print. She had a great, brief taste of what it was to earn her own living as a writer. But it was a matter of pride for men at the time that their wives "didn't have to work," so most women gave up their jobs outside the house once they were married, especially once children were born. Careers for women were mostly not an option, no matter how long the women had studied and dreamed or how excellent they were at their profession.

Instead, Mom helped Dad get his first job as an advertising copywriter by writing all his trial assignments for him on the kitchen table, which he submitted with his applications. Dad had returned from World War II knowing he needed a more secure career than the song and dance comedy team he'd been so brilliant in in college, but he didn't know anything about copywriting. After Mom helped him get his first job, she helped him *keep* his job by rewriting much of what he did at the office during the day when he brought it home at night. She redid his work for months—taught Dad until he was an excellent advertising writer on his own. She still tells the story modestly, not wanting credit or praise now any more than she wanted it then. Dad's the one who's always made sure we knew that

Mom made his career possible. Still . . . Dad went on to become the president of an advertising agency. Mom never had a chance to go back, not to Rike's, certainly not to any form of more personal writing. It's incomprehensible how my father or any man back then would have felt to be married to a woman who fully expressed her feelings on the printed page.

Grandma had a one-letter identity—"X."

Mom got six letters—"Mrs." and "Mom."

Just last year, Mom mentioned for the first time that she went back to school and earned her master's degree in journalism when my sisters and I were in school, but never bothered to fill out the paperwork to get the certificate or even tell us she did it. "Why would I talk about it?" she asked. "I didn't do it for praise or a paper to hang on the wall. I just loved to learn." She briefly tried being a kindergarten teacher but told us that by then, it was too hard to leave her own children to teach other people's children. She lived with all the modern complications of trying to be a working mom at a time when there was almost no support for it.

Mom didn't get a writing or teaching career. She got my sisters and me. She got to be a beloved voice for mothers all over the world as Mom in my comic strip, even though I was the one who got to write the words. It's why Mom always had a bigger speaking part in the comic strip than Dad, because I was always aware that in real life, she had way fewer chances to be heard. I filled in the blanks on her behalf, with a special thrill that I could give voice to some of what she felt. Everything I've ever written, including this, has been a little bit for her.

Mom also got this: her kitchen, where she fed our bodies, hopes, and the possibility that we could grow up to do anything. She's never once expressed resentment or regret; has only always told my sisters and me that we were her most important job. She channeled all her love of working into us and her home; the pots and pans in this room.

I try to imagine what it must be like to be Mom now, with all that behind her and almost out of birthdays. For all the time I spend being upset that things are changing around me, what could it possibly feel like to be the one who's on the edge of leaving? I try to comprehend how it must feel to have a spoiled daughter examining the expiration dates of the ingredients she's using with such care.

I vow to never, ever bring up the expiration date discussion again.

But Mom knows all this. She knows my generation carries our grand sense of entitlement right next to where we carry our profound sense of gratitude for our parents and helplessness that we can't protect them from what's ahead. She knows what this kitchen will be like for me when she isn't in it. She knows that the ways we make each other crazy are part of the ways we keep each other sane. She forgives me for being young and for forgetting she isn't. Forgives me for being an overindulged child of America and forgetting how close I am to a tiny house in a remote village in Slovakia where no one ever threw out a crumb.

Mom sees me looking at a juice carton she pulled from the back of the refrigerator. She puts it down, raises a neurotoxin-leaching plastic cup full of the mystery liquid she just poured out of it, and flashes her beautiful, defiant, ninety-year-old smile: "Here's to 1972!"

If I don't die eating this lunch, I will remember it as one of the best meals of my life.

38.

ATE O'CLOCK

ight o'clock. I stand in the bathroom tonight, too disgusted with myself to floss.

Sometimes it all just swells up in me. Such great intentions to be everything to everyone, including myself. So little done. My one and only accomplishment today was to snap off a public radio show I started listening to about trailblazing women before it made me feel even worse. I didn't need to hear any more inspiring stories. I already have enough examples of incredible women who aren't me in my mind . . .

I imagine dynamic, driven women in their offices tonight, grabbing bites of takeout vegan spring rolls while brainstorming corporate overhauls. I imagine brilliant women in their labs, too absorbed in lifesaving research to notice that the sun went down.

I stare at the dental floss in the drawer. Next to it are steps 1, 2, 3, 5, and 6 of a six-step skin care system, which I also do not care enough about myself to use.

I imagine women rushing to the 24-hour gym for a FlyBarre class before diving into their online master's courses. I imagine women across the world, bent down in fields, babies strapped to their backs, harvesting the grain they'll pound into flour and bake into the bread that will keep their families alive.

The bread image makes me think of the half-eaten bag of Wetzel's Pretzels Bitz in the kitchen. It takes every shred of my nonexistent personal power to not run down the hall and eat some. I repulse myself.

I stare back at the untouched six-step skin care system. Step 4 isn't there because I tossed it in the bottom of my purse to use as hand lotion a while back, its top promptly popped off, and my wallet, keys, and a month of loose receipts and coupons got treated with $15-per-ounce cell-regenerating bio-peptides.

I imagine women in space, women in uniform; women editing films, performing brain surgery, teaching, composing, inventing, discovering, giving, building. Women "just like me" who are raising their own children while launching programs to empower and uplift girls in underprivileged communities.

Every incredible woman I imagine makes me feel worse about myself.

Every reminder that I'm part of the most dynamic group of females in the history of the world—that there are billions of women supporting, encouraging, and cheering other women on—makes me feel more alone.

I tell myself I have to dig deep, but at 8:00 p.m., the deepest I can dig is to the next drawer down in the bathroom cabinet. Twelve varieties of mind-and-body-calming bath soaks, salts, beads, and bubbles greet me with a sick blast of lavender mixed with the aroma of unwritten thank-you notes for the gift baskets in which they arrived.

If I weren't already basically immobile, the bath stuff would stop me in my tracks. I've never understood. The whole bath industry is based on the premise that it's soothing and healing to take off one's clothes and hop into a scented tub. But absolutely no mention of how unsoothing and unhealing it is to get a glimpse of one's unclothed self on the way into and out of the tub, even by candlelight. No mention of how much worse it would be to blow the candles out, navigate the relaxation process in the kindness of the dark, slip, be knocked unconscious, and be discovered in that state by another human being.

Everything in my bathroom—my girl cave, the sacred retreat for pampering and celebrating me—is only making me wish I had all the money back for all these abandoned girlie systems, reminding me how long it's been since I cleaned the drawers, and how very unproductive it is for me to have "me time."

I decide I'll not only not floss, but I won't wash my face, either. Won't brush my hair. Won't sterilize my contacts. The choices come slowly at first, then start flying in: Won't remove my makeup, exfoliate, breathe deeply, or reflect. Won't stretch! Won't read! Won't pick anything up off the floor! The opposite of proactive. I have become pro-passive. Succeeding only in choosing *not* to do things. Except . . .

My mind goes back to the Wetzel's Pretzels Bitz.

"If I eat some, maybe I'll be inspired to stay awake and accomplish something!"

The convoluted logic of this hour: Eight o'clock. Ate o'clock. When the healthy choices of the day are so easily wiped out, and so much damage can be done.

I can't lift a small string of floss to my mouth, but could sprint across the house to the kitchen for a cold, stale chunk of mall dough. It's way too early to go to bed. But also too late to start anything that I could finish except that which I can swallow.

I imagine my foremothers sewing by the fire. I imagine women singing French lullabies to their bilingual triplets. I imagine women working into the night, starting charities, writing Broadway shows, reading poetry to elderly relatives.

Finally . . . I imagine that somewhere in the universe, there's another woman standing in her bathroom at 8:00 p.m., too disgusted with herself to floss. After all the amazing women I've imagined tonight, that's the one who gives me strength. That's the one who makes me smile and inspires me to go on. The one who will wake up tomorrow with a pretzel hangover and periodontal disease.

Tonight, that's the wonderful, wonderful woman who makes me feel okay.

39.

MOTHER'S DAY TEXT MESSAGE

Fairy princesses. A crumbly prom corsage. Flip-flops with six summers ground into them. Boots that barely made it out of the box. Sometimes I open the door to my daughter's bedroom and just stand here, taking it in: the still life of my child. Diploma tassel. Kindergarten tiara. Sleeping Beauty pencil cup. High school yearbook. Tiny plastic golden retriever holding a pumpkin. A faint whiff of the cologne she used to wear for a boy she used to love.

I remember the day she left for college last September when I crawled into that bed and cried myself to sleep curled up with a stuffed Dalmatian named Shaka and the agony of knowing this part was over.

I press my hands to my chest to comfort myself, trying to hold in my heart, pounding so hard it . . .

It isn't my heart pounding.

It's my phone vibrating, announcing a text message. THE message no devoted mother on earth should have to see the first week of May:

> my exams got moved so i can com
> home early 4 the hole sumer. 4 hole
> munths of tv and video gams! can u
> book me a flite and put $900 in my
> acount so i can ship all my stuf?

40.

NOVOCAINE IN THE
WAITING ROOM

I'm sitting in the dentist's office weeping, long before anyone comes near me with a drill. Just sitting in the waiting room, big mom tears plopping down on the pages of the parenting magazine in my hands.

Complicated tears, like mom tears often are. Joy and longing. Hanging on and letting go. Memories. Dreams. Blisses. Regrets. I stare at the article I've been trying to read. How is it possible that my little girl and I never made caterpillars out of egg cartons and pipe cleaners like the giggly mother and daughter in the picture? I flip ahead. What have I been doing that's so much more important than showing my child how to plant carrot seeds in hand-painted paper cups to make a kitchen window garden like the good mom on page 26?

I flip through more pages, searching for all the things parenting magazines always hold: cute ideas, wonderful tips, and confirmation of how completely I've blown it.

Page 34: "Turn Off the TV and Turn On Your Toddler's Imagination!"

I'm a horrible mother.

Page 52: "Make Cleanup Time a Counting Game!"

I taught her nothing.

Page 65: "Boost Self-Confidence at Every Age—Infant, Toddler, Preschooler, Preteen."

My utter failure broken down into life stages.

This is a toxic combination if there ever were one. An overachiever working mom with a stack of parenting magazines and ten "free" minutes in a waiting room. I flip through another magazine, then another . . . compare perfect mother after perfect mother to imperfect me. I clutch the magazines to my chest, hold them way too close to the growing cavity I feel inside. It's as if the hygienist's pointy little metal tool is stabbing me in my decaying sense of well-being. I feel the almost intolerable pain of everything I missed doing with my child.

"NOVOCAINE!" I scream. "I NEED NOVOCAINE IN THE WAITING ROOM!!"

My inner scream is so loud I can't believe the staff hasn't rushed in to sedate me. They shouldn't leave parenting magazines like these out where parents might pick them up and get hurt.

Parenting seemed so doable before I tried to do it.

I almost didn't try at all. When I graduated from college, the women's movement was cheering women on to put off marriage and children until we pursued our careers—to become everything we could be before, if ever, becoming wives and mothers. In the beginning, what I lacked in personal conviction, I made up for in obedience. The other women's voices were powerful, and the instructions were nice and clear. Also, it was easier to fling myself into my job than to find someone to date.

I fell crazy in love with work. Mr. Desk. Mr. File Cabinet. Mr. To-Do List. Those relationships were 100 percent thrilling and fulfilling. I loved the freedom of working late into the night and all weekend. I loved making my own money and decisions. I loved writing about men and dating, but in my real life, I loved living alone with a dog who thought I could do no wrong.

On my thirty-fifth birthday, I announced to my parents that I was so happy on my own I'd decided to never get married and have children. The mom in the comic strip would have gone insane. My real-life mom has a capacity for graciousness I'll never comprehend. She paused for the briefest moment, exchanged a look with Dad, then smiled at me and said, "Your father and I think of *Cathy* in the newspaper as our grandchild. We love her dearly, and couldn't be more proud of the life you've built for yourself." Later that day, Mom presented me with the set of wedding silver she'd been collecting for me, one beautiful spoon, fork, and knife at a time, since the day I was born. Gift-wrapped in wedding paper, in a lovely fabric-lined box.

"You shouldn't have to be married to eat with a nice fork," Mom said with a little wink, handing my wedding silver to me. She said it with so much love, so much incredible, nonjudgmental support, so much respect, and even a little wistfulness, I think, for the different kind of life the women of my generation could have, that she ruined everything. Poked a hole in my whole life plan and in it replanted possibility. How could I not give a real grandchild to that woman? How could I not experience raising a child of my own? The dream of becoming a mom that I'd had before it got pushed down and away by other dreams started growing in me again and didn't go away.

I gave myself a deadline that I had to be in a relationship heading for marriage and children by age thirty-nine. When that didn't happen, I gave myself an extension to age forty. When that didn't happen, I gave myself an extension to age forty-one. When that didn't happen, I began suspecting my lack of success in relationships might have something to do with me, and I gave up on the marriage part of the plan.

A few years earlier, I'd been at an event in Los Angeles and over-heard a woman talking about her vision for her future. She was riveting—confident, cosmopolitan, and unbound by any conventions of the world in general, not to mention the cozy 1950s conventions of Midland, Michigan, where I'd grown up. "If I don't have a baby with someone," I heard her declare jubilantly, "I'll just adopt one on my own!" This was a shocking concept at the time. Women were expressing independence in all sorts of new ways, but not that. I'd never heard of a single person adopting a child before, and neither had the other infinitely more hip L.A. guests in the room. "You can *do* that?" I heard another woman ask. "Why not?!" the first woman answered.

A thousand reasons, I remember thinking to myself at the time. There are at least a thousand reasons to *not do that*. I will never know how that concept, which seemed so bizarre and wrong to me at the time, resurfaced in my mind as something to consider.

Only that it did. Shortly after I turned forty-one, late at night, when the mind wanders and the defenses are asleep, I looked up the names of adoption attorneys in the Yellow Pages. I had all the lights in the house off except the one on the kitchen counter, almost so I couldn't even see myself thinking about it. I quickly wrote down three names, slammed the Yellow Pages shut, buried the piece of paper on the kitchen counter under a pile of bills and newspapers, and went to bed. Did nothing for two months except feel relief that I hadn't done anything. I tested the concept on myself and rejected it dozens of times. I tested it once on my sisters and rejected their enthusiasm and support.

It's never the perfect moment to make a decision that will alter the rest of your life. Especially not when you're all by yourself. I'm not brave and I'm not impulsive. I can't even switch brands of toothpaste without a whole life review. Nothing *ever* would have changed for me . . . Except . . . a few months after that midnight encounter with the Yellow Pages, I had one really good day at the office. One really productive day, at the end of one unusually productive week . . . and I had one of those exhilarating inner power surges, suddenly believing I could take on anything in the world.

That's why I finally dug out the list and called an adoption attorney. Not because I was suddenly ready to be a mom, not because I had some sign from above that it was time. I called an adoption attorney because, for the first time in months, my desk was clean, my purse was organized, my jeans zipped, and I was really happy with the work I'd sent in that week. "When people have a good week, they go get a pedicure, not sign up to adopt a baby!" a friend mentioned to me later. "Oh, right . . ." I answered. But then I'd had a really, really good week.

The first two adoption attorneys I called told me no. "We don't accept single-parent applicants." If I hadn't felt so great about myself, I wouldn't have called the third number, but I did. The adoption facilitator who answered told me to come to her office the next day.

Today, sitting in this waiting room with all these magazines, I can't help but wonder about the chain of unlikely miracles that got me to motherhood. How it is that I, of all people, champion of single, childless career women, would be sitting here crying over articles like "Roberta Made a Puppet Show Booth in Her Home Office."

In spite of all my fears, I knew I had the ideal career to be able to work from home and raise a child at the same time: writing and drawing a comic strip. As I got the house ready, I imagined I could be a model mom for parenting magazine articles myself: arty, maternal, and professional all at once. After all the things I'd already learned to juggle, how complicated could it be to bring an infant into the mix? The plan was that I would take several weeks off from deadlines after my baby was born and then . . .

My baby will nap in the bassinet, I'll write a joke.

Baby will coo in the bouncy chair. I'll draw the art.

Baby will snuggle on my shoulder. I'll color the Sunday comic with the other hand.

I set up a workspace at home for the two of us prepped with everything for our sweet new life.

And then my daughter was born. My life ended and began in

the same second, 8:38 a.m., May 6. The doctor laid this beautiful, perfect, tiny girl in the arms of her birth mother, and after some moments, her birth mother turned and laid her in my arms. I fell completely, insanely in love.

I fed her in the hospital nursery until she was ready to come home. I drove her home by myself, so terrified that she'd wake up and I wouldn't know what to do that I drove twelve miles per hour. Irritated Los Angeles drivers blared their horns. I silently screamed words I never thought I'd ever even think: *"SHHHHH!!! THE BABY IS SLEEPING!!"* At a stoplight on the corner of Sunset Boulevard and Laurel Canyon, I whispered to my sleeping forty-eight-hour-old infant that she was adopted, so it would be less awkward to bring it up later.

Our first weeks together, before I had to go back to work, were surreal. This topped all previous obsessive relationships in my life by such a massive degree, I could barely breathe. This was way, way better than Mr. Desk and Mr. File Cabinet. This made me lose my mind. I couldn't think one coherent non-baby thought if I was anywhere near my baby, even if she was sound asleep. If I was in the room with her, I just stared, transfixed. If I was in the house, but in a different room, every cell of me was listening for sounds of her stirring.

If I was in the house and my baby was awake, it was still insane love, but also pandemonium. That sleep-deprived, nonstop frenzy of diapers, bottles, rocking, walking, onesie changes, and first-time-mom freakouts that no one who hasn't had an infant can comprehend. When she finally took a nap, it meant I had one hour flat to do everything I couldn't do when she was awake, except when she finally took a nap, all I wanted to do was stand over her crib and gaze at her some more.

Getting back to writing and drawing a comic strip wasn't even in the top five thousand things to do on the list. My great big career of expressing the challenges of being a woman, suddenly outweighed by a six-pound, four-ounce girl. I couldn't believe that anyone ever did anything else after a baby was born. Couldn't believe anyone could go back to a job. Couldn't believe I had to.

Couldn't believe how simple it had seemed to work from home with a baby before I tried doing it. My leave ended and I was back on deadline much too soon. After five frantic days of trying my beautiful new "napping-cooing-snuggling" work schedule, I hired a babysitter and moved my work supplies back to an office space in a different zip code.

My mother was right that it felt as if the comic strip was her first grandchild and my first child. *Cathy* was "born" when I was twenty-six years old, and had been the total focus of my life ever since. I had a new child to support now, but I was also definitely not finished raising the first one. Besides the fact that I was under contract to keep doing it, I couldn't pretend the comic strip didn't still need me or that I didn't still need it. It had been part of every minute of my life for sixteen years before my daughter was born. "A teenager." Mom glowed. "Now you have an infant *and* a teenager!"

I also had a licensing company, which I'd set up a few years earlier, that I couldn't simply close. A separate office of several people making all sorts of deals for character merchandise and advertising endorsements, requiring all sorts of other jokes, art, meetings, trips, and appearances. Right in the middle of everything, one friend gently asked if adopting a baby as a single person, with no family members living within 3,000 miles—when I already had the full-time job of running a licensing company on top of the full-time job of doing a daily comic strip, when I was already completely overwhelmed by deadlines and obligations—if becoming a mom on my own just then wasn't a teensy bit overreaching. Even now, when I think back on how 100 percent right my friend was, it's irritating to remember the question.

It was exactly what women had just spent the previous century fighting so hard for—the right to go as far and high as we possibly could in our careers and have a family at the same time. It's what we'd finally won—what, for men, had always been a birthright. Of course I could do it all.

And I did do it all . . . just like a man. Since I became a mother through adoption, someone who wasn't me went through nine months of pregnancy and gave birth to my child. Since I was the bread-winner, I went to the office every day while a woman I supported—ultimately, a live-in nanny—stayed at home with the baby. It's more than a little uncomfortable to think of it this way, but as close to doing it all as I got was doing it all just like an old-fashioned dad would have.

I flip to the "working mom" section of the next magazine.

Page 96: "Make an Animal Magnet Parade on Your File Cabinet to Teach the Alphabet While You Work!"

Page 102: "Peekaboo Tents Keep Little Ones Happy in Mom's Office!"

Another tear plops down. *These* women aren't stay-at-home

moms who made the hard choice of giving up or putting off career dreams to be with their children full-time. They're executives with changing tables next to their printers! Architects with pint-size easels and crayons by their drawing boards! Accountants with playpens in the corner! Working women who look like I thought I would look! Women who figured out how to do what I couldn't do for ten minutes in a row. What kind of concentration superpowers do these modern Wonder Women have?? How is this new generation of moms, who still face all the impossible pressures and choices mine did—who still live in a country where pay isn't equal, flextime rarely exists, on-site day care is rare, parental leave is still a battle—how are they finding the energy and ingenuity to mesh all the parts of their lives in such incredible, inventive ways? How do they even have time to have their pictures taken for the articles?

When I tried bringing my daughter to the office when she was a little older, it was still impossible. "Mom, up!" . . . "Mom, watch!" . . . "Mom, potty!" . . . "Mom, play!" . . . Each "Mom!" would set me back another half hour. I'd have to start all over . . . try to get back into a quiet, creative brain . . . and then there'd she be, my sticky sweetie, climbing up my leg squealing "MOM!" while I tried to write jokes about a childless cartoon character. If I'd ever thought to make a play tent in my office, I would have crawled into it and hid. I always wound up giving up on any work and just playing on the floor with her on our "office" days, shoving everything I was going to do to the next day's list.

I know that if I'd been with my daughter twenty-four hours a day, I'd still be right here feeling as though I hadn't been there enough. I know that every mom does exactly the best she can. That we all have days full of compromise and impossible choices. Every one of us looks back and longs for another chance. Even the very best moms must feel inadequate compared with the perfect moms in the magazines. Still . . . I flip through the pages faster . . . woman after woman finding ways to make a little more time . . . sweet project after project reminding me what I could still do . . .

I'm becoming frantic to make up for lost glue stick time when the hygienist opens the waiting room door and tells me it's my turn. As if having my teeth cleaned is anywhere on the list of things that are important right now. If this were a movie, the heroine would charge out of the dentist's office, race home, scoop up her daughter, and reconnect with what really matters. But I'm the Heroine of My Own Life, and charging out of the office to race home and reconnect with what really matters will incur a $50 cancellation fee, which would make me feel even worse than I already do.

I force myself to follow the hygienist to the Chair. I numb my emotions enough to endure the tooth cleaning by thinking up farm animals my daughter and I could create out of the little vacuum sweeper tube the hygienist sticks in my mouth. I imagine how her scrapy tools would be perfect for modeling Play-Doh.

"How's your daughter?" my hygienist—mother of four—asks, as she always does, right when my mouth is too full of equipment to defend myself. She adds with a little sigh, as she always does, "It must be so wonderful to have a job where you can work out of your house!"

What feels like a lifetime later, I'm finally released, jump into my car, and hurl home.

"Mom's home!" I call, running in the front door. "Wake up, sweetie! We're going to make things! We can paint paper cups and plant carrot seeds! Create egg carton caterpillars! Laminate flower petals onto place mats!"

I see rustling under her fuzzy pink blankie on the couch. My heart rustles in response. There's still time. I didn't miss all my chances!

A foot sticks out and wiggles.

A giant, size 7 foot.

I pull the blankie back. When I left two hours ago, she was three years old and getting tucked in for her nap by a babysitter. Now there's an nineteen-year-old sprawled on the couch covered in potato chip crumbs and electronic devices.

"WHERE'S MY BABY?!," I scream. "WHERE'S THE BABY-SITTER?!!"

My daughter yawns, squints, and laughs.

"Hey, Mom. What's for dinner?"

The only thing about her that still resembles my baby is the fact that she's back on a once-every-two-hour feeding schedule. I plop down on the couch and wrap my arms around the sixteen years that went by on the way home from the dentist. I take a deep breath of her: Victoria's Secret body mist and Pringles. Eau de Nineteen-Year-Old.

I squeeze her to me and announce, "For dinner we're having Silly Sausage Pasta and Smiley Face Squash, and after dinner we're going to make a big, sparkly Summer Reading Goal Prize Box!"

Maybe she's just sleepy enough from her midday, beginning-of-the-summer teen coma to not protest. Or maybe part of her longs for a little of what we missed along the way like I do . . . In any case, instead of the automatic recoil, she hugs me back and rests her head on my shoulder.

I'm grateful for it all. Grateful for her almost-grown-up arms that can hold a laptop, smartphone, iPad, TV remote, and her mother at the same time. Grateful for the million ways that being her mom has made my life fuller and better. Grateful that I had a chance to try. Grateful for how much she loves me even though we never made a fairy tea set out of bakeable oven clay.

Really, really grateful I only need to get my teeth cleaned every six months.

41.

COOL WHIPPED

W here's the Cool Whip, Mom?"

"I had to destroy it."

"Destroy it, as in you threw it out? Or destroy it, you ate it?"

"It was your fault that it was open," I say, defending myself.

"I didn't even know we had Cool Whip until you asked if I wanted some on the strawberries you were trying to get me to eat," she answers in her best self-righteous teen voice.

"Exactly. I opened the Cool Whip so you'd eat some fruit!" I reply with my best self-righteous mom shot.

"I had one blob on a strawberry. Where's the rest of it, Mom?"

"I told you. I had to destroy it."

"And you say *I* have no self-control!" she huffs.

"I have LOTS of self-control!" I huff back. "I let some of it thaw naturally instead of chipping it out frozen solid! I . . ."

I spent nineteen years trying to expose my daughter to art, music, dance, theater, literature, and the wonders of nature. All those conversations in the botanical gardens, she'll forget. All those concerts, gone. This, she'll remember. The big takeaway from childhood: Mother can't be in the house with an open container of Cool Whip.

She stares at me with critical college student eyes. I search them for a flicker of her five-year-old eyes—the ones that saw me as perfect, back when she wanted to be just like me. All I can find are the teen ones, recalculating my standing and reaffirming her superiority.

She shakes her head. "Wow."

I'm not sure if it's because of shame or surrender or just because this scene is so ridiculous, but her "Wow" makes me start laughing, which makes her start laughing. And then we're laughing together, doubled over each other in the kitchen. I'm so far from being perfect, and she's so close to needing me *not* to be perfect. There's relief, I think, that the guard can finally be let down. If she can remember this moment— where her old vision of me and her new vision of me blur into some loving acceptance of Mom as an Actual Human—it's surely more precious than anything they tried to teach her through the self-guided tour headset I forced her to wear at the Natural History Museum.

Still laughing, she turns away from me and scans the pantry. "Where are all the chocolate chip cookie dough granola bars, Mom?"

Then again, it's going to be a long evening.

42.

NEVER, EVER DO WHAT I SAY

T op of the fifth with no outs, a man on first and the pitch is wide and outside . . ." Baseball. Soundtrack of my dad. I'm sitting on the couch in Florida with him, watching a game. The happy, homey whir of the KitchenAid mixer starts up in the background. My ninety-year-old mom is baking, something she hasn't done in years!

This is exactly what I should be doing, I know that now. Just being here with them. Not meddling in my parents' life for once. Not micromanaging like I did on earlier visits. No TiVo. No trying to convince them they wouldn't feel "so overwhelmed with stuff" if they'd just let me help them get rid of some stuff.

There's comfort in their stuff, I appreciate that now. There's security in the basket of Christmas cards that's still in their living room every June, waiting for addresses to be double-checked in the address book, in the pile of magazines "we might still need to clip something out of to send to someone" on their kitchen counter. In their tidy stacks of scrap paper made from the unwritten-upon parts of stationery they cut off and saved. They were raised in a time and a culture that taught them not to waste, so they use the backs of every piece of paper, keep little stashes of "perfectly good" used rubber bands, twist ties, and rinsed-out Baggies. The care they take to "save things for later" implies there will be a "later," and it's deeply, sweetly reassuring.

I have no agenda left except to completely surrender to their system and honor the rules of their home. It's been unbelievably peaceful here so far, which is probably what inspired Mom to bake today after all these years. Nothing, not even the future of one old paper clip, is being threatened by me on this visit.

"Two strikes, one ball, with a man on second and one out . . ." comes the announcer from the TV set. The whir of the KitchenAid . . . Happy, homey, relaxed, perfect.

Dad's loving this too, I can tell. He turns his head toward the sound of the mixer. "Mother's at it again!" he proclaims with a grin.

"What do you suppose she's making for us?" I ask, feeling as giddy as a five-year-old, pretty sure it will be those fudge bars Mom knows I love so much. I snuggle into my childhood. Smooth my hand on the familiar fabric next to me. Along with all the used envelopes, old catalogs, and twist ties, they never got rid of their couch. I'm sitting on the same couch next to the same table next to the same lamp that's been in their living room my whole life. The paintings my sister did in high school are still on the wall. The coasters Mom and Dad brought home from their honeymoon in Niagara Falls sixty-five years ago are still on the coffee table. By hanging on to everything forever, my careful, frugal parents have kept our family's sweet, safe nest perfectly intact.

"Oh, Mom's not baking." Dad laughs. "She's shredding!"

Chocolate? Coconut? "I didn't know you could shred with a mixer!" I laugh happily.

"That's not the mixer." Dad beams. "That's our new document shredder!"

It takes more than a moment to register, but when it does, my happy laugh is over.

"Document shredder??" I repeat.

"Yes!" Dad says proudly. "We finally picked one up last week and have been going to town!"

My happy laugh is definitely over. My surrender's over. My micromanaging moratorium is over.

"Stop her!" I yell, jumping to my feet. "Stop her before it's too late!" I charge down the hall into Mom and Dad's home office and throw my body between my mother and the nice new piece of equipment she and Dad bought without my permission.

"Surprise!" Mom exclaims, trying to reach past me with a handful of papers. "I'm doing what you've been telling us to do for months!"

"Stop, Mom!! What's—in—your—hand??" I stammer, reaching for the papers, trying to not sound as panicked as I sound.

"Oh, these are just some old college things," Mom says, dodging my reach and aiming for the slot in the top of the shredder. "Out they go!"

"NO!" I say, snatching the papers before the shredder does. "You can't throw these out!"

"Ancient history!" Mom proclaims. "Who needs them?"

"I do! It's *your* history!" I look at the yellowed page on top, a college newspaper article with my mother's maiden name in the byline. "You *wrote* these!" I say, clutching the papers to me.

"For heaven's sake," Mom says, reaching toward a tall stack on her desk, "you were right! It's time to unload all this stuff!"

"What stuff??" I ask, horrified. My eyes do a speed scan of the room, searching for familiar piles. I drop to the floor and peer through the little plastic window on the front of the shredder. The shredder is half full. "What have you already shredded??"

"Just some old bills, bank statements, calendars . . ." Mom shakes her head with a laugh.

"*Family calendars??*" I choke. "You shredded *family calendars??*"

"Oh, I've barely gotten started on those!" Mom says.

I yank the top off the shredder, reach in and pull out a handful of shreds.

"We had them going back to 1955!" she adds.

I spread the shreds on the floor, try to match any minuscule scrap with any other. "Nineteen . . . no . . . here's . . . no . . . These pieces are so tiny! I'll never get them stuck back together!"

"You most certainly won't!" Mom says proudly. "Your father was afraid someone would go through our recycling bin and try to piece together our old electric bills, so we got the *micro cross cut* shredder! Burglar proof!"

"What else have you been shredding??" I ask helplessly, the teensy pieces of our beloved family history running through my fingers like confetti.

"All kinds of things! Old medical records! Letters! Pictures of people we don't recognize!"

"You haven't thrown out a rubber band in fifty years and you shredded letters and pictures??"

"We finally listened to you! Ta-da!" she says, opening a file drawer next to where I'm sitting on the floor, a drawer that used to be packed too tightly to add even one paper and is now almost empty.

"What was in there, Mom??" I peer in and ask, even more helplessly.

"Who knows? It's gone now! It feels wonderful to unload some of this stuff!"

I look up from the file drawer, which is nine tenths empty, at my beautiful mother, whose life is nine tenths over. "Please don't unload anything else, Mom."

"Don't be ridiculous!" She shakes her head. "We don't want to leave this mess for your sisters and you! Who's going to go through all this useless stuff when we're gone?"

"My sisters and I are!" I say. "We want all your useless stuff!"

"Oh, for heaven's sake." Mom shakes her head. "You've been try-ing to get us to do this for years and you were right!"

"NO! I was not right! And besides, I didn't mean *this!* I meant you should part with an old envelope now and then . . . throw out a used Post-it Note . . . not *this!* Don't *ever* listen to me, Mom! *Never, ever do what I say!!*"

"I'll get the vacuum cleaner," she says with a chuckle and nod to the pile of shreds in front of me as she walks out of the room.

I crawl right through the shreds to Mom's desk, rise to my feet, grab her desk phone, dial Staples, and start screaming before the poor receptionist knows what hit her.

"YOUR DOCUMENT SHREDDERS SHOULD HAVE PARENTAL WARNING LABELS!" I yell into the big plastic receiver. "GREAT BIG *DO NOT SELL TO ANYONE'S PARENTS!'* STICKERS! NO ONE OVER THE AGE OF EIGHTY CAN BE TRUSTED! THEY MIGHT START LISTENING TO THEIR CHILDREN AND WILL *NOT* USE GOOD JUDGMENT! NOT MAKE GOOD CHOICES! IN THE NAME OF PERSONAL SECURITY AND IDENTITY PROTECTION, YOU ARE WIPING OUT THE IDENTITIES OF ENTIRE FAMILIES! IT SHOULD BE AGAINST THE LAW TO SELL THIS MEMORY HATCHET TO SWEET, THOUGHTFUL, RESPONSIBLE PARENTS LIKE MINE WHO GET IN AN 'UNLOADING' MODE!"

The cool, professional voice on the other end of the phone has been trying to make herself heard since I began my tirade and is still going on and on, utterly unruffled by my outrage. She continues calmly, almost robotically, "For store hours, press 4; for billing, press 5; for corporate accounts, press 6; for all other inquiries visit our website at . . ."

I slam down the receiver without giving her the satisfaction of finishing her big rehearsed speech. Another thing that will be lost if people keep selling new gizmos to old people, I think. The feel and sound of a receiver smashing down on its base. The wimpy click of ending a cell phone call is utterly ungratifying for the hanger-upper, and delivers absolutely no message to the hanger-upee. Only by throwing a cell phone at a wall as hard as possible can a person get anything close to that great old sound and feeling of a phone being smashed off, but as happy a moment as that is, I've learned, it isn't really worth the replacement cost.

I make a mental note to add "Launch a movement to bring back less expensive and more gratifying ways to hang up on people" to my to-do list. But that's for later. For today, I need to rescue all the beautiful pieces of Mom's and Dad's lives they haven't managed to shred yet. Now that it's all been threatened, every single scrap of paper in their house seems special.

The grocery lists written on the backs of car insurance envelopes . . .

The paper bank statements, still checked off by hand against paper copies of written checks . . .

The copies of the copies of the copies of travel plans Dad makes to be sure he remembers to quadruple check everyone's reservations and which he hangs on to years after the trips are done just to review and reverify that it all happened as planned . . .

The rough drafts of notes written by Mom in the lovely cursive longhand they used to teach in school. My mom, who would have been a famous writer if she'd lived in a different century and had a chance for self-expression—all that talent and possibility channeled into beautiful notes to friends and family members, written as eloquently and thoughtfully as a poem . . .

The address book with names and birthdays carefully recorded, deaths gently and respectfully noted in light pencil, not the brutal electronic *delete*, which is how dear friends disappear from address lists now . . .

The basket of handwritten, pancake-batter-stained recipes Mom has thankfully never gotten computer literate enough to type into a nice clean legible impersonal computer file . . .

The worn file folders full of the roasts, toasts, and songs Dad wrote for decades of birthdays and anniversaries and retirement parties . . .

The old files of credit card receipts—who Mom and Dad are right now, where they went last year, what they needed at Walgreens in 1983 . . .

I can't leave them alone with their things anymore, I think. Can't trust them to not try to clean their desks.

I will have to move in and plant myself outside their home office door like a security guard! Install a camera that sets off an alarm in California if a piece of paper nears the trash in Florida so I can supervise from three thousand miles away! Buy boxes, pack up their whole house, and ship it to my house so they can't get rid of anything else!

I'm back in full micromanaging mode. Hyper-hoverer. I need to watch over them *and* guard every little scrap of them in this house *and* do the same for my daughter *and* make sense of all the little scraps of my own life. The job is suddenly, completely overwhelming. I need my mom and dad, I think. I need them now.

I yank the shredder's cord from the wall, wrap it in a rubber band from Mom's ancient rubber band collection, and stuff the shredder behind one of the desks. I hurry to the living room, sit back down next to Dad, and lean my head on his shoulder, lean right back into being five years old.

". . . the crowd is going wild after that last unbelievable catch deep in center field. Two outs and the tying run is at third . . ." I hear Mom fussing with something or other in the kitchen. I pat the familiar couch, breathe the familiar air, look around the familiar room. My eyes land on one tiny shred that got stuck to the knee of my jeans. I lift it off, squint to try to make out any letter or number that might match any of the 500,000 other little shreds I will be rescuing from the vacuum cleaner bag later. I tuck the shred in my pocket for safe-keeping. Nothing's leaving this happy house today. Not on my watch.

43.

LOVE IS IN THE AIR

Back in Los Angeles. I need a moment for me. Just to sit quietly and regroup. I flip through a catalog . . .

It's all so romantic on these pages.

Satisfied women lounging on overstuffed floral pillows in big rattan swings. Serene women in arty tunics snipping basil sprouts from hand-hewn clay pots. Lovely tranquil women in braided sandals and embroidered smocks walking through the gardens of their quaint cottages with pretty mugs of tea.

There are no men in the pages of this sumptuous catalog. Just romance.

Not hot, urgent, looking-for-romance romance. This is deeply contented, "I-looked-I-found-and-now-I'm-just-so-happy-I'm-here-all-by-myself" romance. Romance that's possible without a man's gym clothes strewn all over the beautiful bedroom . . . without a man spitting mouthwash on the pristine granite bathroom counter . . . without manly scorched pans and empty tubs of jalapeño dip in the immaculate girlie country kitchen sink. Romance that's possible when no one's there to question why fifteen pretty decorator pillows are taking up "his" side of the bed.

Romance that's possible when there aren't any men in the picture at all.

These are steamy "after" pictures if I ever saw them. What a woman claims for herself after giving so much to and for someone else for so long. When it's just the two of us: me and my American Express card.

I order up the life on page 32. Item #234, size M. Item #47Q, size 8. Get a little giddy and add Items #309, #457, and #199: periwinkle, blush, and avocado. Pop it all into my cart. I feel the passionate need to spring for $24.95 Rush Overnight Delivery.

Click!

I lean back in my dumpy Saturday morning sweat suit, raise my old chipped coffee cup, and toast myself and the life I so richly deserve. A confirmation bings back almost immediately. Love will be in the air in a matter of minutes, and soon after that, will be on a FedEx truck to my front door.

44.

BARBIE MOM

half-naked princess was hiding behind the china cabinet in our dining room. I found her there twenty minutes ago. Naked royalty was the last thing I thought I'd be dealing with on this busy, busy day, but I did what any mother would do. I dropped all plans I had for the afternoon, tore through the house until I found a box of clothes, dumped hundreds of tops, bottoms, gowns, cloaks, tiaras, and possibly a thousand pairs of shoes on the dining room floor and got that young lady properly dressed.

Before I could stop myself, I rummaged through other cupboards and pulled out another box. And another. In minutes, I was back sitting on the dining room with fifteen other princesses laid out in front of me. Some with less clothing than the first. Some amputees. Some bald, some with faces mauled from when our dog mistook them for chew toys years ago. Some perfect, as if they were just freed from the Barbie package I learned to rip open with my teeth at thirty-five miles per hour for the impatient little princess in the back seat of my car. By the day we bought my daughter's eighth Barbie, I could free the doll, her stitched-down hair, and half a dozen tiny accessories twist-tied to the package, and partially set up Barbie's Pet Care Center on the pull-down cup holder between the seats, all while maintaining perfect eye contact with the road.

Motherhood takes us lots of places we don't expect, that's all I can say . . .

Today, for instance. Instead of rushing around town efficiently checking accomplishments off my to-do list, I'm sitting on the floor of the dining room trying to wriggle Astronaut Barbie back into her silver spandex space suit.

For a beautiful minute, I pause to appreciate something I almost never, ever have: zero inner conflict.

These dolls, with their ridiculous figures, flawless faces, and un-attainable hair . . . their obsession with fashion, parties, and match-ing accessories . . . their inexplicable fixation on a grinning blond surfer dude named Ken who was always sitting in a pink convertible on the side of my daughter's bedroom . . . These beloved, all-wrong role model dolls helped create some of my daughter's and my favorite memories with each other, some of the very sweetest times of my life. I love these girls.

For several more beautiful minutes, I'm back where I used to be when my daughter was six years old—right back in the happy middle of my two personas: Trailblazing Career Woman by day, Barbie Mom by night. My daughter would greet me at the front door after work with a fistful of dolls and, before I could change out of my office clothes, I'd be on my hands and knees in her bedroom—crawling around in my no-nonsense business suit and pumps, helping her stuff Beach Barbie into a tiny bikini. Trying to sit on the floor in my conservative, below the knee skirt, while squashing Neurosurgeon Barbie into hospital-green hot pants and thigh-high operating room booties . . . Lying on my stomach in my blazer, packing Librarian Barbie into a strapless purple tube dress with matching glasses . . . Orthodontist Barbie into a plunging neckline, sequined lab coat . . .

I pick some poodle-print leggings from the pile of tiny clothes on the dining room floor, find Veterinarian Barbie in the lineup of dolls, and stick her skinny little legs into them. An act more satisfying than almost anything I've done all week.

I hadn't been with these girls in a long time, and the reunion is sweet. More sweet, probably, because of what's coming from the other room—the sound of my real-life grown-up princess giggling on the couch with a real-life boy, watching a reality TV show about teens behaving badly. The living room is just close enough for me to be disturbed by what I can hear, but just far enough to not be sure which sounds are coming from the TV and which are coming from the couch. I beam all the motherly disapproval I can their way to cover all possibilities and go back to the dolls.

My job was easier back in our Barbie years, I think, clamping a miniature magenta stethoscope around the hot doctor's neck. Distinctions between what was play and what was real were nice and clear and simple to explain to my child. All I had to do was make peace with the fact that I was crawling around in my career woman power suit helping my little girl dress her Career Barbies in what sometimes appeared to be tiny hooker outfits.

That was nothing, it turns out. Nothing compared to what a mom needs to make peace with today to help her daughter navigate the world. Distinctions between play and real are no longer nice and clear at all. Neither are the distinctions between good and bad, healthy and unhealthy, honest and dishonest . . . Pretty much everything is complicated in a way it wasn't then.

So much had already changed in the world for women by the time my daughter was six, it was impossible not to assume that by the time she got to the age she is now, everything would be completely fixed and wonderful. Work opportunities would be wide open, pay and promotions would the same for everyone, relationships would be completely equal, companies would be set up to embrace parenthood, and rights of all people in all areas of life would be guaranteed. I could spend hundreds of hours helping my young daughter dress princesses for the ball in the Barbie castle without ever worrying that I was endorsing a life goal of being a princess or, worse, marrying Ken. This was *play*. Generations of women had launched a spectacular new kind of *real* for women. A whole powerful new path for my girl had been set.

The giggling from the other room intensifies. I don't like it. I don't like that I need to either give nineteen-year-olds space and privacy in my living room in the middle of the afternoon or risk having them find someplace to go where I can't hear the things I don't want to hear. This is not a new motherly complaint, I know, but it's worse now. This part of the powerful new path has an extremely fast lane and I don't like it one bit.

"Stop doing what you're doing in there!" I yell toward the room when I can't stand it any longer. *"Hands in the air! Feet on the floor!"*

I go back to the dolls on the floor and the less complicated time. I miss Ken, the grinning blond surfer dude in Barbie's pink plastic convertible. Ken was too oblivious to be any kind of threat. Ken didn't have a Snapchat account. No selfies of any part of himself. He didn't even have his own car. That was *Barbie's* pink convertible! I trust absolutely nothing about today's boys or what the world has encouraged today's girls to think is expected in relationships.

I want to see Ken again. I dump what's left in the boxes I brought from the other room on the floor.

Where is he? Where's that oblivious surfer dude? I ask myself silently as I rummage through the pile. *I miss you, you overconfident, undeserving, nonthreatening Romeo! Where are you?? Come out! Come out and let me hug you, little plastic guy!!*

"MOM!" My grown-up princess is standing over me. Apparently I wasn't as silent as I thought.

"Sorry, honey," I say. "I was just reminiscing."

"Seriously, Mom?" she asks, looking down at her childhood spread out on the dining room floor. "Is this what you do when I'm at college? Play with my Barbies??"

"Don't be ridiculous," I answer. "I'm looking for Ken."

"Ken?"

"I'm searching for the clarity of simpler times."

"Mom??" she asks, peering at me curiously.

"I worry about your world, honey. So much comes at you from so many directions all day long—popping up on Facebook . . . swirling on the Internet . . . life coaching by YouTubers with green hair . . . link after link to who knows what after what . . . a constant exposure to . . ."—I point toward the living room—"things like that!"

"It's a *TV show*, Mom!!" she says with an exasperated laugh.

"Exactly!" I answer. "That's why it's dangerous! Behavior that should be shocking is edited into Netflix episodes that start to look normal! The distinction between play and real is gone! I miss Ken. I miss the good old days of Ken!"

"You're funny, Mom," she says, shaking her head with a laugh and giving me a comforting little pat on the head. She turns and walks back to the living room. "And don't worry, I know the difference between play and real!"

I do a quick scan of her teeny shorts, scoopy top, perfect makeup, long flowing hair, and stacked platform sandals as she walks away. I'd be more comforted if she and much of her peer group didn't look like life-size Barbies a lot of the time. I try to imagine all she's already facing and is going to face in the future without calling her mom for help.

Then again, what help would I be? I spent years writing about relationships—reading, researching, trying to condense giant societal shifts into comic-strip-size stories that would help women navigate love, work, and self-esteem with a sense of humor when all the rules were changing.

But at least there *were* rules then. Nothing prepared me to help my daughter deal with what feels like the complete free-for-all of now. I don't know how to shield her from pressures I don't even know about and, when I learn about them, can't comprehend. It makes me crazy when I see freedoms my generation was so proud to win get translated into presumptions and pressures that can make today's young women more, not less, vulnerable to everything: being hurt, misunderstood, taken advantage of. When I learned that what my mother's generation saved for their wedding night can be arranged in a nanosecond with a right swipe on a hookup app, I wanted to put my arms around my daughter's whole generation. Hearts and souls couldn't possibly have evolved at the same pace as electronics. Moms can't possibly keep up with all we need to protect. Young women must be feeling more lost and alone at the exact time in history they should feel more in control of everything.

More sounds from the living room. More sounds back from me: *"I'm serious! Stop whatever you're doing in there! Focus on your wretched TV show!"*

I pick a princess up off the floor and wrap her in a long yellow gown with glittery butterflies on the skirt. I can barely remember what I did yesterday, but I remember that this gown from years ago came with matching long yellow gloves and teensy silver plastic stilettos with an even teensier butterfly on the toes. I dig through the pile of clothes, determined to put the outfit in order.

It isn't only relationships. Everything's more complicated for my daughter's generation. Hanging on to career passion when it's so hard to find a job . . . Feeling that one person's voice can't possibly matter when so many voices together haven't made a difference . . . Knowing who and what to trust . . . Staying connected to humans when so much of life is online . . . Feeling safe when the whole planet feels so fragile . . .

I worry that the bright, blazing possibilities of my generation don't seem possible at all to a lot of young women today. I hear my own daughter say things no women were saying when I was her age.

Things like "Nothing's ever going to change . . . Nothing I do would make a difference."

I never imagined I'd think what I think a lot of the time now, which is that I don't really know how to prepare my own daughter for womanhood in this world.

The sounds have stopped completely in the living room. It's way too quiet in there. I look down at everything that came out of the Barbie boxes on the floor in front of me. The sparkly pink uncomplicated jumble of what was. There's no going back, I know that . . . but I wish I were a little more confident about how things would go forward. I'm feeling more than a little powerless when . . .

My daughter's suddenly back in the room, standing in front of me.

"Here, Mom," she says, pulling something from behind her back and handing it to me, with a compassionate grin and smiling eyes. "I keep him buried in the back of the top shelf of my closet. So I always know where he is."

Same oblivious surfer dude grin. Same blond hair still frozen in place. That overconfident, undeserving, nonthreatening Romeo. That oh-so-welcome unlikely touchstone of innocence. My heart skips a little beat.

"Also, don't worry, Mom," my daughter says, pointing toward the living room, "we're in there laughing about what losers the kids are on that show. I'm not going to turn into one of them! And the guy who's with me . . ."—she rolls her eyes and shakes her head—"believe me, Mom, nothing to worry about with him, either." With that, she leans down toward me and taunts my motherly fears with a big grin of her own and "Not THAT guy, anyway!"

She leaves me with another comforting pat on the head and something even sweeter—a hint of reassurance that she's able to handle things better than I think. I'm heartened by her self-awareness and sense of humor. Maybe along with all the new things coming at her from the outside that I can't control, she has coping skills on the inside that I actually planted. Maybe I put enough in there to help keep her grounded in who she is, no matter what the world brings. I touch my hand to my head where she patted it. Maybe she even wants to take care of me a little, just like I want to take care of her.

I hear her get resettled on the couch with her guy. I gaze at the guy she brought to me from the shelf in her room, and have my second beautiful moment of zero inner conflict for the day: This feminist Barbie Mom doesn't care one speck how happy it makes me to be reunited with Ken.

FIVE WAY BETTER THAN ALL THE OTHER REASONS I DIDN'T EXERCISE TODAY

1. I don't want to get all muscly.

2. I don't want to get all sweaty.

3. My sunscreen is too sticky.

4. My earbuds are tangled up.

5. I've exhausted myself thinking up excuses.

45.

MEDITATIONS ON A SWEAT SOCK

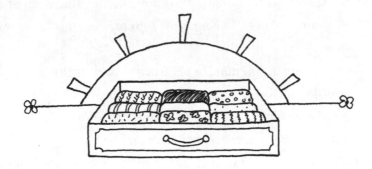

Some sit quietly, listening to the healing tones of the Native American flute. Some meditate to recordings of shorebirds or mountain streams. Eyes closed. Body still. A gentle transport to that beautiful place of serenity from which to gather strength and inspiration for the day.

I sit in front of my sock drawer. I organized the drawer four days ago and it brings me instant peace. One organized drawer in a house full of drawers and closets, in a lifetime of Things to Go Through. It fills me with hope. I come back to it several times a day. All I have to do is pull the drawer open and peek in at my perfectly lined-up socks to feel restored.

It wasn't easy in the beginning. My dog associates the opening of the sock drawer with the possibility that I'm going to put on socks to go for a walk, and he went berserk the first nine times I came in here to be re-inspired. His frantic, hopeful barking, leaping, and clawing at my leg interrupted my journey to stillness. The disbelief in his eyes when he saw me bring a chair into the room, sit in front of the open drawer, and look at the socks instead of putting any on made me question my path. The way he slumped to the floor when he realized there was no possibility of a walk and stared up at me with those pitiful sad eyes, boring guilt into my soul, made me want to give up.

But not succumbing to outside pressure is part of the journey to inner peace. I've glanced at enough mindfulness-seeking links on my Google search for Purpose and Meaning to know that. My personal quest is to own the concept that I can't fix every single thing for every single person. I'm never going to make everyone happy. If I can rally past the guilt of disappointed dog eyes, I know I can learn to say *NO!* to the rest of the universe.

I'm emboldened by my progress. This morning I used some of the new clarity of mind provided by my nice neat sock drawer to present my dog with a choice: did he want to continue staring at me or did he want to chew on a big smelly bone in the other room? He chose the bone.

Surely anything is possible for me now.

46.

MOTHER'S SOUP

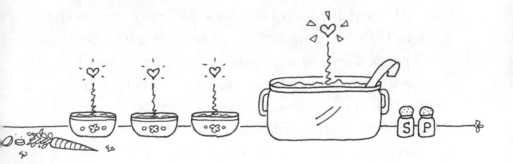

There couldn't possibly be more love packed into this little kitchen. My mom, my daughter, and me. Three generations of women, deeply devoted to one another. Mom is gentle and joyful. She was never overbearing, but she's even more serene now, grateful for each day and the people she loves. I'm more gentle and joyful, too. I quit panicking that I was going to turn into Mom long ago when it became clear I already *was* her. My only worry now is that during all the years I was so resistant to being like her, I blocked a lot of the goodness I could have inherited. As for my daughter, she has one foot in childhood and one in adulthood, and is standing right on that sweet spot in which she mostly needs to be hugged more than she needs to be belligerent. Today we are all best friends.

The kitchen is a special place for everyone in the family, but when it's just the three of us in here, as it is today, it's something more. Something happens. As soon as we get out the pots and pans, as soon as we begin the ancient, honored ritual of making food, all our love and devotion spirals into that *other* ancient, honored ritual of loving mothers and devoted daughters: We drive each other crazy.

It's all so beautiful when Mom, my daughter, and I sit and talk in the kitchen, sharing plans and stories. It's only when we try to cook in the kitchen that trouble happens. Women of our family should never, ever cook in anyone's kitchen. Not together. Not ever. Especially not this one, the kitchen of kitchens: Mother's Kitchen.

Every single fork, saltshaker, potholder, cutting board, glass, measuring spoon, bowl, pan—*everything* has an exact place from which it must be picked up and to which it must be returned. It isn't bossiness—just Mom's sweet, maternal belief that everything has its own little home and should be tucked back into it when it's finished doing its job. Everything also has its own purpose. *This* knife cuts tomatoes; *this* one is for bread; *this* plate is where chopped things go, on *this* side of the stove; *this* is the burner that has to be used with *that* pan. An orderly one-woman monarchy with systems carefully streamlined and perfected over decades to better serve her people. Everything is always just where it should be, including my beautiful mom, whom my daughter and I found standing in her welcoming position a few minutes ago—the Queen right in the middle of her Queendom, arms open wide, lovingly, magnanimously, inviting us in to make the great big mess that will make her insane.

Although . . .

The Queen is beginning this day a little bit on edge because the whole family's in town for a visit this week, and her refrigerator looks as if it's been invaded by aliens. The family currently includes two vegetarians, two carnivarians, a pescatarian, a few flexitarians, two gluten-free people, one low-carb and one orthodox vegan, who won't allow a broccoli floret to be steamed in the same zip code as a hot dog. Before we came, we all emailed Mom our requirements for our morning coffee: whole milk, fat-free milk, lactose-free milk, soy milk, rice-almond milk blend, and non-dairy hazelnut creamer.

I'm a little on edge today because I adore my mom and am supersensitive to how taken advantage of she must feel by all the self-centered, picky members of my family whose obsessive food requirements took over her refrigerator. However, I'm the one who needs whole milk in my coffee, and I'm peeved that Mom either forgot the instructions in my email or simply ran out of room in the refrigerator for me. Coffee with fat-free milk throws my whole system off for the entire day.

My daughter's a little on edge because she's nineteen, and that sweet spot on which she's standing can also feel like a suffocating spot into which she's stuffed. Especially in the morning, especially when I make her get up before 10:30 a.m. *on her vacation.*

Three generations on edge. So many reasons *not* to suggest what I'm about to suggest.

But I am my mother's daughter. I have optimism wrapped around my DNA like a strand of Christmas lights. Surely our love for one another can see us through one happy cooking experience together. Surely my fear that I'm running out of chances to ask Mom things I'll wish I'd asked, the reality that *this could be the last time we're ever in her kitchen together* . . . Surely I can smile and say thank you instead of getting irritated when Mom tells me I'm slicing celery the wrong way.

Surely the understanding that my adopted daughter is at a time in her life when she's struggling to know who she is and needs all the happy family memories I can provide to help make up for all the blanks in her family tree . . . Surely that will inspire me not to attack her for the sloppy way she peels a carrot.

Surely the years and years I spent writing about the beautiful, profound, and tangled relationships between mothers and daughters— literally drawing the mom who's standing in front of me right now as my role model of unfailing forgiveness, love, and good humor . . . Surely some of that will guide me today, in my dual mom-daughter roles, to react with patience and appreciation, and not do what I usually do.

I move between my familial bookends, put an arm around each of them. I am ready to be the loving mother and daughter I know I can be. Ready to embrace this morning of possibility and make it as meaningful as possible for all of us. "Mom," I say, full of emotion, "I'm so happy to have the three of us here together. I would love it if you would spend this special morning teaching your granddaughter and me how to make your amazing chicken soup."

Mom looks at me and smiles.

My daughter looks at me and doesn't smile.

"I'M NOT EATING SOUP IF IT'S MADE FROM A CHICKEN THAT'S BEEN IN GRANDMA'S REFRIGERATOR FOR A MONTH!" she announces.

And we're off.

Mom quits smiling, clearly sensing I've shared some of my concerns about her disregard of expiration dates.

"We have a new chicken!" I hiss to my loudmouthed child. *"I bought it yesterday!"*

"Why would you buy a new chicken??" Mom asks sharply. "I have a perfectly good chicken in the freezer!"

"I thought we should start with a nice fresh one! One we wouldn't have to take time to unthaw!" I answer as brightly as possible, not mentioning that we also wouldn't have to take time for any hospital runs, since her chicken's been in the freezer since 2011.

"I thought you didn't *eat* chicken anymore. Half the family won't eat chicken!" Mom states.

"I will eat your chicken soup, Mom!" I say, giving her a hug, trying to salvage the moment. "I've tried to make it so many times, but your chicken soup doesn't taste like your chicken soup when I make it. I want us to watch, to work by your side, to learn every step from you!"

I reach into the cupboard and pull out a big pot.

"Not that pot!" Mom declares. She gets on the floor, pulls out half the contents of the cupboard, and retrieves a bigger pot from the back. *"This* is the pot the soup goes in!"

I feel the first little twinge of annoyance from being corrected before we even start. Mom hands the pot to my daughter and asks her to fill it with water.

"Where's your water?" my Los Angeles born and raised daughter asks.

"The sink!" Mom points to the sink, showing more early signs of exasperation. "The water comes out of the faucet in the *sink!*"

My daughter shoots me a look.

"The *sink,*" I hiss through clenched teeth. *"Use sink water!"*

"But, Mom, you said the contaminants in tap water can . . ." she starts.

My child only repeats my wisdom when it will get me in trouble. I divert attention by getting out ingredients I know go in the soup—carrots, onions, and celery—and cheerfully ask, "Where do you keep your vegetable wash, Mom?"

Mom looks at me with lowered eyelids. "My vegetable wash is the water that is currently coming out of the faucet which your daughter is now putting into the pot," she answers curtly.

I can't stop myself. "But water alone can't get rid of pesticide residue, airborne toxins, and microbial—"

"If you already know everything, why did you ask me to teach you how to make soup??" Mom interrupts, her eyes now in a full stern squint. With that, she turns, gets the fresh chicken I bought from the refrigerator, and hands it to my daughter, saying, "Here, honey. You need to remove the chicken from the plastic and rinse it under the faucet, making sure to stick your hand inside the cavity and remove the little pouch of organs and neck bones."

"I'M NOT STICKING MY HAND INSIDE ANY CAVITIES ARE YOU OUT OF YOUR MIND GRANDMA AND ALSO I AM NEVER TOUCHING ANY ORGANS OR NECKS! EVER!" my little city girl shrieks.

"Maybe you should show us how to rinse the chicken this one time, Mom," I offer.

The chicken finally makes it into the pot. Mom tosses in seasonings while I try to calculate how much flies from her hand into the water.

"How much was that, Mom?"

"I don't know. Just toss in what it needs."

"How do we know how much what it needs?"

"You just know!"

I move on to something measurable, like how many wrong things I can do while I try to cut up the vegetables.

"No! *This* is the knife for onions," Mom says, correcting me.

"No! *This* is the plate for the pieces." Mom corrects me again.

"No! The plate should be on *this* side of the stove . . ."

I turn it on my daughter.

"No! *This* is the way to peel a carrot!" I snap at her.

"No! *This* is how big to make the pieces!" I snap again.

"No! The scraps should go *there!* . . ."

Before long, every helpful suggestion is taken as a judgment. Every comment received as a critique. The daughters get defensive, the moms get frustrated. Perceived disapproval turns into real disapproval. Within minutes the three of us put salmonella to shame in terms of how quickly and completely we're poisoning the happy, healthy attitude that used to be in the room.

"Why are you getting snippy? I'm just trying to help!"

"Why are you attacking everything I do?"

"What attack? I just mentioned you should use the cutting board, not the counter!"

"Exactly!"

Before long, Mom doesn't need to correct, I don't need to snap, and my daughter doesn't need to grumble. It's all done with a glance, a gesture, a sigh. The secret sign language of women—so powerful when we're not directing it at one another, so devastating when we are. In minutes we've gone from being glad to be together to silent irritations flying around the room like Mom's seasonings. No calculations necessary. No need to taste the pot. It was way too much before anyone started. Even completely silent. Everything that isn't being said sounds like "The way you're doing it is wrong."

"What, Mom?? What now??"

"I didn't say anything!"

"You thought it. I heard you think it!"

With mothers and daughters, what's going on in the room is never simply what's going on in the room. One word can call up a whole history of grievances—an incident from childhood, unspoken slights, ancient aggravations. Decades of motherly guidance that got translated by the daughter brain as criticism and rejection. I'm not good enough, I'll never be good enough. One sigh can summon up all the old baggage. Even in my happy family, and I didn't even think we *had* baggage. But one look from Mom, no matter how 100 percent devoted she's been my whole life, registers as some kind of scolding. For some reason, it's always worse in the kitchen when we're cooking. Is it being near food that brings out so much tension? Because the umbilical cord is located so close to the stomach? All I know is, when my mother flips on the under-cabinet light a little too abruptly, as she just did so I can see what I'm chopping, I feel attacked.

"I don't need the light, Mom."

"You can't see what you're doing without the light."

"Yes, I can. I don't need the light on."

"I like to have the light on when I chop things."

"I don't! I like to chop in the complete dark!"

What is wrong with me? Why couldn't "Thanks, Mom. That really helps!" be the first thing I say? Do I really need to win the moment by turning off the light my ninety-year-old mother wants me to use??

No time to figure that out. Mom has expressed her frustration by snapping the kitchen fan on right over my head, which makes me insane. I pick up the parsley my daughter's cutting all wrong and demonstrate how to do it, which makes her insane. Mom picks up the parsley *I'm* cutting wrong and demonstrates *her* way of doing it, which makes me insane. The circle of life played out on a cutting board in a tiny kitchen in Florida.

Not now, I think. Not when our time left is so short. Not when these days are so precious. This is my big chance to not only have this special time with the two of them but model for my daughter how to lovingly receive guidance from Mom, be an example of the respect I hope my child will have for me when I'm older. It's all right here for me to give and take. But I do it anyway. Stay stuck in the middle. I am the worst of both—I'm the bad daughter *and* the bad mother. I overreact to what Mom says to me and turn around and say the exact same things to my child. I revert to being five years old. Stubborn, defiant, reactionary. So irritated with myself I could scream.

The soup has to simmer for a long time. While it's cooking, my daughter and I go to different rooms to regroup. She needs time with her phone. I need a time-out. The smell of the soup fills the entire house. After a while, I hear some of the family return, descend on the refrigerator, and start pulling out ingredients for their microwaved vegan burgers, fried sausages, kale smoothies, and low-carb hummus tortillas. Their happy chatter in the middle of such disparate food plans makes me feel even worse. I go over and over what happened between Mom, my daughter, and me, trying to think how to redeem this day, when I hear Mom's voice coming from the kitchen . . .

"No, honey, *this* is the bowl for salads," she's saying to one of my sisters.

"Here, *this* is a better potholder for that pan," Mom says to my other sister.

"Here, let's turn on the light. You can't see what you're doing without the light on."

I stop searching within and pay attention to what's happening in the other room. Mom's saying the same things she said to me, but her words now don't sound judgmental at all. I hear my sisters start to tense up, even get a little on edge with their own daughters just like I did. I happily note how immaturely they respond. I move to the kitchen doorway so I can enjoy the chain reaction of bad attitude.

"What, Mom? What *now?!!*" . . .

"I *like* cooking in complete darkness!!" . . .

The scent of Mom's soup is overpowering. It fills all the spaces between the people, connects everyone. It's impossible to breathe it in and not be a little bit intoxicated. Impossible to remember what seemed so annoying a short while ago. Impossible to witness all the irritations flying around the room right now and not think of them as spices tossed in the air—literally, the spices of our family's life. I take a deep breath of all of it. It smells like Grandma's house in here. Smells like Mom's house. It smells like a place where everything is forgiven, everyone belongs. It smells like home.

I watch Mom graciously ride out the family chaos, watch her help everyone put away their alien ingredients and clean up their low-carb messes. Even in the cleanup, I see how all the little gestures and glances that make me so defensive when I'm the recipient are infused with Mom's love.

Finally, everyone's dishes are washed, everything's tucked back into its proper home, and the family heads back outside to the beach. The kitchen is quiet again. I find my daughter and wrench her away from her phone. She and I sit back down at the kitchen table. Mom lifts the lid on the big pot on the stove. A giant waft of comfort, reconnection, and reconciliation fills the air. She ladles out a steaming bowl for each of us. I feel happy and grateful and at peace. I get some spoons from the drawer.

"No, use *these* spoons!" Mom corrects, getting out some other ones.

Three generations sit back down at the table. Mom smiles. We smile back.

"And that," my sweet, wise mother says, "is how you make chicken soup."

47.

SUPERMAN VERSUS
THE MEATLOAF

Just in case leaving isn't difficult enough . . .

DAD: Let's get that suitcase out to the driveway!

ME: My plane doesn't take off for six hours, Dad.

DAD: You should be on your way! What if the cab gets
a flat tire?

ME: The airport's only a ten-minute drive!

DAD: What if there's an accident? What if you run out
of gas?

ME: The cab isn't coming for another four hours!

DAD: *What?? That's cutting it way too close! I'll drive you myself! Let's get your bags in the car!*

With that, I call the cab company and reschedule my pickup for two and a half hours from now. That will put me at the small local airport—which never has more than four people in line—three full hours early. Dad checks his watch . . . checks out the window to see if the cab might have arrived early . . . checks The Weather Channel . . . checks with the airline to see if the plane's on time . . . checks with the cab company to make sure they have my new pickup time . . . checks back to make sure they wrote the address down correctly . . . checks the kitchen clock in case his watch is broken . . . checks the bedroom clock in case the kitchen clock is broken . . .

ME: The cab won't be here for another couple hours, Dad. Let's just sit and relax until it comes.

DAD: *What if the cabdriver's watch is broken??*

I don't know why I even mentioned the word *relax*. We've replayed this scene every time anyone's gone anywhere my whole life. We replayed it just yesterday and the day before when the rest of the family, including my daughter, all had flights to catch to other places. Dads don't relax. Not this one. Especially not when there's a plane coming or going. Not until everyone in the family is where they're supposed to be with the front porch light on and the doors bolted.

Mom, who's lived through almost seven decades of this, has ensconced herself in their little home office with the door shut.

("Airplane worry is Dad's department.") I would be irritated by the obsessive triple and quintuple checking if it weren't for the meal we had last night. Instead, I watch Dad go from the kitchen clock to the bedroom clock to the window to the phone to the front door to the kitchen clock to the bedroom clock to the window and feel a little bit of relief. It's as if his superpowers have kicked in and he suddenly has unlimited strength and energy. Nothing will stop this man, I think with a smile. Nothing can stop Superman.

Nothing but a bite of meatloaf . . .

While Dad heads for another front door check, my mind goes to yesterday—to dinner last night . . .

"Did you call a cab for the morning yet?" Dad asks for the fifth time since we sat down to eat.

"Yes, Dad," I say with as much patience as possible considering that he's been asking about my return cab since ten minutes after my plane landed a week ago.

But I'm not concerned with that tonight. It's my last meal of the visit. With the rest of the family gone, I get Mom and Dad for one evening all to myself. So many of my friends have lost their parents or are caring for sick parents in places that are nothing like home. I'm unbelievably grateful to be here with Mom and Dad, at their table in the dining room of their house. I want to freeze this moment in time. I finish the last bite of my dinner and look across the table at my dear parents.

No need to freeze the moment, it turns out. I've finished my meal, but Dad still has his first bite of meatloaf poised in the air, halfway between his plate and his mouth. Mom's taken a few bites, but has gotten up for the third time to go back to the kitchen for something she forgot.

Time has stopped on its own without one bit of assistance from me.

"Um . . . Can I help with something?" I ask lightly, knowing how sensitive they both are to any suggestion that there's something they can't do on their own.

"NO!" they answer together in their super-competent, Mom-Dad Twin voices.

Time hasn't merely stopped; now it's gone backward. When Dad said "NO!" he put his fork down on the plate, so he has to start all over with bite number one. Mom's "NO!" made her forget why she went to the kitchen, so she's come back to the table empty handed and can't start eating again until she re-creates the train of thought that got her up last time.

Is it possible Dad's waiting to start eating until Mom finally gets settled at the table? Is Mom stalling on purpose so Dad will have company when he finally begins to eat? Is their capacity to care for each other still so great after sixty-five years of marriage that dinners go on like this for an hour before anyone—except me—has a bite of food? Each one waiting for the other to be ready to start?

Or were things different on this visit—and it was so busy with the whole family here that I either didn't or wasn't willing to notice? Especially with Dad? Are there changes in him that I'm nowhere near ready to accept?

"How about if I warm your meatloaf up for you, Dad?" I ask, reaching for his plate. I can't stand where my questions are leading. Even more, I can't stand that Superman, who used to sweep me over his head and onto his shoulders, is taking so long to raise a bite of food to his mouth, and that when he finally does, it will be cold and taste terrible.

"No, it's fine!" he answers, gesturing with the midair fork in one hand and reaching for his water with his other hand, which, if I'm completely honest, seems more than a little unsteady.

Not those hands, I think, trying to dismiss what might be the truth—that I'm watching hands that could always do everything struggle to do even the simple things. Not Superman's hands.

Dad was never like the other fathers who came home from the office and sat in the den with a martini. Our dad came home, pulled off his necktie, and jumped into our world. His strong hands taught my sisters and me how to catch a ball, build a snowman, and turn sheets and sticks into backyard tents. They held us while we wobbled on our first bikes and roller skates and hurled down huge toboggan runs.

Dad's hands carried bugs and spiders outside to be reunited with their bug and spider families while my sisters and I screamed. They made huge milkshakes that got all over the kitchen, which made my mother scream. They scraped snow and ice off the car for a thousand early-morning and late-night trips to a barn where, while the family stayed warm at home, his frozen hands hauled buckets of food and water to care for my sisters' horse, pony, and two cows named Huntley and Brinkley.

His hands held the newspaper while he read the funny pages to me at the kitchen table every Sunday morning when I was little, introducing me to what would be my life's work. They wrote letters to my sisters and me almost every week until recently, when I tried not to hear him tell me it was getting hard for him to use a pen. They squeezed bravery into my hands all the way across the Atlantic Ocean not that long ago, protecting me from a few bumps in the air, when we went to visit the field in France where he, at age twenty, spent nights freezing and rain-soaked in the World War II trenches, with gunfire blasting over his head.

I send an encouraging smile to Dad across the table while I struggle a little to swallow my own sip of water.

It's impossible to watch Dad's hands and not think about everything they built, including some of the best memories of my life. "Do we need anything today, Dad?" the seven-year-old me would ask hopefully over Saturday-morning cereal.

His eyes would twinkle. "Oh . . . we might be running low on electrical tape. We'd better go to the hardware store and poke around."

An hour later, we'd drive home with enough rope, pulleys, hooks, wood, and nails to build a tree house. Saturday after Saturday, we spread hardware store treasures out on Dad's workbench and went to work. He taught my sisters and me how to make and fix things just like he did, using the beautiful worn wooden tools he inherited from his father, who taught woodworking to high school boys in Youngstown, Ohio. We fixed faucets and lamps . . . reassembled bicycles . . . made a tiny hospital for the field mice our cat kept bringing home.

I think of the go-kart he and my sister made out of wooden crates and metal roller skates and painted bright pink for my eighth birthday with the same hands that are now trying to maneuver his water glass and fork. I think of the village he and I built together for my electric train, both of us oblivious to the fact that in those years, dads weren't supposed to give trains to girls for Christmas, and even if they did, dads never spent their weekends building things with their daughters. I think of the fortress he turned every apartment and house my sisters and I ever lived into, by installing dead bolts on every window and door.

Not those hands . . .

I look at them now, paused midair. Nothing Dad ever taught any of us can fix this.

"Please let me warm that up, Dad!"

"No! It's fine! I just started working on it!" Dad smiles the reassuring smile of someone who clearly doesn't know he's already been working on it for forty minutes.

"**Can I warm up your meal, Mom?**" I call loudly because she's suddenly nowhere to be seen again.

"*I'll* warm up Mom's meal!" Superman has been startled into action by the call of duty and pushes his chair back from the table to stand. "I'll take care of Mom. You should eat *your* dinner."

"I already ate, Dad!"

"You ate? We didn't start yet!"

"Don't get up, Dad! Seriously! I already ate!"

Mom has reappeared from nowhere.

"You ate?" she asks. "When did you eat? We didn't start dinner yet!"

Now they're both up. Dad's trying to take care of Mom. Mom's trying to take care of me. I'm trying to take care of both of them. Everyone's trying to prove to everyone else that he or she is the one who should be helping the other. Everyone finally gets a warm plate of food and gets situated back at the table.

And we're right back where we started. Dinner with Mom and Dad. I'm so grateful to be here with them at their table in the dining

room of their house. I lift my eyes from the second serving of everything Mom just put on my plate and look across the table at my dear
parents and . . .

—⟨ HONK ⟩—

I'm snapped back to right now by the sound of a cab honking in
the driveway.

We hurry outside. Dad, incredibly, grabs my suitcase with the
same hand that struggled so hard with the meatloaf last night and
tries to show the twenty-five-year-old driver the best way to get it
in the trunk of the cab. Dad's superpowers rise to the occasion again,
charging him with strength and energy, somehow overcoming any
weakness, so he can make sure his girl gets off safely—and quickly!
I wrap my arms around both parents. I'd hug them for an hour, but
I feel Dad triple-checking his watch over my shoulder.

It's impossible to see them waving and blowing kisses from the
driveway as my cab pulls away and not wonder if . . .

I've had the same horrible thought each time I've left their house
for the last thirty-five years, but today is worse. They've both seemed
so invincible until now.

I bawl all the way to the airport like I often do, but this time is
more wrenching. I sit at the gate crying to one of my sisters on the
phone, like I also often do, but it's harder today. I blow a kiss out the
airplane window when we're airborne and imagine that Superman
and his bride are still standing in the driveway, looking up at the sky
and blowing kisses back, as I imagine they do every single time one
of us leaves. I spend half the flight to Los Angeles asking myself
what on earth is so important at home that I have to rush there to

do. I rehash the decision I made a lifetime ago to move across the country.

Two days ago I was frustrated by how long the family visit to my parents' house seemed. I couldn't wait to get back to my life. Now I can't wait to come back to theirs. I check my watch. I check how many more hours until I land. I check how long after that until the cab will get me through L.A. traffic to my home and I can call Dad to let him know the porch light's on and the doors are bolted. I check the clock on the seat-back monitor in front of me in case my watch is broken. I check my seatmate's watch in case my seat-back monitor clock is broken. I dig my phone out of my carry-on and check the clock on it in case my seatmate's watch is broken. I check my watch again in case the clock on my phone doesn't work when it's in airplane mode. I check my seatmate's watch again . . . check my watch again . . .

Even though I'm heading in the opposite direction, it suddenly starts to feel as if Mom and Dad aren't all that far away. I almost feel Dad's hand on mine.

48.

MY CUP WOULD RUNNETH OVER EXCEPT IT WAS FULL OF M&M'S AND NOW THEY'RE ALL GONE

t's 8:30 p.m.

In front of me is a spirit-soothing, sage-scented aromatherapy candle and a laptop full of the starts of ten thousand sentences I haven't figured out how to finish. I'm writing by candlelight because I'm no longer capable of buying a lightbulb. My $1,200 computer came with no instructions, but my $12 desk lamp came with a six-fold pamphlet, with warnings printed in five languages about the fire hazards of using the wrong type of bulb. The new shapes and numbers of all the new energy-efficient bulbs in the store's giant display correlated with nothing on my lamp's pamphlet. The sales associate I finally located peered at the wall of light-bulbs and pointed at one with a shrug. "That one should probably be okay."

I gave up on the lightbulb and lit a candle. Less risk of fire with a live flame than a grounded lamp, it seems. But maybe it's better this way. For a lot of reasons, maybe the candle's more appropriate to-night.

In front of me is the spirit-soothing candle and the laptop full of all those unfinished sentences. Behind me is my life. To my left is my iPhone, in case someone wants to rescue me from an evening of solitary reflection, even though I told everyone I know that I'm busy tonight. To my right is a small cup containing fifty-seven frozen M&M's. Fifty-two is the "serving size," but three M&M's were slightly chipped, so I put five extra ones in the cup to make sure I had the proper amount and also to reward myself for being so conscientious. I banned M&M's from my house years ago, but they used to have such power over me, I thought they might be a portal to the truth, so I invited them back in for the evening. I spent so many years hiding them from myself in the freezer that I came to prefer M&M's frozen solid. Ditto donuts. Ditto Girl Scout cookies. Ditto . . . never mind. Those aren't the truths I'm interested in at the moment.

I would be in my pajamas except I live in Los Angeles and 8:30

p.m. is way too early to be found under rubble in pj's in case the Big One happens tonight. It would appear I had no life. I would be crushed, so I wouldn't have a life, but it would appear that I had no life *before* I had no life. In this town, you need to either fall asleep fully dressed or stay conscious until 10:00 p.m., when you can confidently change into pajamas without worrying that anyone will whisper at your funeral that you went to bed too early. Even all those young, creative TV and film people in town who go to meetings in what appear to be pajamas change into actual clothes in the evening, before changing back into pajamas for bed. Those are the rules.

When I was twenty-five I sat at a kitchen table like this with paper and a pen. Computers and serving sizes hadn't been invented yet, so I wrote my frustrations out in M&M's and ate them one paragraph at a time. I scrawled the first drawing that would turn into my first comic strip on a night just like this, when I was full of chaos and had run out of chocolate.

Tonight's a lot like that except a great big chunk of "What am I going to do with my life?" already got answered. The things filling my mind are different and the chocolate's being rationed . . . but sitting here at a kitchen table—where I've always come to try to make peace with what is and was—feels almost exactly the same. I understand my dad now when he tells me that on the inside he feels just like he did when he was a boy. "I can hardly believe it," Dad says, way too wistfully for me to be able to stand it. "I can hardly believe it when I look in a mirror and I see that I'm ninety years old."

I squint a little to block out the room around me so I can try to imagine I really am twenty-five again. I try to call up exactly who I was and how I felt that depressing night that launched the unbelievably wonderful life I've been so blessed to have. I squint a little more so I can block out how old my hands look now, which is ruining the whole poignant experience. I pull my sleeves down so I won't be distracted by the sight of aging arms.

I think of the sad song I used to listen to over and over back then when I sat at a table just like this, searching for answers and then searching for jokes that would save me from the search for answers. I want to click on YouTube so I can see and hear the soundtrack of that time in my life . . . but I'm way too experienced to fall for that trick tonight. There's no coming back to anything productive after clicking on YouTube at 8:30 p.m. A 30% OFF EVERYTHING! offer pops up in the upper right corner of my laptop screen, but I delete it without even peeking. I am a rock.

As for the M&M's, they've already proven to be a portal to nothing tonight except how much I want more M&M's. I anticipated that trick too, and destroyed the rest of the bag before I sat down at the table. The only thing left to eat in the freezer is a bag of frozen lima beans, and hungry as I am for distraction, I'm not remotely tempted to leap up and refill my treat cup with a serving of those.

I watch the candle and let the song I used to listen to play in my mind.

I remember exactly who I was and how I felt that night when I was twenty-five, when I did that first frantic drawing: I was a success in the advertising business and a failure in relationships. I was proud to be on my own and miserable that I wasn't with someone. I was confident, competent, and unbelievably insecure. Strong *and* submissive. Brave and terrified. Focused and confused. I sought guidance from the vending machine. Refuge in the refrigerator. I gained everything but clarity.

I was thrilled to be part of a dynamic new generation of career women, but I couldn't stand to look at myself. I grew up with the most loving, supportive parents on earth and was ashamed to tell them how bad I felt about myself. I had wonderful sisters and good friends and was embarrassed to let them know I was having a hard time. I couldn't admit to anyone how complicated everything was. I don't think I knew how complicated it was. I was too tangled up in the middle of a great big cultural shift to have any perspective at all. At the exact time in history when women were demanding respect, equality, and independence, I let my sad love life define my existence and ate my way into solitary confinement. I felt completely alone.

Mom taught me to express my feelings by writing them down. Dad taught me there's humor in almost every situation; that when things seem their worst, there's almost always a different way to look at them that can rescue you from feeling horrible. The misery of that night wound up as a journal entry because of my inner Mom . . . and then turned into a scribbled self-portrait that was so pitiful, it made me laugh out loud because of Dad. The combination made me feel so much better, I spent the next thirty-four years doing pretty much the exact same thing every single day.

I take a long, spirit-soothing breath of sage-scented air. I try to imagine how I would have felt that night if I'd known what would unfold from that first miserable scribble. How the drawing that saved me from feeling bad would start something that would connect me so deeply to women who felt exactly as alone as I did. Women I've never met to whom I will feel bonded like best friends for the rest of my life. Soul sisters. Anonymous confidantes, lots of times, because it was hard to admit weakness at a time when our generation was fighting so hard for women to be perceived as strong, equal, and able. The comic strip syndicate urged me to give the main character my name so the words would seem more authentic. Many, many, many days, I wished she was called *anything* else so I could at least pretend it wasn't as authentic as it was.

I try to imagine how I would have felt back then if I'd known how many women will open diaries, drawers, or scrapbooks sometime in the future, find faded comic strips they've tucked away, and smile, as I do, at everything we went through together:

All those now-unimaginable early battles over whether women should be allowed to work and girls should be allowed to play sports . . .

All that money spent to look professional only to be criticized if we wore men-style suits or ogled if we wore skirts. And no matter what we wore, still having to spend part of our workdays explaining why it wasn't our job to wash the cups in the coffee room . . .

All that fighting to be as successful as a man only to have to act less successful than men if we wanted one of them to be interested in us . . .

All those traditions we were suddenly free to break that emboldened us to walk through so many new doors, but kept some of us from even peeking in some of the old doors—not getting married, not having children, not living near family . . .

All those dreams of having it all that deteriorated into having all of a Sara Lee cheesecake, with all the doors locked and the blinds pulled down . . .

All those insane miracle diets and all the ways we continued to blame ourselves when they didn't perform miracles . . .

All those paychecks surrendered to the shoe department, all those magnificent muscle-cramping, toe-crushing pedestals upon which we made our stands—to be respected, noticed, loved—the glorious confidence we had from the ankle down . . .

All our brave, devoted dads, who had to learn to juggle being their daughters' protectors while helping launch us into a world that felt so new and unsafe.

And all our beloved, mortified mothers, who were so excited for us to do all those things they hadn't been able to, but were afraid for what it all meant. Who worried like our dads, exactly like we do now with our children, about all the new ways they were powerless to protect us.

It was humbling to get to be a voice for a little bit of what a lot of us shared, and unbelievably reassuring when I heard from readers. Letters were like full body hugs. Lots of them made me cry. "Thank heavens," I'd think reading them, "thank heavens there's someone else in the world who did that . . . or thought that . . . or felt just like that . . ." It made everything infinitely more bearable to know I wasn't the only one. It made it possible for me to keep doing my job for as long as I did because so many other women let me know we were in it together.

My eyes move to my empty treat cup. These emotions are too much for a sage candle to handle. I need comfort food. I get up and pour some frozen lima beans into the cup. Utterly unsatisfying. I try the refrigerator: leftover stir-fry, fat-free yogurt, mini carrots. The pantry: low-sodium garbanzo beans, high-fiber bran flakes, organic quinoa. I remember that in a recent life-affirming, protein-boosted, power-smoothie rush, I recommitted to healthier habits and did a full kitchen cleanse, getting rid of everything that might lead me to do what I want to do right now. The kind of take-charge act that's so exhilarating at 9:00 a.m. and so irritating to revisit at 9:00 p.m., when the day settles down and there's nothing left to eat.

I return to my chair with a glass of natural berry-flavored spring water and take an uncomforting sip. I add *Go to the grocery store and restock everything* to my list. We're not quite done, I think. Not quite done at all.

This time of life is beyond unnerving and unsettling. I'm having conversations with friends that include words that used to refer only to people my parents' age. Old people words. *Knee replacement. Hearing loss. Osteoporosis.* And much, much worse. I've lost dear friends decades before I thought I'd have to say goodbye to anyone my age. Attended funerals before I even had time to send a get-well card.

Just like that. My whole generation is reeling from the stunning truth—that we, who are way too young and hip to ever look or act old, are not too young to pass away.

I had a six-month period last year in which so much started failing and changing in such a short amount of time, it got scary to get out of bed. Rattled to the core. As if the earth were actually moving, as if I—along with most of the people I know—was and am in a great big life shift, a rearrangement of all that's familiar. Many mornings still make me want to grab the trash bag and just start throwing things out, to take charge in any way I can of anything I can.

If it weren't enough to have cherished people, places, and things disappearing, other things keep *not* disappearing. Things that are still on the to-do list a lifetime later. All kinds of problems my generation thought we'd solved for the next generation that aren't solved at all.

There are superstar role model women in every walk of life now, who will help our daughters and granddaughters believe anything is possible. There are wonderful enlightened men who are 100 percent equal partners in everything, who are redefining what it is to be a man for our sons and grandsons. A whole new generation of girls and boys who are being raised with a whole different set of expectations for themselves and one another.

But there are also still great big inequalities that prevent a lot of women from being all they can be or even feeling sort of good about who they already are. Very few women have time or energy at the end of the day to take care of themselves as lovingly as they take care of everyone else. There are still thousands of things that chip away at women's sense of competence and confidence. Things that use up our days and will use up our daughters' and granddaughters' days, things that subconsciously erode feelings of self-worth and achievement.

There are still impossible choices that most women have to face, which most men don't have to face, when they want to start families and careers at the same time. Still huge differences in what men can earn, how much time they have, and how they feel about themselves—like how men can expect man-size pay and promotions . . . how a successful man is usually revered and a successful woman is still often suspect . . . how men can be confident that the pants they're wearing when they board an airplane for a cross-country flight *will still fit by the time the plane lands.* Great big imbalances still, in many families, over who does what.

There are still unthinkable inequalities between races, cultures, and lifestyles that we thought we were stomping out in all our marches on the U of M Diag, way back in those heady days of promise, back in those first pairs of liberating jeans.

There's the profound grief that the planet we thought everyone was surely on board to protect feels so utterly unprotected, the helpless feeling that my little donations, recycling bins, and vegan lunches aren't going to save the world.

And hovering over the frustration of everything we can't fix, the awareness my generation has of the big looming deadlines—that we're all in some version of being on the brink of Something Else.

Even though we all surely know we're in this together, there will be many, many days and nights to come in which we feel completely alone all over again. We're way more aware that every second of these days should be treasured, even as so many of them speed past and seem out of our control.

Days so full of being the guardians of others.

Days with so many, many dreams still on the list.

Days wasted feeling bad about what we didn't do in the previous 20,000 days.

Days in which, on top of everything else, we should be "reimagining and reinventing ourselves for chapter two."

I blow out my spirit-soothing, sage-scented candle and shut my laptop full of unfinished sentences. I sit in the dark, wrapped in gratitude for the wonderful life I've gotten to have. Thankful beyond comprehension for my parents—Superman and Supermom—who raised me with such devotion and embedded a sense of humor so deeply, it will help me experience everything the rest of my life brings—even all the things I just said—with hope and optimism.

I'm thankful to the bottom of my heart for my daughter and stepson, who expanded my world with love and joy a billion times over.

And for my sisters—the wonderful ones in my family and the universe of women who feel like my sisters. All those dear women

I've never met—and all their beautiful mothers—who helped me feel so relieved that I wasn't the only one during all those years I sat in a room by myself drawing a comic strip. Who helped me keep my sense of humor and sense of purpose, helped me know I'm connected to something way bigger than myself.

We all have stories of our past boxed up in garages, storage rooms, and cupboards. It's liberating to unload what's there. But we also all have stories of our past boxed up in our hearts, and those are even more difficult to sort. Stories based on crumpled-up moments we've collected since childhood: the mean thing someone said . . . the dances where no one asked us to dance. Moments we translated into "facts": I'm too ugly, too weird, too awkward. "Facts" verified by just enough as we got older that they grew into stories about ourselves that had a stronger grip on us than our DNA. Stories we've repeated for so long they can still work on us, holding us back at a time of life we should feel most free. Stories enhanced by women's beautiful impulse to take responsibility for anything, which can leave us blaming ourselves for everything.

I'm deeply thankful for all the ways other women continue to lift me out of all that and let me know I'm not alone. For women's bravery, compassion and inspiring examples of how to rise above, persevere, and create new life from tiny specks of possibility. For the support that will help all of us let go of what was and take on what's ahead.

That's the truth I needed to revisit tonight, when so much is changing and there's still so much to do. How important all those connections have been to get us this far, and how much we need them now. The love of family and friends . . . a smile between strangers at the mall . . . the gift of seeing another woman do the impossible . . . the shared grief of all those lines and non-functioning sinks in all those ladies' rooms . . . the way we can look across a room of women and recognize a little bit of ourselves in a hundred different faces . . . the powerful bonds between us.

That's the beautiful truth to carry right now, when we feel crushed for time and squashed in the middle of everything—that all those hearts are wide open to help one another through what's next. We can give one another strength to raise the trash bags and empty all the storage boxes of what holds us back. The perspective and permission to declare the many, many things that aren't our fault.

I remember that other truth, too . . . that thing all those especially great women—our moms—told us: "Just do the next thing," Mom always said. "You don't have to figure it all out right now. Just do the next thing."

I stand up, walk to the sink in the dark, dump out the rest of my uncomforting berry-flavored spring water, and smile. It's 10:00 p.m. in Los Angeles. It's safe to put on pajamas.

In Loving Memory of Superman

Acknowledgments

I dreamed of writing a book of essays for a really long time.

Dan Lazar, my agent at Writers House, not only made this book possible, but made it much, much better. His thoughtful insights helped me turn the pieces I'd started to write into what I was trying to write. He gave me the bravery to weave my past into my present and tell more personal stories. Dan inspired me with his grand vision and great ideas and has cheered me on with a belief in me matched only by that of my mother. Along with Dan, Steven Malk, Torie Doherty-Munro, Maja Nikolic, and Peggy Boulos Smith at Writers House got behind my book with the full force of their support. I am very grateful to each of them for their wonderful input, hard work, and help.

Sally Kim, my editor at Putnam, gracefully guided me to the heart of things. She helped me find truths and balance. Her ability to see the big picture from a lot of little pictures made it possible to create a whole out of the many pieces of things I wanted to say. Sally embraced this project with a wide-open heart, a wonderful sense of humor, and a deep appreciation for the power of winding hope through the piles of the day. She surrounded me with the world's most enthusiastic and hard-working team at Putnam: Ivan Held, Danielle Dieterich, Ashley Pattison McClay, Alexis Welby, Emily Ollis, Brennin Cummings, Gabriella Mongelli, and Christine Ball. And on the production and design side: Meredith Dros, Sandra Chiu, Monica Cordova, Anthony Ramondo, Marie Finamore, Nancy Inglis, Claire Vaccaro, and Meighan Cavanaugh. Each has made every step of this book a very special experience.

Thank you to Todd Doughty for being a champion of possibility and opening doors with his encouragement and generosity.

Thank you to Jerry Scott and Marla Frazee for their part in ruining my retirement.

Thank you to my sisters: Mickey Guisewite is my one-woman sounding board—the only person I've ever shown anything to before submitting it. Mickey's taken every frantic long-distance phone call through a lifetime of deadlines to help me write and rewrite, with nothing in return except smeared mascara from thousands of hours of laughing and a great big phone bill. Mary Anne Nagy is an artist whose beautiful paintings have been a role model of how to create something that's very personal and universal at the same time. Her passion for her art and commitment to sharing a meaningful, uplifting message have helped me stay true to mine.

Thank you to Lee Salem, Jim Andrews, John McMeel, and my friends at Universal Press Syndicate. At a time when there were no other voices of real women in the comic pages, they boldly put mine out in the world and formed a great big family of support around me. They gave me the gift of trust, time, and freedom over decades to develop the kind of self-expression that I got to continue in a longer form in this book. I deeply appreciate everything they've made possible.

I am very grateful to all these dear people. Thank you from the bottom of my heart for helping me finish this book before my 100th birthday.